Lincoln's Continuing Revolution

Lincoln's Continuing Revolution

Essays of M.E. Bradford and Thomas H. Landess

John Devanny, Editor

Lincoln's Continuing Revolution:
Essays of M.E. Bradford and Thomas H. Landess
Copyright© 2024 by John Devanny

ALL RIGHTS RESERVED. No part of this publication may be reproduced, distributed, or transmitted in any form or by any means, including photocopying, recording, or other electronic or mechanical methods, or by any information storage and retrieval system without the prior written permission of the publisher, except in the case of very brief quotations embodied in critical reviews and certain other non-commercial uses permitted by copyright law.

Produced in the Republic of South Carolina by

SHOTWELL PUBLISHING LLC
Post Office Box 2592
Columbia, So. Carolina 29202
www.ShotwellPublishing.com

ISBN 978-1-963506-10-5

FIRST EDITION

10 9 8 7 6 5 4 3 2 1

Contents

Foreword vii

M.E. Bradford On Lincoln

1. Lincoln's New Frontier:
   A Rhetoric for Continuing Revolution 1

2. The Heresy of Equality 9

3. Dividing the House:
   The Gnosticism of Lincoln's Political Rhetoric 39

4. The Lincoln Legacy: A Long View 71

5. Lincoln and the Language of Hate and Fear:
   A View from the South 89

6. Against Lincoln: A Speech at Gettysburg 115

7. Lincoln's Republican Rhetoric:
   The Development of a Political Idiom 125

8. With the Lion and the Eagle 157

9. From the Family of the Lion 161

Thomas H. Landess on Lincoln and Bradford

10. Abraham Lincoln and the Rhetoric of Love 169

11. With Malice Toward Many:
    Washington, Lincoln, and God 185

12. Bradford's Argument on
    "Continuing Revolution" 195

13. Mel Bradford, Old Indian Fighters,
    and the NEH 201

14. Harry Jaffa and the Historical Imagination 211

Editorial Note and Acknowledgements 219

About the Editor 221

Foreword

IN THE FALL OF 2022, Dr. Clyde Wilson approached me about putting together a collection of M.E. Bradford's essays on Abraham Lincoln. In addition, Dr. Wilson suggested including some essays by Thomas Landess, a close friend and former colleague of Bradford's at the University of Dallas. Dr. Wilson's idea for this collection is, to some degree, long overdue. Bradford was among the most important scholars of the late twentieth century. Landess was, in his own right, an insightful and perceptive literary and social critic, and his knowledge of the price paid by Bradford for his views on Lincoln and other matters sheds an important light into the world of conservatism in the 1980s and 1990s. Unfortunately, little of Bradford's work is still in print, a situation that this volume seeks to rectify, at least in the matter of Bradford's assessment of Mr. Lincoln.

Seven decades ago, historian David Donald attributed Abraham Lincoln's status as national hero to "his essential ambiguity."[1] Professor Donald's Lincoln was the ambitious American pragmatist and opportunist, a man without an ideology. Lincoln's malleability rendered him every man's hero, be that man Republican, Democrat, Northern, or Southern. Today, Lincoln is now so much more. He is an untouchable demi-god, the embodiment of Amer-

---

1 David Donald, *Lincoln Reconsidered: Essays on the Civil War Era,* expanded edition (New York: Random House,1961), 18.

ican principles and values, the law giver, the new "Founder" of America upon the principle of Equality. To subject Lincoln to any sort of critical examination is viewed by the academy and those who control the centers of power in the United States as a species of apostasy.

As Bradford documents in his essays, few scholars contest Lincoln's role as a revolutionary, indeed most applaud Lincoln's rerouting of the course of American history. This presents no problem for scholars and others who identify with the Left. *Pietas* was never cultivated as a virtue among them. For conservatives, Lincoln and his legacy present a real conundrum. The Lincoln dilemma—the current version of Donald's "getting right with Lincoln"—hinges upon Lincoln's status as the revolutionary, penultimate founder of the postbellum American regime. Lincoln was the first president to openly and brazenly seize powers delegated by the Constitution to the Congress, the two outstanding examples were his calling out the militia and his suspension of *habeus corpus*, powers reserved to the Congress under Article One, Sections Eight and Nine (respectively), of the Constitution. Lincoln placed Maryland under martial law and jailed many of that state's lawmakers and leading citizens without due process. He suppressed opposition newspapers in the North in violation of the First Amendment. The list goes on. Bradford is diligent in recording the outrages.

That Lincoln committed these outrages is not in dispute. To suggest Lincoln's gross enlargement of the powers of the executive branch or his disregard for the Constitution in his crusades to save the Union and free the slaves (so the mythology asserts), is in any fashion conservative stems from either ignorance or duplicity. Almost to a man, the attendees at the Philadelphia Convention and their opponents, the Antifederalists, feared standing armies, dreaded the enlargement of the powers of the executive branch and never applauded the marriage of big government with big capital. Lincoln, as most scholars believe, was the father of these trends. When Lincoln's less than progressive racial attitudes and beliefs are mentioned to his defenders, "conservatives" rush to his defense claiming Lincoln knew he must pander to the biases of his day to get elected, as if duplicity and cynicism were virtues.

In the eyes of the American "conservative" establishment, Bradford's unforgivable sin was his thorough assessment of the actions, character, and rhetoric of Mr. Lincoln and the inescapable conclusions the evidence confirmed. Bradford viewed Lincoln as a gifted orator and man of unusual political skill. These laudable gifts, however, were placed at the service of Lincoln's overwhelming ambition to secure his place in American history as the nation's second founder, a revolutionary who internalized the radical values of secular Puritanism and gave it expression through "a rhetoric for continuing revolution."[2] Bradford introduced these themes in two essays on Lincoln, "Lincoln's New Frontier" and "The Heresy of Equality." His later essays were more complex and detailed analyses of the relation of Lincoln's rhetoric and policies, revealing the rupture Lincoln created with the men who framed the Constitution.

Bradford's was a direct attack upon the Lincoln *mythos*. What made it more outrageous to the adherents of this *mythos* was that Bradford was not easily dismissed. Bradford was a man of letters, educated in that venerable tradition at Vanderbilt by the eminent poet and social critic, Donald Davidson, and other gifted scholars. His mastery of rhetorical analysis was of the first rank, and Bradford was widely read and formidable in his command of the fields of history and political theory. Bradford possessed an agile mind and understood complex matters on a profound level. He was daunting in scholarly debate. As the leftist scholar Garry Wills relates, Bradford was not wrong about Lincoln, he was

---

2   For Bradford's study and assessment of the rhetoric of Secular Puritanism see "Lincoln, the Declaration, and Secular Puritanism: A Rhetoric for Continuing Revolution," *A Better Guide Than Reason: Studies in the American Revolution* (LaSalle, IL: Sherwood Sugden & Company, 1979), 185-206.

merely "suicidally frank."[3] And as Thomas Landess tells us, for all the above sins, he was never forgiven.

Bradford understood the stakes were high. Any sort of "conservatism" that embraced Lincoln embraced revolution and ultimately rejected many of the principles of the men who framed the Constitution. This has certainly occurred and has in part resulted in a conservative movement unable to achieve any of the basic premises justifying its existence: limited government, the rule of law, fiscal responsibility, a return to the moral principles of Western civilization. The late, esteemed political theorist, Willmoore Kendall, understood well that Mr. Lincoln and the Framers did not keep house together; Conservative Inc. shudders at making the same and obvious admission. This is why Bradford's work on Lincoln is desperately needed today. For unless we can turn a "cold, cold eye" upon Mr. Lincoln and his legacy, then we shall be continually tossed in the revolutionary whirlwind.

---

3 Garry Wills, *Lincoln at Gettysburg: The Words that Remade America* (New York: Simon Schuster, 1992), 39.

M.E. Bradford On Lincoln

1.

Lincoln's New Frontier:
A Rhetoric for Continuing Revolution
(May 1971)

Though Americans have never been "a people" in the received and historic sense of that term, it is a commonplace of scholarship that we make up the most self-confident and least self-conscious of modern societies. For nearly two hundred years it has been our imagination that we "knew" our nature and destiny. Unequivocally, we affirmed that the obvious truth of who-and-for-what we were was contained in a set of sacred (but generally extra-legal) documents—Declaration, Constitution, *Federalist* and the rest. Their authority was no more subject to question than that of the tablets given upon the mountain. Neither has a detailed inquiry into their formal properties (and therefore their intrinsic ambiguities) been encouraged. For our truth was "one and indivisible."

Of course, we sometimes quarreled over the meaning of these *a priori* guarantees of our future well-being—quarreled even as we agreed upon their canonical stature. But whatever side of the disagreement the earlier American took for his own, his explanation of the dispute he had joined was always the stupidity and obscurantism of his antagonists. Moreover, until after World War II, the breathtaking pace, institutionalized good fortune and periodic convulsiveness of our record prevented any single view of the matters contested from being pursued into the hard divisions of a nationwide and nation-effecting conflict between permanent orthodoxies. (Of course, I must except the South from these generalizations. And even there the hardening process did not achieve completion until the conclusion of the Civil War when the South was near voiceless and discredited, so far as political doctrine was concerned. Furthermore, before this localized hardening could effect the general "We," the ongoing flow of the national "business" had caught up the unruly children of secession and mitigated their "otherness" into the exception which proves the rule: In any case, even if Dixie had remained to the present in obdurate, and principled rebellion of the spirit, it could not have altered the national self-assurance of the Union and its grounds. For the rest of the republic has always expected the South to be something like "another country," a heresy *bound* by geography and therefore beside the point in a discussion of America at large.)

But in the last few decades experience has shaken our self-confidence and intensified our self-consciousness: we have reached a point where easy assumptions about our nature and destiny are no longer convincing. There is, in fact, a widespread sense among Americans that a process of disabusement of such assumptions by disaster is near to fruition. Thus it is now possible to consider the ambiguities of texture and design in our national weave that make fair to divide us beyond all powers of healing. For the first time in a century (since Gettysburg, when we were *almost forced* to learn how many we could be), the generality of our countrymen have had some intimation of their subjection as a body to the ordinary laws of group mortality: some inkling that any number of circumstances in combination might insure that they would cease forever to be anything recognizable as the United States.

We are, in short, prepared as never before to doubt our secularized eschatology: to examine the "roads taken," the evangels heeded, and the prophets deputized to lead forward the march. And for similar reasons, there is an urgency to our retrospection on once "safe assumptions" which resembles not so much the curiosity of the antiquarian or the animus of the partisan as the anguished confession of the damned.

It is my purpose to accept the opportunity for reflection suggested above by focusing *as a practicing rhetorician* on certain internal contradictions of thrust and presupposition in an illustrative sample of the sanctified American writings. I must from the first admit that my sampling is nothing like a full one. Fortunately, some materials in this collection are more sacred (because more rhetorical) than others. Three in particular, I think, demand close inspection in any survey of the lot—the Declaration of Independence, the Gettysburg Address and "The Battle Hymn of the Republic." (I except the Constitution from my analysis, as it is a rhetorical instrument of law qua law.)

After the example of the poets, I must begin in the middle. For the significance of this procession comes clear only there, in Lincoln's Gettysburg Address. To state my argument briefly, what the Emancipator accomplished by confirming the nation in (or "institutionalizing") an erroneous understanding of the Declaration of Independence made possible the ultimate elevation of that same error in Mrs. Julia Ward Howe's "war song" and set us forever to "trampling out the grapes of wrath." More importantly, the proof of this synopsis—and the proper instruments for extricating our country from the now evolving political and intellectual impasse which it explains—are *available* in a conjunction of the ancient rhetorical distinctions between levels of style and kinds of discourse. There, and not in the straightforward dismemberings of the political philosophers.

Our three documents are illustrations of what the older rhetoricians called a "mixture of the modes" and therefore sources of confusion having much to do with our present peril, The Declaration of Independence is a lawyer's answer to lawyers, a counterplea to the English government's explanation *cum* apologia of its American policy—a forensic counterplea in tone *and* organization. The Gettysburg Address is an unmistakable memorial oration in the high epideictic (declamatory, demonstrative) vein prescribed for such solemn moments. And finally, "The Battle Hymn of the Republic" is certainly a "practical poem," of the Dorian variety, an exhortation to action which would have created no surprise had its numbers sounded through the ranks of Cromwell's Ironsides. Consistent with the pattern which produces all such "landmarks," everything to be identified in (and complained about) each of these singular writings is available in other sources contemporary with them; a cluster of related speeches, histories, essays in opinion and poems surrounding and supporting their separate splendors. History did not give them to us in isolation or according to the order of time and importance which they have assumed. Their *form* finally determined their meaning, their "family tree" as we presently conceive of it. The Declaration, Address and Hymn are therefore epitomies, hallowed by usage (and confirmed by their own internal logic) into a millennialist and gnostic injunction to the country (and indeed the species) at large: an injunction which can never rest easy with the given social and moral nature of the poor souls whom it enjoins. The reason behind this movement of mindless rehearsal into myth is then the success of Mr. Lincoln's battlefield performance. On such a fulcrum history is easily remade. For Lincoln's Pennsylvania miracle is visible in the shape and surface of its accomplishment, a retreat from proposition, discussion and argument into oracle and glorified announcement: an advance from discourse of what is *believed to be* into an assertion of what *must be and yet forever remain in the process of becoming.*

The most important formal property of Lincoln's great address is the biblical language in which it is cast. For Americans the effect of this epideictic encapsulation is what the Greeks called Asiatic, after observing its prevalence and usefulness among nations living beyond their eastern boundaries. It is a pre-rhetorical rhetoric, suited to judges, prophets and priest/kings who instruct and command without explaining: that is, suitable to a "closed" world. As no dispute concerning the materials it enshrined was imaginable, the end to which it was employed was obviously very different from that of the deliberative and forensic discoursings of which the Athenian philosophers approved. Probably its intent was the affirmation of a common bond—often *in* its user, but always shared by those who heard or read after him. Of course, as long as there have been "authorities" among or over their people, the style has remained a part of every Western rhetorician's equipment, a magic to be used whenever what was there for the saying was less important than the saying itself. Now, we may at first reasonably resist this association of Lincoln and Oriental despotism, but before we resist too strongly let us look at what the biblical style implies (and conceals) in his address.

Among Americans in the middle years of the previous century there was one authority above all others. Revival and frontier had deepened a relationship established with settlement. We were a fellowship of "the Book" and took all government and political philosophy—even the Constitution—to be practical and unworthy of mention in the same breath with Holy Scripture. Politics might (within reason) be tested against revealed truth. But we never imagined more than a tangency for the political and the sacred— never a holy beginning or conclusion *by* politics. In putting away our Englishness—and in adopting the First Amendment—we made these distinctions plain. We were thus a religious "community" as opposed to a divinized state, a polity with no god's son to make us and no god's city to build. (That is, except in New England—of which more hereafter.)

Now, the proper voice of this communal orthodoxy—its style, if you like—was that of the King James Version. Therefore anything spoken to us that hoped, in South Carolina *or* Massachusetts, to suggest the transcendent had to sound and feel like "a Daniel come up to judgment." Lincoln's strategy in the first sentence at Gettysburg is to lift beyond discourse, away from the political and into the "moral" order, what stands in the Declaration (despite its reference to the Deist's "Creator") to be proved and argued. The world of the epideictic, of "four score and seven" (instead of 87), of "our fathers," is an ultra-prescriptive realm which claims God for a sponsor and a sanction from out of time for what is done within it; a sponsorship through a "righteous blood" or genealogy (of fathers, as opposed to founders) and according to partially mysterious purposes (as opposed to reasonable ends). Certain men belong to that world by *a priori* definition; they *know* it is theirs. Others join the dispensation through the loaning of the established blood: hence "brought forth"—an equivocal phrase, again implying a source other than "our fathers" themselves for the "new nation" which they "birthed." (The image, it is worth remarking, runs with a full set of corollaries throughout the speech. Its final result is sacrilege by submerged metaphor: a phony "new testament," out of a phony "old," with dead soldiers for a bridge.)

In contrast, the remainder of this opening sentence is not of Mosaic or "pre-classical" (as political philosophers use the term) stock. With "liberty" we enter the English Whig commonwealth of slowly earned and evolved rights and law, and with "equality" the French Jacobin satrapy where men are dignified by abstract "proposition" and loud musketry. However, since liberty and equality are hieratically marked as "brought forth" by "fathers," their doctrinal status as emulsible elements in a settled, blessed, patriarchal and republican solution are thus certified with finality. Moreover, the fundamental question of the irreconcilability of these terms of honor is left aside—yea, forbidden.

The biblical note is sustained—and our problem with it compounded in the following sentences of the speech: "consecrate" and "hallow" for the "new birth" and "dedication." Finally this confusion issues in a peroration even more confusing. Collectively the red tide of battle is to redeem us—though this time we will midwife our own regeneration. The godly work of the fathers will be completed in a joining of three in one; government "of, by and for the people." But, like Lincoln's first baby, this final monster is a bit puzzling. For government "by" the people might not be "for" the people (see Plato on "elected" physicians and ship captains). Likewise, government "of the people" is possibly neither "by" nor "for" them (remember Disraeli on "Tory Democracy"). "Four score and seven" or "fathers" can be reconciled to "for the people"; equality alone consorts well only with "by." And "of" implies representatives, courts, and the "system of liberty"—not inheritance. (To see what is most mischievous in this "new birth" and "baptism" we should recall that Lincoln had promised a "new founding" as early ' as his 1858 speech at the Springfield Lyceum—the "House Divided" speech.) But let us forget the paradox and oxymoron before us and look back at liberty and equality in the

Declaration of Independence and then forward to "The Battle Hymn of the Republic."

I have already mentioned the quality of counterclaim (or legal "charge") in our manifesto of '76. Only the opening sentences of paragraph two of that special pleading—"We hold these Truths to be self-evident," etc.—do not belong in the Declaration's forensic whole. And, as the epideictic/beatific swallows up, liberty and equality in Lincoln's Civil War speech, here also the disposition and weight of other components in the total apologia—their historic and prescriptive appeal to the customary and English, to the inherited rules governing prince and subject—cancel out the vanity of "self-evident" and "all men." Perhaps the peculiar lines are a concession to the Revolution's leftmost wing. Or they may be no more than what Mr. Jefferson was able to "sneak in" (in satisfaction of his *philosophe* streak) because his compatriots in the Continental Congress refused to read into his composition any more than was anticipated in the "Glorious" turnover of 1688. The reader should look elsewhere for a history of the Whig doctrine and idiom which could "neutralize" such words: only as much equality as is consonant with liberty and necessary to a modest minimum of human dignity; and only that liberty recommended by the English experience and enjoyed by the Saxon forbears. But—and this is my point—the dominance of that Whig temper is evident, especially in the deletions from his original draft which the Congress imposed upon their young spokesman. We can presuppose it.

Now what is a solicitation *from* a given Whig law and *for* a good repute among the nations? First of all, it is a bill of particulars against the royal government, making plain that the Crown—in violating its well-defined prerogatives—has forfeited all purchase upon its creations, the American colonies. (It is noteworthy that the Declaration speaks for the independence of the *separate* individual colonies and thus belies Mr. Lincoln's purposively mistaken chronology.) Following the pattern of another variety of legal instrument, it says "you, not I, destroyed our connection." For under a rule of law, leigemanship and lordship are indeed like man and wife: neither role exists unless both are observed with some strictness. Portions of Jefferson's catalogue of the King's sins—especially in the author's original version—are a reaching after visceral influence on natural (not reasonable) and emotional men: persons of distinctive temper and culture. Often overlooked, they add both racist and Christian/traditionalist appeal to the case at law. Certain lines evoke the horror of "servile insurrection" and black overpopulation; others refer to mercenaries and kindred affronts to the "common blood," and still others complain of British involvement with "merciless Indian savages." Elsewhere we read of the impropriety of resemblance to the conduct of "Infidel powers" in the policy of a "Christian King." Lastly, all of this in-view-of-paragraph-two surprise is hedged with a disclaimer that the colonies intended no revolution when they first grew restive and is coupled with an admission that political restiveness and innovation are, in most circumstances, to be avoided. The close goes the same way—a retreat into "sacred honor."

Prescriptive law and kings and honor have nothing to do with "self-evident" and "metaphysically" proved first principles. Their "legitimate" ancestor is, rather, history: trial and error, reputation and disrepute, sifting and selection stand behind Jefferson's appeal. In weight, this teleological argument from the record will not replace revelation or anointment by Samuel. But it is far removed from the abstractions of the Encyclopedists or the mechanical universe of their perpetually absent "Creator." And therefore it does not pretend, despite "self-evident," to bespeak his will. Respected only for what it is (and with its explosive sentences "held down" and converted into "mere argument" by a Whig rhetoric), the Declaration is agreeable enough. But its denial that there was "a founding," its complexity and dialectic (recognised by most responsible American leaders who invoked the document before 1860 and acknowledged by the very different language of the 1787 Constitution), were inverted by Father Abraham four score and seven years later. And the forces which he thus released in manufacturing his "political religion"—Lincoln's own phrase in the Springfield Lyceum speech—found their tongue in "The Battle Hymn of the Republic."

2.

The Heresy of Equality (1976)

I

Let us have no foolishness, indeed.* Equality as a moral or political imperative, pursued as an end in itself—Equality, with the capital "E"—is the antonym of every legitimate conservative principle. Contrary to most Liberals, new and old, it is nothing less than sophistry to distinguish between equality of opportunity (equal starts in the "race of life") and equality of condition (equal results). For only those who are equal can take equal advantage of a given circumstance. And there is no man equal to any other, except perhaps in the special, and politically untranslatable, understanding of the Deity. Not intellectually or physically or economically or even morally. Not equal! Such is, of course, the genuinely self-evident proposition.[1] Its truth finds a verification in our bones and is demonstrated in the unselfconscious acts of our everyday lives;

---

* This essay is a direct response to Harry Jaffa's "Equality as a Conservative Principle," *Loyola of Los Angeles Law Review*, VIII (June, 1975), 471-505, which is itself a critique of *The Basic Symbols of the American Political Tradition* by Willmoore Kendall and George W. Carey. Lincoln's reading of the Declaration of Independence is the central subject of this entire exchange. Jaffa's piece invites direct comparison with mine.

1 When pressed in debate by the righteous minions of Equality, an antebellum Northern congressman once called sentence two of the Declaration a "self-evident lie." Consider also *The Federalist,* No. 10.

vital proof, regardless of our private political persuasion. Incidental equality, engendered by the pursuit of other objectives, is, to be sure, another matter. Inside of the general history of the West (and especially within the American experience) it can be credited with a number of healthy consequences: strength in the bonds of community, assent to the authority of honorable regimes, faith in the justice of the gods.

But the equality of Professor Jaffa's essay, even in the ordinary sense of "equal rights," can be expected to work the other way around. For this equality belongs to the post-Renaissance world of ideology—of political magic and the alchemical "science" of politics. Envy is the basis of its broad appeal. And rampant envy, the besetting virus of modern society, is the most predictable result of insistence upon its realization.[2] Furthermore, hue and cry over equality of opportunity and equal rights leads, a fortiori, to a final demand for equality of condition. Under its pressure self-respect gives way in the large majority of men who have not reached the level of their expectation, who have "no support from an inclusive identity," and who hunger for "revenge" on those who occupy a higher station and will (they expect) continue to enjoy that advantage. The end result is visible in the spiritual proletarians of the "lonely crowd." Bertrand de Jouvenel has described the process which produces such non-persons in his memorable study, *On Power*.[3] They are the natural pawns of an impersonal and omnicompetent Leviathan. And to insure their docility such a state is certain to recruit a large "new class" of men, persons superior in "ability" and authority, both to their ostensible "masters" among the people and to such anachronisms as stand in their progressive way.

Such is the evidence of the recent past—and particularly of American history. Arrant individualism, fracturing and then

---

[2] See Helmut Schoek, *Envy: A Theory of Social Behavior* (New York: Harcourt Brace Jovanovich, 1970).

[3] Bertrand de Jouvenel, *On Power: Its Nature and the History of Its Growth* (Boston: Beacon Press; 1962).

destroying the hope of amity and confederation, the communal bond and the ancient vision of the good society as an extrapolation from family, is one villain in this tale. Another is rationalized cowardice, shame, and ingratitude hidden behind the disguise of self-sufficiency or the mask of injured merit. Interdependence, which secures dignity and makes of equality a mere irrelevance, is the principal victim. Where fraternity exists to support the official structure of a government, it can command assent with no fear of being called despotic or prejudiced in behalf of one component of the society it represents. But behind the cult of equality (the chief if not only tenet in Professor Jaffa's theology, and his link to the pseudo-religious politics of ideology) is an even more sinister power, the uniformitarian hatred of providential distinctions which will stop at nothing less than what Eric Voegelin calls "a reconstitution of being": a nihilistic impulse which is at bottom both frightened and vain in its rejection of a given contingency and in its arrogation of a godlike authority to annul that dependency.[4] As Robert Penn Warren has recently reminded us, distinctions drawn from an encounter with an external reality have been the basis for the intellectual life as we have known it: prudent and tentative distinctions, but seriously intended.[5] With the reign of equality all of that achievement is set at peril.

II

So much in prologue. Concerning equality Professor Jaffa and I disagree profoundly; disagree even though we both denominate ourselves conservative. Yet this distinction does not finally exhaust or explain our differences. For Jaffa's opening remarks indicate that his conservatism is of a relatively recent variety and is, in substance, the Old Liberalism hidden under a Union battle flag. To the contrary I maintain that if conservatism has any identity

---

4 Eric Voegelin, *Science, Politics and Gnosticism* (Chicago: Henry Regnery Co., 1968), 99-100.

5 Robert Penn Warren, "Democracy and Poetry," *Southern Review,* XI (January 1975), 28.

whatsoever beyond mere recalcitrance and rationalized self-interest, that identity must incorporate the "funded wisdom of the ages" as that deposition comes down through a particular national experience. Despite modifications within the prescription of a continuum of political life, only a relativist or historicist could argue that American conservatism should be an utterly unique phenomenon, without antecedents which predate 1776 and unconnected with the mainstream of English and European thought and practice known to our forefathers in colonial times. Jaffa of course nods toward one face of Locke and, by implication, the chiliastic politics of Cromwell's New England heirs.[6] And I have no doubt that he can add to this hagiography a selective (and generally misleading) list of earlier patrons of his view. I cannot in this space encounter the full spectrum of Straussian rationalism. To specify what I believe to be lacking in Jaffa's conservative model (and wrong with the intellectual history he uses in its validation), it will serve better for me to concentrate first on how I read the Declaration of Independence and then append, in abbreviated form, my estimation of Lincoln's lasting and terrible impact on the nation's destiny through his distortions upon that text. This of course involves me incidentally in Jaffa's quarrel with Kendall/Carey and *The Basic Symbols of the American Political Tradition*. But it must be understood that my object is not to defend these worthy gentlemen. To the contrary, my primary interest is in a more largely conservative view of the questions over which they and Professor Jaffa disagree. And therefore, incidentally with the operation and quality of my adversary's mind which lead him to conclusions so very different from mine. With those concerns I propose to organize and conclude my remarks.

III

Professor Jaffa begs a great many questions in his comment on the Declaration. But his greatest mistake is an open error, and

---

6 See my "A Writ of Fire and Sword: The Politics of Oliver Cromwell," in No. 3 of *The Occasional Review* (Sumer, 1975), 61-80.

supported by considerable precedent in both academic and political circles. In truth, his approach is an orthodox one, at least in our radical times. I refer to his treatment of the second sentence of that document in abstraction from its whole: indeed, of the first part of that sentence in abstraction from its remainder, to say nothing of the larger text. Jaffa filters the rest of the Declaration (and later expressions of the American political faith) back and forth through the measure of that sentence until he has (or so he imagines) achieved its baptism in the pure waters of the higher law. He quotes Lincoln approvingly that "the doctrine of human equality was 'the father of all moral principle [amongst us].'"[7] Jaffa sets up a false dilemma: we must be, as a people, "committed" to Equality or we are "open to the relativism and historicism that is the theoretical ground of modern totalitarian regimes." The Declaration is, of course, the origin of that commitment to "permanent standards." And particularly the second sentence. The trouble here comes from an imperfect grasp of the Burkean calculus. And from the habit of reading legal, poetic, and rhetorical documents as if they were bits of revealed truth or statements of systematic thought. My objections derive primarily from those antirationalist realms of discourse. For I assume, with Swift, that man is a creature capable of reason, *capax rationis*, but not a rational animal. Therefore the head and heart must be engaged together where instruction is attempted. The burden of poetry and rhetoric is inherent in the form through which that idea is embodied: its meaning *is* its way of meaning, not a discursive paraphrase. And it achieves that meaning as it unfolds. According to this procedure we are taught from of old that the soul may be composed, the sensibility reordered. Reason enters into this process with modesty and draws its sanction for

---

[7] Doctrine is a loaded word. It is here suggestive of theology, revealed truth; though Lincoln means by it the kind of demonstrable "abstract truth" of the sort Jefferson "embalmed" into a "merely revolutionary document." See Lincoln's letter to Messrs. Henry Pierce & Others, April 6, 1859, on 374-376 of Vol. III of *The Collected Works of Abraham Lincoln* (New Brunswick, N. J.: Rutgers University Press, 1953). The usage is thus a device for "having it both ways;" as does Jaffa when claiming that the commandments of Sinai are knowable by unassisted human reason. For the commandments are explained only in Christ, a scandal to the Greeks.

whatever new truth it may advance from cooperation with sources and authorities that need produce no credentials nor prove up any title with the audience assumed. For in poetry as in law and rhetoric all matters are not in question. There is a prescription, or something equivalent to what Burke calls by that name. And usually a theology to channel and gloss the prescript. Tropes and figures, terms weighted more or less by usage, norms of value configured and dramatic sequences of associated actions discovered through an unbroken stream of place and blood and history operate in this mode of communication as something logically prior to the matter under examination. And likewise the law, especially where the rule is *stare decisis*. Where myth or precedent or some other part of the "wise prejudice" of a people is presupposed and identity therefore converted into a facet of ontology, a providential thing ("inalienable" 'in that word's oldest sense, not to be voted, given, or reasoned away), there is nothing for mere philosophy to say. And that philosophe abstraction, political Man, who once theoretically existed outside a social bond, nowhere to be seen. As a wise man wrote, "Where the great interests of mankind are concerned through a long succession of generations, that succession ought to be admitted into some share in the councils which are so deeply to affect them."[8] For the "moral essences" that shape a commonwealth are "not often constructed after any theory: theories are rather drawn from them"—the natural law, made partially visible only in the prescription, but made visible nonetheless.[9]

IV

To anyone familiar with English letters and the English mind in the seventeenth and eighteenth centuries, the Declaration of Independence is clearly a document produced out of the *mores majorum*—legal, rhetorical, poetic and not a piece of reasoning or systematic truth. No sentence of its whole means anything

---

8   Edmund Burke, *Reflections on the Revolution in France* (Chicago: Henry Regnery Co., 1955), 240.
9   *Ibid.*

out of context. It unfolds *seriatim* and makes sense only when read through. Furthermore, what it does mean is intelligible only in a matrix of circumstances—political, literary, linguistic, and mundane. Nevertheless, no one trained to move in the rhetorical world of Augustan humanism would take it for a relativistic statement any more than they would describe Dryden's *Religio Laici*, Addison's *Cato*, Johnson's *Rasselas*, or Burke's *Reflections on the Revolution in France* in that fashion.[10] Jaffa revives the error of his master, Leo Strauss, in speaking of the bugbear historicism and of "mere prescriptive rights."[11] For it is in our day the alternatives which carry with them a serious danger of the high sounding despot. Radicals (to use his term, meaning the Liberals who see in politics a new "Queen of the Sciences" and employ a sequence of private revelations to exalt her condition) believe in a "higher law"—have done so at least since the politics of secularized Puritanism first appeared in European society.[12] Even Marxists finally worship the—demiurge of history—and rest the remainder of their argument upon that authority. And the goddess Reason is still with us, available to sanction whatever her hand finds to do in erasing all that survives from what Peter Gay rightly labels the mythopoeic vision.[13] I agree with Professor Jaffa concerning the danger of relativism. A Christian must. And

---

10   I borrow from the title of Paul Fusell's, *The Rhetorical World of Augustan Humanism* (Oxford: The Clarendon Press; 1965). In the same connection see J. R. Bolton's, *The Language of Politics in the Age of Wilkes and Burke* (Toronto: University of Toronto Press, 1963).

11   See Jaffa's *Equality & Liberty: Theory and Practice in American Politics* (New York: Oxford University Press, 1965), 122; and Leo Strauss' *Natural Right and History* (Chicago: University of Chicago Press, 1953), 1-9.

12   Jaffa accepts the Puritan typology for the American venture. There are, we should remember, alternative formulations (*Equality & Liberty*, 116-117) formulations less infected with secularized eschatology. And if Jaffa pursues his analogue, he should remember that there was slavery in Israel and among the ancient Jews a racism so virulent that they considered some neighboring peoples too lowly even for enslavement and fit only for slaughter. Or too wicked (Indians, the Irish at Drogheda, etc.).

13   Peter Gay, *The Enlightenment: An Interpretation* (New York: Alfred A. Knopf, 1966), ix-xiv.

also about behavioristic political science. Such study is description only, or else mere manipulation. But, hunger for the normative aside, we must resist the tendency to thrust familiar contemporary pseudoreligious notions back into texts where they are unlikely to appear. Any Englishman of 1776 (colonial or not) should not be expected to construe natural rights so rigorously as Justice Black— except perhaps for hyperbole and in argument. In between our day and that first July 4 stand a number of revolutions; especially the French. And also two hundred years of liberal and radical thought. We are bemused by the spectre of Locke (an authority to some of the revolutionary generation, but read loosely and in the light of Sir Edward Coke and William Petyt, and the 1628 Petition of Right, and the 1689 Declaration of Rights).[14] The legacy of English common law is lost upon us. And in the process we have forgotten, among, other things, that Edmund Burke is our best guide to the main-line of Whig thought: *not Locke or Paine, or even Harrington, but Burke*. It is, of course, a truism that all colonial Americans did their political thinking inside the post1688 Whig legal tradition.[15] Some years ago Professor Jaffa attempted to counter this line of objection to his Lincolnian construction of the Declaration by setting Paine and Locke (plus an irrelevant bit of Blackstone) upon Daniel J. Boorstin's excellent *The Americans: The Colonial Experience*. But in so doing he only evaded his antagonist and obfuscated the question of what is typically Whig and behind our "revolution."[16] For Locke is not so consistent a source of equal rights as Jaffa would lead us to believe. Indeed, that worthy theorist of liberty was an eager part to the creation of

---

14   See Maurice Ashley, *The Glorious Revolution of 1688* (New York: Scribner's, 1966), 97-106.

15   And this of course includes certain established rights, plus a balance between the values of liberty and community. I do not mean to minimize the value of these achievements. Clearly I identify with them.

16   *Equality & Liberty*, 114-139. For correction (in some respects),see Leonard Woods Labaree's *Conservatism in Early America* (Ithaca: Cornell University Press. 1959), 119-122; and Clinton Rossiter's *The Seedtime of the Republic* (New York: Harcourt, Brace & World, 1953), especially 345; also Ashley, *op. cit.*, 193:198.

a slaveocracy in South Carolina.[17] And on occasion he justified the peculiar institution with nothing more sophisticated than an appeal to race or right of conquest.[18] Blackstone, for his part, was a high Tory and a poor sponsor for equality of any sort. And Paine relates to very little that became American in our Constitution of 1787. Recent scholarship on early American history has, by and large, exhibited an anachronistic tendency to ignore all patriot utterances that do not sound like Locke in his highest flights of freedom or Paine before the Mountain: like the Whig "Left," in other words.[19] They have ignored the problems in logic set up by "all men are created equal" when understood as one of Lincoln's beloved Euclidian propositions and the larger problems for libertarians determined not to call for equality of condition when they start from such a postulate.[20] Along with the political philosophers they have approached the task of explication as if the Declaration

---

17 "David Duncan Wallace, *South Carolina: A Short History, 1520-1948* (Columbia: University of South Carolina Press, 1966), 25.

18 John Locke, *Two Treatises of Government: A Critical Edition with Introduction and Apparatus Criticus*, edited by Peter Laslett (Cambridge, England, 1960), 159.

19 For examples consider Bernard Bailyn's *The Ideological Origins of the American Revolution* (Cambridge, MA: Harvard University Press, 1967); and Gordon S.Wood's *The Creation of the American Republic, 1776-1787* (Chapel Hill, University of North Carolina Press, 1964). Somewhat better are H. Trevor Colhoum's *The Lamp of Experience: Whig History and the Intellectual Origins of the American Revolution* (Chapel Hill: University of North Carolina Press, 1965); and Merrill Jensen's *The Founding of a Nation:The American Revolution, 1763-1776* (New York: Oxford University Press, 1968). These last two books are especially good on the "reluctant rebels," who were Burkean, not Lockean Whigs, postualting law, not a state of nature (*i. e.* where a full scale, new contract can be drawn). See also Wallace (*op. cit.*, 273) for an account of the prescriptive South Carolina patriot—William Henry Drayton.

20 In strict logic there is a problem with quantification if the proposition is supposed to be universal: a universal proposition would read "every man is created equal to every other man." Jefferson's phrase is merely a loose generalization, when seen in this light. For the libertarian the trouble goes the other way around: if all men are by nature equal (morally, in will, intellect, etc.) then only circumstance can explain the inequalities which develop. And these circumstances are thus offences against nature and the

existed *sui generis*, in a Platonic empyrean.[21] A gloss upon what transpired in a real (i.e. intellectually "messy") convention in a real Philadelphia seems not to interest these sages: what with reason could be expected to occur.[22] With a non-Lockean Whig machinery (and as a practicing rhetorician) I will attempt to draw the inquiry down toward such probabilities.

V

Contrary to Professor Jaffa, it is my view that the Declaration of Independence is not very revolutionary at all. Nor the Revolution itself. Nor the Constitution. Only Mr. Lincoln and those who gave him support, both in his day and in the following century. And the moralistic, verbally disguised instrument which Lincoln invented may indeed be the most revolutionary force in the modern world: a pure gnostic force.[23] The Declaration confirms an existing state of affairs, even in its announcement of a break with George III. For the colonies existed as distinctive commonwealths with (and out of) English law. Yet they were English with a difference. It required only a fracturing of spiritual bonds that it be made official. In the spring and summer of 1776 things came to a head. As Jefferson wrote, a British army was descending upon Long Island: an army bent on putting an end to petitions, inquiries, declarations, and all such irritants. The King had declared the members of the Continental Congress rebels, without the law. And likewise those who thought themselves represented by that body. No security

---

Divine Will—offences demanding correction. What some libertarians try to get out of "created equal" is "created unequal, but given an equal start." Jefferson's phrase will not submit to this.

21 An exception is Russell Kirk's *The Root of American Order* (La Salle, Ill.: Open Court, 1974).

22 One has the temptation to say, as Socrates did of the rhapsode in Plato's *Ion*, that they understood the subject not by art or knowledge but by "inspiration."

23 I began to develop this view in "Lincoln's New Frontier: A Rhetoric for Continuing Revolution," *Triumph*, VI, No. 5 (May 1971), 11-13 and 21; VI, No. 6 (June 1971), 15-17. I use the term from Eric Voegelin's *New Science of Politics* (Chicago: University of Chicago Press, 1952).

from deportation for trial, summary executions and confiscation were the alternatives to unconditional submission and allegiance outside of the law.

Rhetorical criticism begins with a careful description of circumstances antedating composition.[24] For without that information well established, the meaning of language is uncertain; and a piece of literature may be treated as if it had been prepared only for the gods. Connection of a document with a set of writings made and/or exchanged before or after its appearance is certainly necessary information. There is no Declaration apart from it. Effacing himself, Thomas Jefferson wrote what completed a conversation concerning the law which had gone back and forth across the Atlantic years before exhausting its purpose. Everything in this sequence appeals to the *consensus gentium* of sensible men (common reasonableness, but not philosophy) and to English law. James II had set himself outside that rule, using the dispensary powers to invent a new equality of rights. This usurpation resulted in a royal "abdication" and a new king who promised to uphold the charters and ancient laws and thus to preserve to Englishmen and their posterity the rights they had inherited through a providentially blessed history. This was the common understanding of that period. It is implicit in the dialogue between Philadelphia and Whitehall and in the antecedent quarrel between the Crown and various colonial assemblies after the Stamp and Declaratory Acts and the Albany Congress. The American "parliament" first convened in September of 1774 and soon issued its "Declaration and Resolves of the First Continental Congress, October 14, 1774." Even there it is unmistakably clear that a composite identity is addressing a related composite identity, that the mode of address is forensic (determining praise or blame between respective parties in dispute over the meaning of a "given" phenomenon), and that the point of reference is not divine revelation or a body of doctrine maintained according to the precepts of philosophy, but rather a

---

24 For a chronicle of these events see Jensen (*op. cit.*) and Lawrence H. Gipson's *The Coming of the Revolution, 1763-1775* (New York: Harper & Brothers, 1954).

wisdom inherited as prescription, to be applied reasonably, but not in *Reason's* name. This particular declaration makes it plain that Englishmen are in dispute with Englishmen, groups with groups, and on English grounds. The colonial charters set up this situation. At law they connect the colonies to a paternal source, even while, they set them apart. They create an ambiguity in relations with the English parliament and the independent reality of other governments. And they leave law and king and common enemies to hold the mix together.[25]

In their first declaration we learn that the remonstrants are entitled to "life, liberty and property"; that these basic rights come from their ancestors (God perhaps acting through them); that removal over the sea can involve no alienation of such inherited rights; that such alienation is now proposed by way of taxation and by the machinery for enforcing that tax; and, finally, that kindred offences against "immunities and privileges granted and confirmed" by royal charters and "secured by their several codes of provincial law" are in prospect. Here and in the later (and similarly argued) "Declaration of the Causes and Necessities of Taking up Arms, July 6, 1775," we can recognise the lineaments of a position finally developed in July of 1776. And also a line of thought coming down directly from the Great Charter of 1689—or even more remotely from Bracton and Fortescue. The king is the king, the subject the subject, only within the law. The American colonies are by blood and law part of the English *res publica*, set apart from the old Island Kingdom by England's destruction of that organic relationship. To repeat, it is well to remember that the king declared them "rebels" (Prohibitory Acts, August 1775) well before they accepted that title for themselves. As they insist, it is for no "light or transient causes" that they make his appellation official. Their charters have become mere paper. By virtue of relocation across the seas they have been defined as alienated Englishmen, without security even in such fundamental matters as life, liberty, and the fruits of their labors. And all men recognise these rights

---

25 Charter and compact are usually synonyms in the language of the Whigs and usually imply a relation of unequals.

as being the precondition of submission to any government. Their fathers had, of course, grown violent over much smaller affronts. But the "authors" of the Declaration are determined to keep within the law and to appear as unusually conservative men. Only when the king denies them all representation, asserts his right to bind them *collectively*, to seize their goods *collectively*, to quarter an angry army upon them, and to punish their entreaties that he restrain his servants to observe the Bill of Rights—only then will they close with a last "appeal from reason to arms."

VI

We are now prepared to ask what Mr. Jefferson and his sensible friends meant by "all men" and "created equal." Meant together— *as a group*. In rhetoric, it is a rule to ask how the beginning leads through the middle to the end. If end and beginning consort well with one another, if they point in one direction, that agreement defines what may be discovered in between.[26] The last three-fourths of the Declaration (minus the conclusion, its original draft) is a bill of particulars.[27] The king (their only acknowledged link with England) has decapitated the body politic and hence is no longer king on these shores. The law/prescription cannot otherwise be preserved. And these men intend such a preservation. Something in existence declares itself in possession of "honor" and "sensible of the regard of decent men," prepared to draw a new charter out of those it possesses, to act as an entity in forming a confederal government. But first these commonwealths must file an official bill of divorcement, designed to the pattern of a countersuit in an action already initiated on the other side. The generation of a new

---

26 There is no room for "secret writing" in public declarations.

27 I cite volume I of Julian P. Boyd's edition of *The Papers of Thomas Jefferson* (Princeton: Princeton University Press, 1950), 315-319 and 414-433. Carl Becker in his valuable *The Declaration of Independence: A Study in the History of Politics and Ideas* (New York: Vintage Press, 1958), argues unreasonably that this bill of particulars is not really important to the meaning of the Declaration. He was, however, as we should remember, an admirer of the *philosophes*—and no rhetorician.

head for this body is not yet, but will, we can assume, present no problem when a necessity for its creation is made explicit.[28]

The exordium of the Declaration begins this appeal with an argument from history and with a definition of the voice addressing the "powers of the earth!" It is a "people," a "we" that are estranged from another "we." The peroration reads the same: "we," the "free and independent states," are united in our will to separation—and prepared to answer to high and low for that temerity. They act in the name (and with the sanction) of the good people whose several assemblies had authorized their congregation. This much formally. No contemporary liberal, new or old, can make use of that framework or take the customary liberties with what is contained by the construction. Nor coming to it by the path I have marked, may they, in honesty, see in "created equal" what they devoutly wish to find. "We," in that second sentence, signifies the colonials as the citizenry of the distinct colonies, not as individuals, but rather in their corporate capacity. Therefore, the following "all men"—created equal in their right to expect from any government to which they might submit freedom from corporate bondage, genocide, and massive confiscation—are persons prudent together, respectful of the law which makes them one, even though forced to stand henceforth apart: equal as one free state is as free as another.

Nothing is maintained concerning the abilities or situations of individual persons living within the abandoned context of the British Empire or the societies to be formed by its disruption. No new contract is drawn. Rather, one that exists is *preserved by amputation*. All that is said is that no component of a society can be expected to agree, even though it is part of that society by inheritance, that it is to be bereft of those securities that make life tolerable simply by geographical remoteness. And, if even the Turk and infidel would not as a people submit to a government

---

[28] The image here is drawn from one of the Fathers of English law, from chapter 13 of the *De Laudibus Legum Angliae* (1471) of Sir John Fortescue (Cambridge, England: Cambridge University Press, 1949), the edition and translation by S. B. Chrimes.

such as George III proposes to impose through Lord Howe's army, how can Englishmen be expected to agree to that arrangement? So much is "obvious" to everyone, in other words, "self-evident." Thus even if the law of nature and of nations is drawn into our construction of "endowed by their Creator," what is left to be called "inalienable" with respect to American colonials and demonstrative of a certain minimal equality of rights in their collectivities is not so much. What happens in the remainder of the Declaration, following sentence two, is even more depressing to the contemporary Jacobin who would see in the new beginning a departure from the previous political history of Western man. Note particularly the remarks concerning the part played by the king's servants in encouraging a "servile insurrection," the xenophobic objections to the use of foreign mercenaries, and the allusion to the employment of savages as instruments of royal policy. Note also Jefferson's ironic reference to "Christian Kings" and anger at offences to the "common blood." These passages draw upon a received identity and are not "reasonable" in character. Certainly they do not suggest the equality of individual men. But (and I am sure Professor Jaffa will agree with me on this), even though racist, xenophobic, and religious assumptions have no place in the expression of philosophic truth, they can readily operate in an appeal to prescriptive law. And therefore, I say, in our Declaration of Independence.

VII

Though I agree with Kendall/Carey that there is a distance between the Declaration and the Constitution of 1787, and that silence on equality in the latter reflects a conscious choice, I agree also with Professor Jaffa that the two are not in conflict. The Constitution, like the Articles of Confederation before it, built a structure of common government (to handle all difficulties made by being one and thirteen) upon a common legal inheritance, common origins, and an established unity of purpose. It is a limited contract, resting on an external and prior bond of free and independent states, perfecting or improving their union.[29] It does not abrogate what it rests upon. The Declaration was a necessary prologue to it's adoption. But, in logic, the Declaration is not implicit in the Constitution except as it made possible free ratification by the independent states. In truth, many rights are secured under the Constitution that are not present in the Declaration, however it be construed. Yet not equal voting rights in state or federal elections. Or economic rights in taxation. Or rights for women. Or even equal footing for various religions—or species of irreligion. To say nothing of slaves. All of this is well known. But, if we reasoned as do some gifted scholars, it might be maintained that the Constitution takes us even further away from equality for slaves than does the Declaration.[30]

---

29   Jaffa's argument that one national Union was decided upon in 1774-1776 or before is easily refuted by John R. Alden's *The First South* (Baton Rouge: Louisiana State University, 1969), in Alden's *The South in the Revolution, 1763-1789* (Baton Rouge: Louisiana University Press, 1957), and in Donald L. Robinson's *Slavery in the Structure of American Politics, 1765-1820* (New York: Harcourt Brace Jovanovich, 1971), 146 *et passim*. More than one Union has always been a possibility to be entertained by deliberate men. See Staughton Lynd's "The Abolitionist Critique of the United States Constitution," in the *Antislavery Vanguard: New Essays on the Abolitionists*, ed. Martin Duberman (Princeton: Princeton University Press, 1965), 210-239.

30   For instance, Professor Jaffa in forcing the notion of a Union before the Constitution into the "We the People" of the Preamble. Few scholars deny that the people acted through the states to ratify—as they had to form a Constitutional Convention. To this day they act through the states to amend. They existed at law through the maintenance of their several freedoms in battle. They formed the Confederation. The Declaration was only a negative precondition to a Union and to the firmer connection that followed. Underneath all of this may stand an unwritten Constitution, joining the partners of the Declaration in more ways than are specified in 1787. And perhaps also committing them to other ends: ends which Professor Jaffa would not care to consider. That compact was the prescription which sanctioned the Continental Congress—a creature of the chartered colonies. If the Declaration commits to anything, it is to that prescription—a compact of "the living, dead, and yet unborn." The continued operation of a society united in such a compact constitutes assent, regardless of official legal relations. New members were the only ones who were "sworn in."

For in Article I, Section 9, provision is made that no law shall be passed by Congress to restrict the slave trade prior to 1808. Slavery exists by acknowledgment of the same document. Yet it encourages that there be more slaves in the Republic than are present in 1787. More in a proportion that twenty-one years can be expected to provide. Hence this provision can be described in logic as presenting Negro slavery as a positive good. For reasons of history I do not insist upon this commentary. The evidence of what lies behind the text suggests another view.[31] And for the same reasons I cannot follow the practical advice of the late Everett McKinley Dirksen and "get right with Lincoln."[32]

VIII

It would be unreasonable for me to attempt to develop in this essay all that I wish to say in objection to the politics of Abraham Lincoln. For it is a great deal and will perhaps involve some years. Therefore I must, in returning the courtesy of this review, raise only my primary objections, most of them proceeding from Lincoln's misunderstanding of the Declaration as a "deferred promise" of equality. I am of course close to the late Professor Kendall in these matters and have learned much from him and from Professor Carey.[33] For one thing, I agree with those gentlemen that Lincoln's "second founding" is fraught with peril and carries with it the prospect of an endless series of turmoils and revolutions, all dedicated to freshly discovered meanings of equality as a "proposition." I do not, however, look so much

---

31 For instance the 32 acts passed by colonial Virginia's House of Burgesses which called for a restriction of trade, all of them negated by the Crown at the behest of Northern traders. Reports of the Constitutional Convention of 1787 indicate the same sort of pressures, resolved there by reasonable men determined to close out a divisive subject.

32 See "Getting Right with Lincoln," 3-18 of David Donald's *Lincoln Reconsidered* (New York: Vintage Press, 1961).

33 And especially from Kendall's "Equality: Commitment or Ideal?" *Phalanx* I (Fall 1967), 95-103, which answers some of Jaffa's complaints about Kendall's silences. I find it curious that Jaffa does not mention this piece.

as they do to New England. It is not my preference for a colonial precedent to the national identity.[34] The millenarian infection spread and almost institutionalized by Lincoln (and by the manner of his death) has its impetus from that "other Israel" surrounding Boston.[35] And its full potential for mischief is yet to be determined. What Alexander Stephens called Lincoln's "religious mysticism" of Union, when combined in "cold, calculating reason" to the goal of "equal rights" and an authoritarian (that is, irrational) biblical rhetoric, constitutes a juggernaut powerful enough to arm and enthrone any self-made Caesar we might imagine: even an unprepossessing country lawyer from Illinois. For by means of that mixture and solution a transfer of authority and energy is effected, from the Puritan dream of a New Jerusalem governed by an elect to the manifest destiny of American democracy led by keepers of the popular faith. Both are authorized from on High to reform the world into an imitation of themselves—and to lecture and dragoon all who might object. Both receive regular intimations of the Divine Will through prophets who arise from time to time to recall them to their holy mission. And both operate from that base to paint all prospective opposition in the darkest of colors, the rhetoric of polarity being a fundamental correlative of all genuinely Puritan activity, with no room for shadings in between and no mercy for the wicked.

This is, of course, not to minimize the role played in Lincoln's rise to power by the tireless "engine" of his ambition. Nor his political gifts—for which I have an ever-growing admiration. As is announced obliquely in the "Address Before the Springfield Young Men's Lyceum, 1838," Lincoln was, very early, touched by a Bonapartist sense of destiny. His papers (all ten volumes, plus a recent supplement) reflect a steady purpose, an inexorable

---

34   Except for reasons of strategy (guilt by association), I cannot see why Jaffa identifies *Basic Symbols of the American Tradition* with the South. For Kendall and Carey begin with Massachusetts and Connecticut.

35   See 226 of Jaffa's own *Crisis of the House Divided*.

will to rise, to put his stamp upon the world.³⁶ Yet there was always another side to his nature—glum, ironic, pessimistic, self-deprecatory: in a word, inscrutable. It has deceived and puzzled many. Yet, as is ordinary in a Puritan, this meandering reflected private doubt of the wisdom behind personal choices and (perhaps) the status of motives which directed him toward their enactment: self-doubt, but not doubt of ideals. And he knew how to cure the ailment—by "striving to finish the work." He had his ends in mind, his religion of Union *in* Equality, but he left it to the "providential" flow of history to carry them to realization. However, after 1854 he condescended to give that flow a little help. The Kansas-Nebraska Act made the political career of Abraham Lincoln, opened the door for the "Reign of Reason," made it possible to put behind the "living history" of the revolutionary generation ("oaks," an organic image), and provided for an opportunity to roll out the big guns of priestly language to give what he meant by "freedom" that "new birth" he came to speak of at Gettysburg. He played with consummate skill the circumstances of free-soil reaction in '54 and then the tumult surrounding the campaigns of '58 and '60. Nor are there many scholars who do not find some mystery or subtle craft in his first months as President, to say nothing of his subsequent conduct. But that story, as I read it, is a large book—larger than Professor Jaffa's. Suffice it to say that Lincoln was indeed a man whose "policy was to have no policy."³⁷ He loved to quote from Hamlet that "there is

---

36 See Edmund Wilson's *Patriotic Gore: Studies in the Literature of the American Civil War* (New York: Oxford University Press, 1962), 99-130. Surely Wilson cannot be mistaken in arguing that Lincoln saw himself in his portrait of the "new founder." For Lincoln clearly knows the animal he describes on a more intimate basis than mere speculation or observation could provide. Wilson compares Lincoln (pp xvi-xx) to Bismarck and Lenin—the other great founders of our age. Another useful analogue (a firm higher-law man, and no legalist or historicist) is Adolph Hitler. For he writes in *Mein Kampf* that "human rights break state rights," calls for illegal as well as legal instruments in "wars of rebellion against enslavement within and without," observes that all governments by oppression plead the law, and concludes, "I believe today that I am acting in the sense of the Almighty Creator ... fighting for the Lord's work." (I cite the edition of 1938, published in New York by Reynal and Hitchcock, 122-23 and 84).

37 Donald, *op. cit.*, 31.

a divinity that shapes our ends,/Rough-hew them how we will/."[38] And from the total pattern of his conduct we can extract the following formula: Wait, set up or encourage pressure, then jump, and call it God. The original behind this procedure could be any one of a dozen historic tyrants, all of whom announced a noble purpose for their acts. But when the pattern is encapsulated by the high idiom of Holy Scripture (the authority of which no man can examine), the Anglo-Saxon prototype emerges as Oliver Cromwell, the Lord Protector. And in searching for what is significant in that analogy, the logical point of departure is the House-Divided speech to the Illinois Republican convention of June, 1858.

IX

Lincoln's political gnosticism does not come to a head in the House-Divided speech, and does not begin there. For even in the Springfield Lyceum, address (made when he was twenty-nine), he concludes on a Puritan note: Let us refound the Union, and "the gates of hell shall not prevail against it." The new founder, having propped up the temple of Liberty/Equality on the solid pillars of "calculating reason," will therefore be, in relation to the powers of evil (*i.e.*, those who do not care for the arrangement) as was the faith of Peter to the Christian church after its foundation. And God is thus, by implication, the security for the quasi-religion of Equality. In a similar fashion Lincoln finds God as a verification for his rectitude as President in his address to Northern moderates, men who loved the old "divided" house, which we find in his Second Inaugural. Here is the heresy of a "political religion" at the beginning of Lincoln's political career, and also at its end. But one prudent shift is observable. Except for an occasional mention of "propositions" or their equivalent, the debt to European rationalism (the source of Lincoln's puzzling theological heterodoxy), fades into the background once Honest Abe appears on the center of the national stage in Peoria, Illinois (October,

---

38   Roy P. Basler, *The Touchstone of Greatness: Essays, Addresses and Occasional Pieces about Abraham Lincoln* (Westport, Conn.: Greenwood Press, 1973), 206-207.

1854). And in the opposite direction the biblical element grows to be more and more dominant after 1858. But we should not infer from this that Lincoln's design changed after he got the Republican nomination against Douglas. Only his perception (drawing from the abolitionists) of the proper instrument for its execution.

The House-Divided speech was, beyond any question, a Puritan declaration of war. And therefore also Lincoln's election on the basis of its contents as transcribed in the Republican platform of 1860. A Lincoln admirer, Don E. Fehrenbacher, in his *Prelude to Greatness: Lincoln in the 1850's*, calls it "Garrisonian."[39] The South saw it that way, as did much of the North. And neither forgot those words:

> A House Divided against itself cannot stand. I believe this government cannot endure, perpetually half slave and half free. I do not expect the Union to be dissolved—I do not expect the house to fall—but I do expect it will cease to be divided. It will become all one thing, or all another.

Yet we should not abstract the speech from the intellectual milieu to which it belongs. By means of his political manipulation, Lincoln, in the words of his one-time friend, Alexander Stephens, "put the institution of nearly one-half the states under the ban of public opinion and national condemnation." And, continued Stephens, "this, upon general principle, is quite enough of itself to rouse a spirit not only of general indignation, but of revolt on the part of the proscribed."[40] Other people in these days made noises like Lincoln. After 1854 they got a good hearing. One of them, old John Brown, received beatification from the Northern newspapers which supported Mr. Lincoln in 1860. What this juxtaposition sig-

---

39   Jaffa praises Fehrenbacher's work.

40   *A Constitutional View of the Late War Between the States* (Philadelphia: National Publishing Co., 1868), Vol. II, 266.

nified, despite certain cluckings of disapproval among Republican stalwarts, no one could mistake.

Of course the central motif of the House-Divided speech, as quoted above echoes the Bible (Mark 3:25): Christ speaking of the undivided hosts of Satan.[41] Lincoln's authority is thus, by association, elevated to the level of the hieratic. But he adds something to the mixture. The myth that slavery will be either set on its way to extinction by an official gesture on the part of the federal government or else all states will eventually become slave-states establishes a false dilemma, describes a set of conditions which, once fixed in the minds of his freesoil audience, was certain to create in them a sense of alarm. Thus he participates in what Richard Hofstadter calls the "paranoid style" in politics.[42] Fear of the slave power (Southern political and economic domination) and racist hostility to the idea of massive Negro influx, free *or* slave, into the North made predictable that one of these alternatives would be perceived as intolerable—and we can guess which one. Thus the size of the Republican Party might be augmented from the ranks of persons who despised Abolition and all its works.

For Lincoln to say after 1858 that the Constitution and the laws were sacred to him, that he would "preserve" the "old Union of the Fathers," is mere window dressing. For to argue that your enemy is evil incarnate (the burden of his rhetoric) in league with Satan, and then add that you respect him and his legal rights is to indulge in pietistic arrogance—as Alexander Stephens specified in the passage I quoted just above. Jaffa confuses matters no end in maintaining that Lincoln addressed a real danger in his imaginary "division." As the South perceived the question, the real issue in Kansas and Nebraska was whether or not there could be a federal policy on

---

41   Lincoln's use of this passage is curious. For, as the context makes clear, Christ's point in setting up the dichotomy is that the devil would not help his servants to ruin his own plans.

42   See David Brion Davis's *The Slave Power and the Paranoid Style* (Baton Rouge: Louisiana State University Press, 1969), especially 10-11.

the "morality" of its conduct in any connection not covered by the original federal covenant: whether they could stay under the gun.

For *houses are always divided, in some fashion or another.* And, no doubt, should slavery be gone, some new infamy was bound to be discovered by the stern examiners whose power depends upon a regularity in such "crusades." A law prohibiting slavery in the territories; in that it affected the ability of a new state to grow to maturity as a child of the total Union, would define the South as outside of that communion. Furthermore, it would set in motion a chain of circumstances that could be used against the region in any connection where antinomian morality could be read into law—could touch slavery or any other "peculiarity," unless a Constitutional amendment (requiring a three-fourths vote of the states) existed to protect it. A Union of this sort was not the old Union. Nor was its issue, a Union by force—in 1865 or *now*. Whatever the intent of armies in blue it could not be the same—not the contract ratified by all the states who were party to it. Rather, it involved Lincoln's worship of the law as the Constitution *with the Declaration drafted into (and over) it*—Lincoln's Declaration: and therefore (*vide supra*), no worship of the law whatsoever, but instead devotion to perpetually exciting goals, always just beyond our reach. Thus, under the aegis of a plurality president, the principle of assent is put aside for the sake of an idea (read ideology) which only a small minority of Americans could be expected to approve, either in 1860 or today. And the entire project accomplished by rhetoric—Kendall's "magic." On the record of American history since 1858, Lincoln stands convicted as an enemy of the "founding."[43] Which is to say, as our new Father— even though many of us still refuse to live in the cold uniformitarian temple he designed.

Of course, military resistance to radical Union (i.e., statism covered by a patina of law) ended in 1865. Lincoln saluted these developments at the beginning of his second term. And I must

---

43 I use quotation marks because I deny that they were ever founded, in the term's strict sense.

conclude my remarks on Lincoln's politics with some observations on that address. His conduct in using the presidential powers has been treated to my satisfaction by Gottfried Dietze.[44] What that conduct amounts to is the creation of an Eastern priest/king—an epideictic personage such as we hear in the voice at Gettysburg. Speech and deeds together did change the country—and in respects more important than the abolition of Negro slavery: together opened the door to portentous changes that finally touch even liberty.[45] The argument of this essay is, in sum, that what Lincoln did to preserve the Union by expanding and enshrining equality left the prescription of the revolution of law in our national beginning and the "unwritten constitution" of our positive pluralism very much in doubt. Such was his purpose. But (and I again repeat) this plan is something which he concealed until he prepared the Second Inaugural—where in victory he became a scripture in himself.

X

There is of course a clear conflict between the Cooper Union speech, the First Inaugural, Lincoln's letters of the time, and the posture Lincoln assumed a few weeks before Lee's surrender. If we would discover in Father Abraham the "crafty Machievel," the conflict between his assent to a constitutional amendment making slavery "perpetual" where established and the House-Divided speech is our point of departure. But the Lincoln who kept Kentucky and Missouri from secession is hard to penetrate. It is wise to assume that he followed the times. For it cannot be demonstrated that he ever really attempted to pacify Southern anxieties without reconstituting the Republic. Certainly he wanted

---

[44] *America's Political Dilemma: From Limited to Unlimited Democracy* (Baltimore: Johns Hopkins University Press, 1968), 17-62. He is supported by papers published in the *National Review* by the late Frank Meyer (Aug. 24, 1965; Jan. 25, 1966).

[45] Liberty is clearly the American value of greatest traditional authority—meaning "liberty to be ourselves," a nation which assumes an established, inherited identity. On the part played by the Gettysburg Address in this process see my *Triumph* essay cited above.

no peace on any grounds but unconditional surrender. And in 1865, he looked back his five years as national leader, "scanned the providences," and "found himself approved."

When seen in the context of his career after 1858 and within the pattern of lifetime of deliberate utternaces, Lincoln's Second Inaugural turns out to be something very different from what most America have believed it to be: a completion of a pattern announced in the House-Divided speech, unfolded in its fullness at Gettysburg, and glossed in a letter to Thurlow Weed written just before his death. Historically, the misconception of this performance may be attributed to a disproportionate emphasis upon the final paragraph of the Second Inaugural treated (once again) as if it had an independent existence outside the total document. Furthermore, what Lincoln means by "malice toward none" and "bind up the nation's wounds" is, even within this single paragraph, modified beyond recognition by "as God gives us to see the right." For he means here revelation, not conscience. Americans are so accustomed, since Lincoln's time, to a quasi-religious rhetoric in their public men that the combination has passed without notice for a century and more. But to discover its full meaning we must look up into the body of the speech. There it becomes clear what Lincoln is about behind his mild forensic tone.

Said another way, what I here contend is that the attribution of his own opinions to an antinomian revelation of divine will as regards America's political destiny more completely and intensively visible in this particular Lincoln document than in any other. For what he does in the Second Inaugural is to expand the outreach of his rhetorical manicheanism beyond the limits made familiar to us in a thousand expressions of piety toward the Union (and most particularly at Gettysburg) to include not only his obviously beaten enemies in the South but also all those who accepted the Union as it had existed from the Founding until 1860. Indeed, the targets of his rhetoric on this occasion are all moderate Unionists who did not aforetimes recognise, as did their prophet for the day, the necessity for a greater perfection in their bonds. The war was long, says Father Abraham, not simply because the rebels were wicked but furthermore because many of their adversaries were reluctant. In the letter to Weed (March 15, 1865) Lincoln observes, in speaking of the unpopularity he expects to be the fate of the remarks in question, that "men are not flattered by being shown that there has been a difference of purpose between the Almighty and them. To deny it, however, in this case, is to deny that there is a God governing the world."[46] Since no Southerners were present to be offended by the Second Inaugural, and since Lincoln's teaching in that address refers chiefly to those who had been patient with the divided house, it is evident that his targets in interpreting long war and heavy judgment are those who did not see *before secession* the necessity of conflict. How this reading of the American teleology could be expected to bind up wounds in any conventional sense is difficult to determine. But the end result is to give Lincoln a rhetorical upper hand he had not sought at any point in his presidency and to prepare him to do whatever he means by "finish the work." It is to leave him, finally, alone as the agent of his master, beyond the most ultra-Republicans as an instrument of providence and with an authority few mortal men have ever aspired to hold in their hands. Death confirmed him (or rather, his design) in that condition. Consider for an illustration Edward M. Stanton's words after reading the Gettysburg Address to an 1868 political audience in Pennsylvania: "That is the: voice of God speaking through the lips of Abraham Lincoln.... You hear the voice of Father Abraham here tonight. Did he die in vain?"[47] Such politics are beyond reason, beyond law, though they may embody a rationalist objective. They are also Jaffa's model—from authority and passion. And with consequences I shall now consider.

XI

"Style," Sir Herbert Read once observed, "is the ultimate morality of mind." By style I would understand him to mean all the elements that go into the composition of a piece of rhetoric, its

---

[46] Lincoln, *Collected Works*, Volume VIII, 356.
[47] Donald, *op. cit.*, 8.

structural elements as well as its textural; and, in examining the "style" of this particular essay, I find an extraordinary laxity—which suggests that Professor Jaffa is not at his best. Indeed; I can hardly recognise here the consummate and ethical rhetorician of *Crisis of the House Divided*, a work which I obviously admire—though from a certain distance. The argument of this later essay is loose and meandering, like some ancient river that is constantly winding back on itself. Lincoln as a young legislative candidate once advocated (like a good, moneyminded Whig) the straightening of such rivers by cutting off the neck of the loops. In closing, I shall attempt to do the same for Mr. Jaffa's argument, if only to indicate the tortuous nature of the "moral" impulse which lay behind its composition.

In the first place, as my metaphor suggests, this is an old river, an ancient argument which need not be developed again in detail since everyone is familiar enough with its tenets (i.e., the equation of the social-contract theory with some theory of equality). What is new in this lengthy diatribe is no more than the ostensible targets of Professor Jaffa's' attack, Kendall and Carey. And indeed they could be a valid point of departure for an egalitarian like Professor Jaffa, since Kendall and Carey do define the true American political tradition as both conservative and hostile to Equality.

But unfortunately Kendall and Carey do not raise their standard on that spot of polemical ground where Professor Jaffa would like to do battle. They do not become overly preoccupied with slavery; and for obvious reasons Professor Jaffa would rather talk about slavery than the political documents which are the announced topic of *Basic Symbols*. And so he does, curving around obstacles to reach the sacred subject, turning his argument in that direction by charging that Kendall and Carey never mention the word in their study and that such an omission avoids the essential question of the American political experience.

He repeats this charge several times during the windings of his thesis, despite the fact that it is unfounded (pp. 479, 486 and 491). For an instance, he ignores the following comment on page

92 of *Basic Symbols*, a passage that raises perhaps a most difficult question for him to consider:

> However, the assembly that approved the Declaration would not subscribe to the denunciation of slavery that Jefferson sought to include, so that we might be led to believe that the signers were talking of equality of men in a sense far short of that which modern egalitarians hold.

Small wonder that Professor Jaffa's rhetorical river veers sharply away from this high ground. Was it forgotten or ignored in order to avoid the issue it raises? Whatever the reasons, it flows off in that direction, attacking Kendall's review of *Crisis of the House Divided*, a Kendall essay in which the issues are relevant to slavery and furthermore a matter of historical interpretation. Soon we are curling and gliding through familiar territory, much of it mythic in nature and therefore simpler and purer than life. In Jaffa's imaginary history of the United States, Jefferson is the drafter of the Declaration, but not the slaveholder who wrote in *Notes on the State of Virginia* of his suspicion that blacks "are inferior to the whites in the endowments both of body and mind" and that this "unfortunate difference of colour, and perhaps of faculty, is a powerful obstacle to the emancipation of these people"; and *certainly not* the Virginian who called "Equality" a "mere abstraction" and its devotees a "Holy Alliance." There, Locke is the philosopher of *The Second Treatise*, but not the man responsible for *Fundamental Constitutions for Carolina*. Antebellum slavery is a kind of Buchenwald;[48] and the United States Constitution is drafted with a tacit understanding that "all men are [really]

---

[48] This analogy smacks of Stanley Elkin's now discredited theory in *Slavery: A Problem in American Institutional Life* (Chicago: University of Chicago Press, 1959). For correction see Eugene D. Genovese's *Roll, Jordan Roll: The World the Slaves Made* (New York: Pantheon Books, 1974). Also consider the fact that Jews were proscribed under Hitler—all Jews, in the same way—while antebellum Southern blacks could be slaves or freemen or even slaveholders.

created equal," that this is a proposition with "constitutional status," in spite of the fact that the Constitution itself recognised the established legal institution of slavery and discouraged interpolation into its provisions of what is not clearly there. All of these oversimplifications ignore one overriding question, the question that Kendall and Carey raise and which Professor Jaffa is careful not to consider. Some "truths" are more important than the Truth. Even the Truth that we have a political tradition that is conservative and contrary to Lincoln. Thus, though the river of Professor Jaffa's argument seems erratic, its wanderings (like the wanderings of a real river) have a predictable pattern; they follow the course of least resistance. And it is in the pattern—tortuous and circuitous—that one can see the relationship between his "style" and his "ultimate morality of mind."

Yet we cannot entirely blame Professor Jaffa for these aberrations, this great falling away from scholarly rectitude and right reason. His errors are endemic among his kind—such Old Liberals as identify their politics with the Lincolnian precedent. As I have tried to indicate, such errors constitute what amounts to a "genetic flaw" within that intellectual tradition, a fracture impossible to heal. Trying to preserve property, secure tranquillity, and promote equal rights, all at the same time, insures that none of these purposes will be accomplished. And insures also a terrible, unremitting tension, both among those in power and among those whose hopes are falsely raised. Especially with persistence in thinking of men outside of all history that is not Lincoln, and apart from the durable communions of craft and friendship, faith and blood. It has been, however, a distinctive trait of American political thought to do its worst as it touches upon the Negro: to break down when unable to make it through the aforementioned impasse of objectives. Class struggle has been the result, to say nothing of race conflict. And that failing attaches by definition to the Republican identity, flawing it perhaps forever as a viable conservative instrument. Said another way, the more a people derive their political identity from Lincoln's version of Equality, the more they are going to push against the given and providential frame of things to prove up the magic of the phrase. And, therefore, the more they will (to repeat one of my favorite images) kick the "tar baby."⁴⁹ And we all know how that story ends.

---

49 "A Fire Bell in the Night: The Southern Conservative View," *Modern Age*, XVII (Winter 1973), 9-15. In these pages I maintain that an expansive view of "natural rights" with respect to Negroes has undermined our inherited constitutional system.

3.

Dividing the House:
The Gnosticism of Lincoln's Political Rhetoric
(1979)

After over one hundred years it continues to be almost impossible for us to ask certain basic questions about the role of Abraham Lincoln in the formation of a characteristically American politics. At every appropriate point of inquiry the Lincoln myth obtrudes. Since 1865 no one has denied the extraordinary purchase of that imaginative construct upon the idiom and character of our public life. Yet few Americans of any influence have attempted to counter this effect, even though in the works of the biographers and historians, material for such a negation has long been available. The truth about the life and death of Lincoln seems to matter very little when it is confronted by the myth. Indeed, the iconic presence of the Emancipator, wrapped up in religious imagery, tends to swallow up any simple narrative of the facts. Writes Don E. Fehrenbacher:

> Lincoln's symbolic importance transcends his own life and time. He has been abstracted from history to serve as the representative American, and as a consequence much of the nation's self-image is visible

in the image of Abraham Lincoln, that successive generations have fashioned.[1]

The poet James Russell Lowell called him our "first American."[2] And for his devoted secretary John Hay—in this speaking for millions—he was "the greatest character since Christ.[3] In the life and death of Lincoln the rest of our common experience as a people finds its sanction and authority. Father Abraham overshadows our perception of the legitimate origins of the Republic in the era of the Revolution. He is also the measure applied to all of our leaders who have appeared on the national stage since the violent conclusion of his career, which makes of him the only viable symbol of authority in our political discourse—plus something else beyond mere questions concerning policy and the best regime. Yet all of this "inflation" has come to pass even while we were beginning to recognise the dangers inherent in such quasi-religious myths, the abuses and disruptions in our civic life which have found in their hegemony a magic for converting reflexive disorder into a "positive good," or perhaps even into an obligation. It is thus fortunate that recent studies of the nature and origin of millenarian thought have put into our hands the rhetorical and theoretical instruments necessary to a belated reduction or "delusion" of Mr. Lincoln's

---

1   This article is based on a paper given at the conference on Gnosticism and Reality, held at Vanderbilt University in April of 1978 under direction of Dr. Richard J. Bishirjian and Dr. William Havard. Sponsors were the Earhart Foundation, the Vanderbilt Research Council, and the Intercollegiate Studies Institute, Inc. This article will subsequently appear as a chapter in a book to be published by the Louisiana State University Press.

Don E. Fehrenbacher, *The Changing Image of Lincoln in American Historiography* (London: Oxford University Press, 1968), 3-4.

2   Quoted from Lowell's "Ode Recited at the Harvard Commemoration, July 21, 1865," line 208. I cite the edition of Harry Hayden Clark and Norman Foerster, *James Russell Lowell: Representative Selections, with Introduction, Bibliography and Notes* (New York: American Book Company, 1947), p.145.

3   Quoted on 93 of Richard Hofstadter, *The American Political Tradition* (New York: Alfred A. Knopf, 1948).

baleful example to its rightful proportions—instruments which enable us to ask what he has really "done for his country."

There is of course a part of the Lincoln myth which is, on its face, harmless enough: the legend of the shy young man who did his reading by firelight, who was unlucky in love, and who learned from his grief. In this version there is some truth and much fancy.[4] But what signifies is its relation to the basic American story of the youth who "made something of himself," on the model of Horatio Alger, with a lost sweetheart included for sentiment's sake. The remainder of the Lincoln narrative draws much of its authority from some of these homely materials. But the legend of the poor boy who is self-transformed becomes another kind of model when it is generalized in a certain way: when it is merged with other, essentially gnostic myths of "self-invention," and detached from the traditional pattern in which a providentially given set of talents is developed and employed. We should remember that the mature Abraham Lincoln was a man who had abolished his past. He cut his ties with family, kept always from his father's house, and refused with nauseating unction to go there when summoned at the time of Thomas Lincoln's death.[5] Very early he set out to join another tribe.[6] And, as he moved forward, there were many of his friends who noticed that he sometimes "forgot the devotion of his warmest partisans as soon as the occasion for their services had passed"[7] As his biographer and law partner tells us, Mr. Lincoln was a cool customer, "led mankind by a profound policy," and

---

4 The Ann Rutledge story hides the coldness and calculation, the lineaments of the country hustler, and the darling of the rich.

5 See Richard H. Luthin, *The Real Abraham Lincoln* (New York: Prentice-Hall, Inc. 1960), 141-144.

6 I refer here to the early admission of Lincoln into the best social circles of Springfield, and thereafter into the elite, largely Southern in origin, of his state. This commerce led to the charge that he was the mouthpiece of "aristocracy." Lincoln followed the example of his law partner, the austere Kentuckian, John Todd Stuart.

7 See David Donald, *Lincoln's Herndon* (New York: Alfred A. Knopf, 1948), 269. He quotes Lincoln's faithful friend, Ward Hall Lamon.

"would have *lost*—lost all, *all*," if he had had a heart.[8] From the shadowy records and recollections of the Illinois years we can infer nothing less, though, as must be admitted, he usually concealed these gifts of calculation under a rustic exterior. The great common denominator of his pre-presidential career was simple ambition, the little "engine" which knew no rest. By it he was propelled to act upon a larger and larger stage, and not by Christian rectitude which requires us to be good stewards of our given abilities or to answer a special "call." For it was not to serve God that Abraham put the Lincolns out of his way, sought office, moved to Springfield, and set out to practice law.

There is God's plenty of evidence to assist us in developing an image of Lincoln as backcountry *philosophe*, as "secularist intellectual," and "rational, progressive, superman" of the variety described in Professor Voegelin's *The New Science of Politics*.[9] But in a study of this scope there is a convenient locus for treating this phase of his development. The address which Lincoln delivered to the Springfield Young Men's Lyceum in January of 1838 is a summary statement of his thought as Whig progressive and moderate disciple of Paine *and* Hamilton, Volney *and* Henry Clay.[10] In it he introduces the theme of a "political religion" or civil theology so important to the rest of his career. He anticipates a refounding of the Republic. He assigns a particular role to reason and language in this process, and he sketches out in brief a theory of American history and of its probable consummation in the appearance of a new

---

8 *Ibid.*, 205 and 210.

9 See *The New Science of Politics* (Chicago: University of Chicago Press, 1952), 124-132.; also 96-98 in Voegelin's *Science, Politics, and Gnosticism* (Chicago: Henry Regnery Company, 1968) for the precise language which I quote.

10 See 108-115 of Vol. I of Roy P. Basler's edition of *The Collected Works of Abraham Lincoln* (New Brunswick, N. J.: Rutgers University Press, 1953). Further references in this paper to Blaser's edition will be abbreviated to *Collected Works*. My reading of this speech is in some respects a reply to Harry V. Jaffa's commentary on it, found on 183-232 of his *Crisis of the House Divided* (Seattle: University of Washington Press,1973).

"leader" or "towering genius" of a particularly dangerous variety. That is, unless the nation follows something like his advice, and, by implication summons to leadership a man of his views. The great theme of the Springfield Lyceum speech is the "preservation of our political institutions." Or at least that is its "official" theme. As we must learn to recognise, Lincoln's habit of rhetorical duplicity is present from the beginning of his public life. What Lincoln here declares is that the established things are now in peril. After only fifty years of independent existence, the nation has already passed through phases convenient and then conventional, is approaching its "third age" and therefore its crisis of development. However, the young legislator, speaking to the citizens of a town whose future he has helped to secure, adds to his version of the familiar gnostic formula a special neo-Puritan twist.[11] For the stage to come, according to his political eschatology, may augur *either* a final perfection *or* an apocalypse, a complete inversion of the fortunate American unfolding already accomplished. That which comes soon may be either the kingdom or the beast. Lincoln mentions riots and social irregularities which point toward the latter prospect. They are the occasions of his remarks. But his strategy in exploiting this antithesis raises the question of his true purpose for speaking on this subject at this particular time. Upon examination of his entire text, it becomes quite clear that what the orator attempts through the arts of language is not preservation but change: radical alterations in the basis and organization of American society. His deliberative procedure at this point is one that he will practice with greater and greater skill in the decades to come. First of all he erects a false dilemma, this time using as a bugbear the likelihood that the enemies of "government" will prevail and that, in response to the excesses of local self-expression, an "Alexander, Caesar or

---

11   Lincoln was a leader in the successful effort to move the capital of Illinois from Vandalia to his new home, Springfield. This relocation was voted in 1837 and accomplished in 1839. There is some evidence of that political horse trading made a part of the transaction. Apocalyptic prophecies concerning disorders caused by the localism of the Democrats was a part of the rhetoric of Federalism.

a Napoleon" will come to power.¹² That is, unless we agree to put behind us our anterior devotion to nomocratic politics, to leave the collapsing shelter of the grove in order to escape the anger of the mob, and to relocate the seat of our "political religion" in another sanctuary—a house unlike any we have known.

I emphasize the part played by certain images in the progression of Lincoln's effects, for these tropes are behind the thrust of Lincoln's rhetorical dilemma, and explain the especial significance assigned to "reason" in the normative system by which it is informed. The forest of "great oaks" which made for a "living history," a compact society first generated by common enemies and fed subsequently by common tasks and shared memories, is too gothic and passionate a source for patriotic feeling and public virtue. Furthermore, it is here defined as frail. Lincoln asserts that a polity connected to its forms by nothing more than the knowledge of what "our people," family and friends, have accomplished will lose its cohesion once its heroes die. That their example might be kept alive through emulation, or through the poet's song, seems to him unlikely.¹³ The idea that it could survive under the pressure of untrammeled democracy is a notion he refuses even to consider. But there is more to this posture than at first appears, since Lincoln must have recognised that such a traditional, old-fashioned republicanism would stand in the way of the evolution which he has in mind. Probably for this reason he makes of it the unacknowledged antagonist of his entire argument. The political antichrist of the following passage has his importance through association with the unstable arrangements that will give him scope:

---

12   Throughout his life Lincoln was fascinated by the careers of great dictators, and especially by the career of Napoleon. The absence of a strong central authority in the France of the Directory had certainly helped along that self-made emperor.

13   Even though Lincoln speaks constantly of Washington as a living force in his own generation. And in particular in the conclusion of his speech, thus confirming a truth he systemically denied.

Many great and good men sufficiently qualified for any task they should undertake, may ever be found, whose ambition would aspire to nothing beyond a seat in Congress, a gubernatorial or a presidential chair; *but such do not belong to the family of the lion, or the tribe of the eagle,* [.] What! Think you these places would satisfy an Alexander, a Caesar, or a Napoleon? Never! Towering genius disdains a beaten path. It seeks regions hitherto unexplored. It sees *no distinction* in adding story to story, upon the monuments of fame, erected to the memory of others. It *denies* that it is glory enough to serve under any chief. It *scorns* to tread in the footsteps of any predecessor, however illustrious. It thirsts and burns for distinction; and, if possible, it will have it, whether at the expense of emancipating slaves, or enslaving freemen. Is it unreasonable then to expect, that some man possessed of the loftiest genius, coupled with ambition sufficient to push it to its utmost stretch, will at some time, spring up among us? And when such a one does, it will require the people to be united with each other, attached to the government and laws, and generally intelligent, to successfully frustrate his designs.

Distinction will be his paramount object; and although he would as willingly, perhaps more so, acquire it by doing good as harm; yet, that opportunity being past, and nothing left to be done in the way of building up, he would set boldly to the task of pulling down.[14]

---

14   *Collected Works*, I, 113-114. Lincoln clearly knows the breed he describes too well to be writing on the basis of mere speculation. The ironic prophecy of these lines is difficult to mistake. Though he disguises his fascination with such figures by speaking of his favorite excuse for emulating their example, in the role of a patriot concerned with "the capability of a people able to govern themselves." That is, with the proper direction.

It is the speaker's plan that, in terror of such a radical threat, a transformation more extreme than the innovation which came with national independence, his audience will agree to replace a regime of experience informed by piety with "pillars hewn from the solid quarry of sober reason...." The remembered "blood of the Revolution" will not suffice: "Reason, cold, calculating, unimpassioned reason, must furnish all the materials for our future support and defense.[15] It is true that he also draws very positive portrait of the millennium which his version of the "Faustian intellect" can actualize, once it is obeyed. It is a fine house made of words. But he does not expect that this image will persuade. Only through a connection of the customary with the onset of a tyranny could his countrymen be drawn to forswear their natural preference for an essentially prescriptive, familiar order, for building upon what their immediate predecessors have achieved, and tolled away from their inherited place to live under the auspices of Enlightenment speculation, symbolized here by the spare classical temple. Yet that is the appeal which Lincoln employs. It is, of course, ironic that this rhetoric does nothing to preserve the Republic invoked through a concluding salute to the living memory of Washington and that it draws almost none of its authority from reason in proposing ostensibly reasonable change.[16] This is trickery enough, but Lincoln is not through. He has saved something for last, a contradiction to the tenor of his entire address, which he expects to round off his sequence of conflations and elevate his matter beyond the reach of close inquiry. Even in concluding, Lincoln says one thing while he means another. For his last words as healer, prophet, and "founder" of the new regime are

---

15 Lincoln here verges on "ideological" politics. What he rejects is a regime of custom, based upon loyalties, habits and a common memory—what Professor Michael Oakeshott calls "nomocratic" politics. See his *On Human Conduct* (London: Oxford University Press, 1975), 199-206. See also Professor Voegelin's remarks on Roman "compactness" on 86-92 of *The New Science of Politics*.

16 Washington here is conflated with the rationalist philosopher. As he is in Lincoln's "Temperance Address" of February 27, 1842, Collected Works, I, 271-279. Lincoln's connection of moral and political reform is here very curiously drawn.

that, if it be faithful to Reason, "the gates of hell shall not prevail against it." This language is, of course, from the promise made by Christ to the Church.[17] But its guarantee belongs not to the mind but the spirit. Here the national society of High Federalism, where liberty has its altar in the temple of philosophy, draws authority from its institutional antitype. This may seem surprising. Yet we must believe that Lincoln knew what he was about. His strategy reflects not mere confusion or opportunism but conscious choice. A successful political religion must replace Church with State, or else must absorb the former into the latter, and borrow the sanction for its sacrilege from the *civitas dei*. In the secular Puritanism of New England political thought something of this sort had taken root during the first years of our national existence. The pattern of transformation was already an old one when Lincoln appeared. His special achievement was in institutionalizing it as the American political rhetoric for occasions of greatest moment. In this craft he was the master—with consequences we shall subsequently explore.

But this is to anticipate. It is another sixteen years, or perhaps another twenty, before Abraham Lincoln loses himself completely in an idiom for calling forth the New Jerusalem. In that interval, while he remains a rather conventional "right-wing gnostic" or "progressive," he perfects his skill in the use of the more conventional persuasive tools—forensic and deliberative weapons

---

17 Matthew 16:18. Upon the rock of such faith as that of Saint Peter the Church is thus secure. A few lines above, his description of the history of the Revolution of 1776 as a scripture he hopes will be equivalent to that in the Bible in its hold on the reverence of Americans further foreshadows the role of secularize religious rhetoric in his "political religion." In this fashion the Declaration of Independence may be elevated into the status of a dogma, with the statesman as "theologian," unfolding its hidden significance. See *The New Science of Politics*, 136: "If a movement, like the Puritan relies on the authority of a literary source, the leaders will then have to fashion 'the very notions and conceits of men's minds in such a sort' that the followers will automatically associate scriptural passages and terms with their doctrine, however ill founded the association may be, and that with equal automatism they will be blind to the content of Scripture that is incompatible with their doctrine." (Voegelin is here quoting Richard Hooker.)

which he will later combine with the epideictic assertion of his righteous Republican maturity.[18] It is easy to forget when we read the life of Lincoln backward, from the martyrdom, that for most of his political career he was an "orthodox Whig" who "accepted his party's principles: high tariff, internal improvements financed by the national government, a national bank, protection of the interests of property and of people of wealth, land policies which served the advantage of speculators rather than settlers, and general sympathy with the business and professional classes."[19] The idea that property, political order, and personal liberty come "down from the top" was, from the beginning, a part of Lincoln's chosen intellectual inheritance. Add to this the romantic doctrine of Union, a highly charged nationalism of the variety preached by Daniel Webster,[20] and you have a highly volatile mixture.

As a promising young centralist, Lincoln played the role of champion for what Professor Oakeshott has called the "enterprise association" theory of the state.[21] While serving as the elected representative of Sangamon (1834–1842), he first made a name for himself by enacting this part. Joining with other soon-to-be forefathers of the Republican Party, the youthful projector had his first political victory with the ten-million-dollar Internal

---

[18] See *The New Science of Politics*, 175. "In every wave of the Gnostic movement the progressivist and utopian varieties will tend to form a political right wing, leaving a good deal of the ultimate perfection to gradual evolution and compromising on a tension between achievement and ideal, while the activist variety will tend to form a political left wing, taking violent action toward the complete realization of the perfect realm."

[19] Quoted from 16 of Donald W. Riddle's *Congressman Abraham Lincoln* (Urbana: University of Illinois Press, 1957); also G. S. Borit, "Lincoln and the Economics of the American Dream: The Whig Years, 1832-1854" (Ph. D. dissertation, Boston University, 1968).

[20] For a survey of this teaching see Paul Nagel's *One Nation Indivisible: The Union in American Thought, 1776-1861* (New York: Oxford University Press, 1964).

[21] *On Human Conduct*, 114-118, 157-158, and 315-317. As opposed to what he calls a "civil association."

Improvements Act of 1837.²² In effect, this legislation borrowed Illinois into an immediate bankruptcy, and left upon the shoulders of each citizen of the state an obligation greater than his average annual income—a debt not finally retired until 1882. It was difficult for Lincoln to give up this dream of terrestrial beatitude brought about through fiat money, as, to be fair, was the case with many of his neighbors.²³ A peculiar feature of the legislation was that it actually discouraged free enterprise and private effort, though, thanks to its operations, many enterprising, private men (mostly Whigs) got rich. In the Illinois General Assembly Lincoln's preoccupations were special interest and local bills, log rollings and other things that government could "do for a community of people, [that] they need to have done, but cannot do, *at all*, or cannot, so well do, for themselves...."²⁴ In this helpful spirit, Lincoln loved a friendly bank, and learned how a pork barrel might best be filled. He became a master of patronage and influence. But his special concerns were roads, railroads, and canals. These works remained (in most cases) unfinished; or, if partially completed, they were underused and then sold at a loss. Yet by these disappointments the "improvement" Whigs were not soon deterred. The power of the legislator was a veritable cornucopia, running on the formula of "tax and tax, spend and spend." Lincoln mocked those who saw danger to the commonwealth in such adventurous, progressive schemes, calling their anxieties a "bugaboo."²⁵ His eyes were fixed on the bright shape of Young America in the making—a composite personage whom he later describes in his "Second Lecture on Discoveries and Inventions":

> We have all heard of Young America. He is the most current youth of the age. Some think him conceited,

---

22   Paul Simon, *Lincoln's Preparation for Greatness: The Illinois Legislature Years* (Urbana: University of Illinois Press, 1971), 48-53.

23   Though not true of thoughtful men like Governor Joseph Duncan.

24   *Collected Works*, II, 220.

25   Simon, 262. As he later mocked those who saw in his campaign a threat to the Union. See his speeches from Nov. 1860-April of 1861.

and arrogant; but has he not reason to entertain a rather extensive opinion of himself? Is he not the inventor and owner of the present, and the sole hope of the future? ... He owns a large part of the world, by right of possessing it; and all the rest by right of wanting it and *intending* to have it. As Plato had for the immortality of the soul, so Young America has "a pleasing hope—a fond desire—a longing after" territory[sic]. He has a great passion—a perfect rage—for the "*new*"; particularly new men for office, and the new earth mentioned in the revelations.... In knowledge he is particularly rich. He knows all that can possibly be known; inclines to believe in spiritual rappings and is the unquestioned inventor of "*Manifest Destiny*." His horror is for all that is old, particularly "Old Fogy"; and if there be any thing old which he can endure, it is only old whiskey and old tobacco.[26]

The tone of this passage is somewhat arch. But the content is a serious account of Lincoln's perception of the nation in his day, especially when it is examined in the light of the prototype of his address, the earlier "First Lecture on Discoveries and Inventions."[27] There he begins, "All creation is a mine and every man a miner. The whole earth, and all *within* it, *upon* it, and *round about it*, in his physical, moral and intellectual nature, and his susceptibilities, are the infinitely various 'leads' from which man, from the first, was to dig out his destiny." From this image he moved swiftly to describe the peculiarly human enterprise as a work of refinement *after the original extraction is complete*. We are reminded of innumerable gnostic tracts, each in its own way concerned with the transformation of reality by "discovery" of what is hidden and

---

26 *Collected Works*, III, 356-357. Young America was a progressivist movement, expansionist, chauvinistic, and usually Democratic.
27 *Collected Works*, II, 43-442.

the "invention," through that discovery, of what is new. According to Lincoln's Whig calculus, the alchemical transformation of the modern world by America is to be accomplished by applied science, ethical culture, and governmental manipulation: but especially by the last of these three, as directed by Whig statesmen who are able to sell their countrymen on the *theologia civilis* of high tariff, the Bank, and Mr. Clay's "American System." Only through their agency will the nation reach the "third age" of the Springfield Lyceum speech, the "Happy day when ... *mind*, all conquering *mind*, shall live and move the monarch of the world." Or come to declare in unison, "Reign of Reason, all hail!"[28]

This Lincoln, the genial prophet of expansion, modernization, and commercial progress never really disappears, even when the man is absorbed into the myth. But if the prophet is to be also the agent and harbinger of these changes, the ultimate miner and refiner, then an attractive meliorist rhetoric must be developed to enforce his designs. And the key to that rhetoric would have to be the mythic articulation of a tempting vision of delights to come—or likely to come, if just a few attendant suggestions are honored by a bemused electorate. Lincoln's language in this period is, it is true, better suited to persuasion than to coercion. It is more carrot than stick, appeals less to order and strength and more to mendacity and opportunism than its model, the nationalist rhetoric of the old Federalist forefathers. But the constitutional progressivism of Whig doctrine required that it be so and also that it disguise some of its essential implications, lest their conflict with basic assumptions given authority by the Democratic opposition be recognised by the many Americans devoted to another view of the functions of the state. Lincoln did not give up on this idiom until he was convinced that the Whig cause was forever lost.

The basic tactic of Lincoln's discourse as Whig loyalist was the argument from character, *ad hominem*. Its theoretical justification was a simple one: that it is difficult to market reason among unreasonable men. But its adoption by many Western Whigs has an

---

28   *Collected Works*, I, 279. The peroration of the "Temperance Address."

even simpler explanation. I refer to the success of the Democrats in their perpetuation of the antistatist momentum of the Revolution. As popular leaders since Jefferson have realized, Americans will accept some direction if they do not sense in the background an *a priori* design—an ideology whose agent shall be government, and whose authority shall be law. Lincoln became a specialist in the populist touch, in formal obeisance to "the genius of the people." But there was a difficulty. For his use of the trope of affected modesty involved him in an endless series of deceptions and finally failed to launch him toward the eminence which he desired.

A summary example of Lincoln's use of this device is available in his first reported speech. It is best to examine it in full, in a version preserved by one of his supporters:

> Fellow Citizens, I presume you all know who I am. I am humble Abraham Lincoln. I have been solicited by many friends to become a candidate for the Legislature. My politics are short and sweet like the old woman's dance. I am in favour of a national bank. I am in favour of the internal improvement system and a high protective tariff. These are my sentiments and political principles. If elected, I shall be thankful; if it will be all the same.[29]

As Richard Hofstadter has observed, Lincoln was a "complex man, easily complex enough to know the value of his own simplicity." Therefore he seldom "failed to strike the humble manner that was peculiarly his"—even though his adversaries recognised the demagogy of this self-dramatization and labeled him Uriah Heap.[30] Moreover, he kept it up to the end, describing his life as "the short and simple annals of the poor" and advising

---

29 Conveniently available on 65-66 of Lord Charnood's *Abraham Lincoln* (New York: Henry Holt and Company, 1917).

30 Hofstadter, 94; see also Luthin, 37.

his campaign biographer in 1860, "I wish it to be modest."[31] In this vein we should understand the cultivated image of the rail-splitter, the teller of bawdy or racist tales, the tall, ungainly figure in the rusty hat and worn shawl.[32] Our point is that the matter hidden behind this Jacksonian exterior belonged to another politics—a system in harmony with the Federalist/Whig model—and involved Lincoln in a persistent deception. Many Whigs had disguised themselves in the same way, particularly after the successful campaign of William Henry Harrison.[33] But none had done so with greater skill than the prairie lawyer from central Illinois.

Yet the problem of conflict between tenor and vehicle in the speech and writing of Abraham Lincoln goes well beyond conventional political obfuscation by the party of privilege and imposed national reform in a traditionalist, socially conservative and closed republican regime. In the record of Honest Abe, deceit by conflation is everywhere, all of it asserting innocence, either of motive or of design. Consider, for an instance, his last letter to Mary Owen, where he offers marriage in such a way as to sever their connection forever.[34] Or his claim to James Shields, a prominent Democratic politician, that a newspaper attack directed at him was in no way "personal" and had been made "wholly for political effect."[35] Even though the piece describes Shields as a "fool" and "liar"; as a "dunce" who can be identified by his smell; and, through his suborning perjury, as a source of political corruption.[36] Or perhaps his handbill on religion, issued at the time of his race for Congress: an open disapproval of scoffers (overt skeptics, as

---

31 See 4 of Stephen B. Oates, *with Malice Toward None: The Life of Abraham Lincoln* (New York: Harper & Row Publishers, 1977); also *Collected Works*, III, 511.

32 See Luthin, 229.

33 Those who did not failed—belated Federalists like Lincoln's sponsors, Ninian Edwards and John Todd Stuart.

34 *Collected Works*, I, 94-95; Letter of Aug. 16, 1837.

35 *Collected Works*, I, 301; "Memorandum of Duel Instructions to Elias Merryman," Sept. 9, 1842.

36 *Collected Works,* I, 294-296. "The 'Rebecca' Letter," Aug. 27, 1842.

opposed to secret unbelievers like himself), which he means to be read as a profession of his own Christian orthodoxy.[37] Or, finally, his antislavery law for the District of Columbia—a measure which did to death a serious Congressional effort to outlaw the peculiar institution in that jurisdiction.[38] Lincoln's conduct in this piece of business, his principal legislative venture during his only term in the House of Representatives, infuriated the antislavery men in that body, released him to oppose other antislavery legislation, and caused one of his Northern colleagues to write that he had, in the entire dispute, "placed himself squarely on the side of the South."[39] Yet he often identified himself as a "free soil" man, and managed to get his share of the "Yankee" vote in the seventh congressional district.

If we are careful to read the public life of Lincoln from the beginning, forward, this unfriendly report by an abolitionist should not surprise. In these years the future Emancipator ran always with Southern Whigs. His presidential preferences were always for slaveholders who helped cut down the Democratic majority in the South—for Clay and White, Taylor and Scott. In 1852 he praised his party for pacifying Southern fears, for refusing to claim a special understanding of the Divine Will, and for avoiding all arguments from definition, direction by abolitionists, or original uses of presidential power.[40] Moreover, he did not scruple at condemning Martin Van Buren for entertaining too advanced a view of the rights of Negroes,[41] or at bringing actions for the recovery of

---

37 *Collected Works* I, 382; July, 31, 1846. See also Luthin, 169, where we see Lincoln pretending rigid Christian orthodoxy, for effect.

38 *Collected Works*, II, 20-22; see also Riddle, 162-180.

39 See 260 of George Washington Julian's *The Life of Joshua Giddings* (Chicago: A.C. McClung and company, 1892). The book is very useful to students of Lincoln's views on slavery.

40 *Collected Works*, II, 135-157, "Speech to the Springfield Scott Club," Aug. 14, 1852—perhaps Lincoln's finest speech.

41 Simon, 36. In this campaign Lincoln made race-baiting speeches all through "Egypt"—the lower counties of Illinois. See also *Collected Works*, I, 209-210.

runaway slaves in Illinois. Devotees of the Lincoln myth have a dreadful time with his role in the celebrated Matson Slave Case of 1847. Their trouble is that they identify his politics with freedom of the Southern Negro. And that belief leads them to misconstrue what was his larger purpose, from the first.

It was no inconsistency for Lincoln the orthodox Whig, the protege of John Todd Stuart and the aristocratic Edwards clan, to go down to Coles County and seek there his fee for returning Jane Bryant and her four children to Kentucky: a place of bondage from whence (we are led to believe) they would soon thereafter have been shipped "down the river" in punishment for the inconvenience they had caused.[42] These Negroes were property. And for any good Whig, respect for the primacy of property rights was an absolute article of faith. Equality was no important part of their teaching, and received their lip service only in passing, when it was time to vote. For the ordinary Whig, equality signified economic opportunity for citizens, with the meaning of that status being defined by law. Slavery agitation divided American citizens and precluded the development of a more perfect unity through commercial exchange: a development encouraged by a benevolent government authority. The Whigs recognised that slavery itself had fostered sectionalism. Therefore, they expressed a pro forma interest in systems of voluntary manumission, if linked (where necessary) to compensation and also (in every case) to African repatriation. The Whigs were uniformitarians to the core. And once the Negroes were gone, the South might be less uneasy about concentration of federal power and more concerned with commercial expansion: less provincial and agrarian. Local feeling and variety were the enemies of the Whigs. They connected both with the passions; and passion forestalled the evolution of the Union which, in standard progressive fashion, they defined more by what it could be than by

---

42 See 130-149 of John J. Duff's judicious *A. Lincoln: Prairie Lawyer* (New York: Rinehart & Company, Inc., 1960). This is an instructive narrative of the entire 1847 case for those who are inclined to take seriously Lincoln's statements on one man "living by the sweat of another man's brow." Lincoln tried his best to do a bit of that living.

what it was or had been. But the Constitution had made us "half slave and half free." And to argue from definition against a part of that settlement could only aggravate the situation which they officially deplored.

It is true that the Whig vision of the national future had more in common with Pleasure Island in *Pinocchio* than with the old Puritan City on a Hill. (At times, in speaking of it, even Lincoln sounds like the poor boy with his face frozen against the window of the candy store.) But as a secular utopia, it commanded the allegiance of many Americans, certain that destiny was on their side, that our nation could bring all history to a rational apotheosis. Therefore, they could afford to wait. Accommodation was their watchword in dealing with certain unreasonable particularities. In the end, rational arguments of enlightened self-interest would prevail. They were ready to describe their conservative opponents as wrong, but they would not call them wicked. For such "high profile" arguments heated up the political atmosphere and turned attention away from the considerations to which they gave priority—away from trade. Unlike their rhetorical *modus vivendi*, these contentions delayed the destined surrender of their countrymen to the teleocratic state, kept alive centrifugal impulses in the body politic, and kept the Democrats in power. The political rhetoric of Abraham Lincoln prior to 1854 conforms entirely to these Whig presuppositions. He had played the game by their rules. But by that time the sectional issues had clearly ruined the hopes of the Whigs in the South. They could not outbid the hated "Locos" there, for these astute enemies had done their best with the raw material of Southern ambition and Southern fear. The alternate strategy was to build a party with a regional base in the North, drawing its strength from former Whigs and former Democrats who resented what Southern "demands" had done to the "house of their fathers": to make capital out of what appeared to be a disadvantage.[43] This procedure would involve an almost total violation of the reasonable precepts

---

[43] Also part of the plan was to push the Democrats still further South, by driving the Southerners to make greater and greater demands upon "their party."

of the Whigs. It would work openly on the passions and diminish national feeling—at least for a while, until one side had won a total victory. Yet as an extremely partisan politician, a man who would do almost anything to defeat the Democrats, Lincoln was not likely to ignore this situation, or to misjudge where it led.[44] As early as 1848 he had agreed with William Seward that "if one had no hope of getting elected on the internal improvements issue, one other issue offered opportunity. 'I reckon you are right, Senator. We have got to deal with this slavery question and got to give it more attention hereafter than we have been doing.'"[45] The Kansas-Nebraska Act gave him that opportunity.

Stephen A. Douglas, United States Senator from Illinois, was the author of the Kansas–Nebraska Act. Douglas was Democratic leader in Congress. The bill was a Democratic measure, repealing the Missouri Compromise of 1820, and leaving the status of the undeveloped territories to be settled by popular sovereignty—first upon their organization, and then again upon their application for statehood. It denied any role to the federal government in making these determinations, and thereby it attempted to close out the possibility of future political debate over the institution of slavery. Senator Douglas hoped that it would launch him upwards, into the White House. Instead, it revived the faltering political career of Abraham Lincoln, and gave him the issue he required to become the *politicus* of his youthful speculations.[46] The method employed by Douglas's old adversary in exploiting the anger of the people of the North at the opening to Southern development of lands which they thought were reserved for their use was extremely artful. It seized upon the fact that the issue in dispute was one of cultural identities, and that slavery was only the circumstance which allowed for its unfolding. And it exploited that opportunity to the hilt.

---

44 See for instance *Collected Works*, III, 330—Lincoln's letter to Norman B. Judd, Oct. 20, 1858. There he advises his associate on how to steal *illegal* Irish votes.

45 Quoted by Riddle, 246.

46 *Ibid.*, 245-249.

Northern outrage at the Kansas-Nebraska Act developed swiftly. Lincoln recognised its dimensions almost at once. And he began to convert it to Douglas's (and the Democrats') disadvantage, to the development of a Northern sectional party, in his Peoria address of October 16, 1854.[47] Though it sounds many new notes, its rhetoric is in some respects transitional. It makes a conventional nod to the example of his "beau ideal," Henry Clay and to the moderate example of his Springfield preceptors. Their opinion is acknowledged in Lincoln's reference to "compromise," and "concessions" or "equivalents" as a normative concept in previous quarrels between the sections.[48] Lincoln admits that the Constitution itself rests upon that principal—in recognition of the original, unnegotiable variety of the United States.[49] It is therefore Stephen Douglas and not his critics who has broken with the authority of precedent. The rest of Lincoln's argument in this pivotal address does not consort well with this complaint against innovation, though he pretends here to be only the "honest citizen" alarmed at change—the forensic "good man, speaking well" of Cicero's definition.

For the great difficulty with Lincoln's Peoria presentation is that it finally refuses accommodation, the sacrosanct principle of Clay and of the Founders, and in its place threatens apocalypse if the alternate principle of exclusion is not applied to all the Western territories of the Republic. To accept the notion that there is any policy superior to these alternatives is called both "monstrous"

---

47 *Collected Works*, II, 247-283.

48 *Ibid.*, 259 and 272.

49 *Ibid.*, 272. It is to the point that Northerners, in 1787, had *without moral outrage* agreed to slavery in the South. And could not thereafter develop an outrage with that portion of the contract between the states without acknowledging that their anger "broke the bond." Especially if this belated morality was to their political and economic advantage. And had come upon them only after they were convinced that the Union was not subject to dissolution. Under the pressure of such convenient outrage, Southerners were quite naturally distrustful of attendant assurances that the letter of the contract would be observed. The form of these disclaimers of innovative intent was their meaning. Had the North in 1787 accepted slavery in this way, there would have been no union.

and worthy of "hate." We are now returned to the false dilemma. Ordinary persuasion is forsworn. A new political religion is implied. And though Lincoln still pretends civility and claims not "to question the patriotism or to assail the motives of any man, or class of men," we are well on our way to a full-fledged Puritan rhetoric of perpetual war against the "powers of darkness": "two universal armed camps, engaged in a death struggle against each other."[50] The speech is rambling, full of historical errors, and, as Professor Riddle has observed, more distinguished for its intensity than for the muddle of what it contends.[51] But its burden cannot be misunderstood: the Northwest Ordinance of 1787 should be applied to all the undeveloped portions of the United States, in the spirit of the Wilmot Proviso, and therefore the balance of the sections forever destroyed. Otherwise, according to his new bugbear, slavery will be released and encouraged to spread throughout the land. And all of this to come to pass because of Stephen A. Douglas and his "declared indifference, but as I must think, *covert* zeal" for such a change.[52]

Thus, Lincoln cries "conspiracy,"[53] a note which becomes stronger and stronger in the speeches that are still to come. We are diverted by his tone, as we are by the stridency of his censure upon a people toward whom he has "no prejudice," and against arrangements that are "in the Constitution."[54] Yet it points us toward what was finally at stake in his effort to repeal the Kansas-Nebraska Act and in the entire discussion of the territorial expansion of the slave power. As I noted above, Lincoln makes use of a fallacious argument from history, and a particular appeal to the authority of the Northwest Ordinance. These new politics undertook to threaten the sense of identity in the people

---

50   *Collected Works*, II, 248; *The New Science of Politics*, 151.
51   Riddle, 249.
52   *Collected Works*, II, 255.
53   See David Brion Davis, *The Slave Power Conspiracy and the Paranoid Style* (Baton Rouge: Louisiana State University, Press, 1969).
54   *Collected Works*, II, 254 and 269.

of the Midwest. They felt that the lands to their immediate west were symbolically marked as theirs by the old line of compromise and the label "free soil." Such had been the true purpose of the Northwest Ordinance at the time of its adoption.[55] But in the dialectic set in motion in Peoria that promise could not be made secure unless all open lands were covered by the Ordinance, or its near equivalent, with the balance of power designed by the Fathers tilted northward and against the Democrats. At times Lincoln seems to moderate this demand in his first attack on slavery as polity, but the *concessions* are only for effect, particularly as he approaches the Illinois senate race of 1858.

The "House Divided Speech" is the watershed of Lincoln's political career.[56] In this address, given to the Republican state convention that nominated their tall compatriot from Springfield to take the Little Giant's place, there are no echoes of Henry Clay. It was the opening gun of Lincoln's campaign to deprive Douglas of his seat. Here he begins to reach after the biblical note. He calls for the first time for the "ultimate extinction" of slavery—which Southerners, upset by the propaganda of the serious abolitionists,

---

[55] See 231-232 of *The Antislavery Vanguard: New Essays on the Abolitionists*, ed. By Martin Duberman (Princeton: Princeton University Press, 1965). The passage which I cite is from Staughton Lynd's essay, "The Abolitionist Critique of the United States Constitution." In it he observes *that most* of the Fathers expected the south to outgrow and outpopulate the North. The South also held rights to most of the Western territories. To set aside the Old Northwest for non-slaveholders was a way of giving the North a reason to "join the Union—a stake in its future and a way of extending the principle of balance of the sections into the future, while at the same time assuring that the new nation (with the slave trade still in operation) would not become altogether surfeited with slaves, to the decrease of their value and the increase of social danger. The very Southerners who adopted the Northwest Ordinance spoke repeatedly of their expectation that slavery would go into the West. And so voted, with many Yankees, in the Southwest Ordinance. (Jefferson himself endorsed such a distribution.) Lincoln's reading of these events is ridiculous—and borrowed from Salmon Chase of Ohio. To argue that the South voted to extinguish itself in 1787 is to ask that we believe a thing not in nature.

[56] *Collected Works*, II, 461-469: "A House Divided": Speech at Springfield, Illinois," June 16, 1858.

translated to mean their absolute subjection to government by a hostile majority. Slavery was a way of marking a boundary between political philosophies and ways of life. It could mean very little else in a debate between cultures which agreed on the inability of the Negro to become a part of the political, economic, or social life of the nation.[57] The central passage in this address flies directly in the face of the Northwest Ordinance and the letter of the Constitution.[58] For, as Lincoln had earlier admitted, there was no provision for the ultimate extinction of slavery there. But the Emancipator leaves as the alternative to war on slavery possibilities even worse than those outlined at Peoria: The spread of bondage (and Negroes) throughout the free states and, therefore, the political and social subjection of the North to Slave power. For, as he had suggested four years earlier, if slaves (hateful in their own right, in being Negroes) entered Nebraska and Kansas, the spirit of despotism would come with them, excluding other people who did not own slaves, increasing the influence of the South in Washington. And

---

[57] On the racial attitude of the North in the 1850's, I recommend V. Jacque Voegeli, *Free but Not Equal: The Midwest and the Negro During the Civil War* (Chicago: University of Chicago Press, 1967); Eugene H. Berwanger, *The Frontier against Slavery: Western Anti-Negro Prejudice and the Slavery Extension Controversy* (Urbana: University of Illinois Press, 1967); James A. Rawley, *Race and Politics: 'Bleeding Kansas' and the Coming of the Civil War* (Philadelphia: J. B. Lippincott Company, 1969); and Leon F. Litwick, *North of Slavery: The Negro in the Free States, 1790-1860* (Chicago: University of Chicago Press, 1961). This is only a sample of a growing literature demonstrating how nonegalitarianism and racist all of the effective opponents of slavery had to appear to be in the years before the conflict came. Which raises serious questions as to what the antislavery cause was all about. With only a few apolitical abolitionists as exceptions. The problem of the Republican was in being against both the slave-holder and the slave—the latter in particular, should he become free; the former in that he must be *forced* to free the latter, and still keep him in the South. Their posture shifted between 1854 and 1877, depending on which of these two they hated the most. Hence abolition could only be a war measure.

[58] Max Farrand writes on 130 of his *The Father of the Constitution: A Chronicle of the Establishment of the Union* (New Haven: Yale University Press, 1912) that the architects of the Republic "regarded slavery as an accepted institution, as part of the established order." Lincoln's argument that the Fathers put slavery on the road to extinction rests on almost nothing.

this influence could, in its turn, be converted into control of the entire country. The equation came down to this: where slavery went, power followed.

This amounts, to be sure, to a dreadful illustration of scare tactics. It led to Douglas' charge that Lincoln was trying to "abolitionize the old-line Whigs."[59] And Douglas was correct, though Lincoln would accomplish that purpose with an anti-abolitionist electorate only by his usual conflation of one thing with another. In particular, his scenario frightened foreign immigrants to the upper Midwest, and the new settlers from the Northeast who were, unlike the early inhabitants of this region, easily alarmed by the proximity of Southern modes and orders, the prospect of a Southern hegemony.[60] For, as Lincoln recognised, Illinois and the other states above the Ohio were rapidly changing in their political composition. The Southernization of the Democratic Party under Pierce and Buchanan accelerated the process. As did the High Court's decision in the case of Dred Scott. But to finish the job of alienating them from a Democratic position owing too much to the influence of the South, he sharpened the dilemma of his intended audience even further, and finally forced it upon them by predicting that a failure to confine and abolish the institution of slavery would result in the enslavement of white men.[61] Reinforcing these demagogic humbugs was the lofty flavor of the speech's opening lines:

---

59   Douglas, as quoted on 5, *Collected Works*, III: from Aug. 21, 1858, debate at Ottawa, Illinois.

60   Even though they had lived under such an hegemony—unknowingly—throughout the antebellum period.

61   The kind of thing he could most easily tell immigrants—especially through his German language newspaper, the *Illinois Staats Anzeiger*, whose support Lincoln bought in 1859. See *Collected Works*, II, 341, 385, and 553; III, 95. On the impact of immigrants in Midwestern politics, see Donnal V. Smiths "The Influence of Foreign-Born of the Northwest in the Election of 1860." *The Mississippi Valley Historical Review*, XIX (Sept. 1932), 192-204.

> If we could first know *where* we are, and *whither* we are tending, we could then better judge *what* to do, and *how* to do it.
>
> We are now far into the *fifth* year since a policy was initiated, with the *avowed* object, and *confident* promise, of putting an end to slavery agitation.
>
> Under the operation of that policy, that agitation has not only, *not ceased*, but has *constantly augmented*.
>
> In *my* opinion, it *will* not cease, until a *crisis* shall have been reached, and passed.
>
> "A house divided against itself cannot stand."
>
> I believe this government cannot endure, permanently half *slave* and half *free*.
>
> I do not expect the Union to be *dissolved*—I do not expect the house to *fall*—but I do expect it will cease to be divided.
>
> It will become *all* one thing, or *all* the other.
>
> Either the *opponents* of slavery, will arrest the further spread of it, and place it where the public mind shall rest in the belief that it is in course of ultimate extinction; or its *advocates* will push it forward, till it shall become alike lawful in *all* the States, *old* as well as *new*—*North* as well as *South*.
>
> Have we no *tendency* to the latter condition?

After such a notable beginning it seems curious that Lincoln devotes most of the remainder of the speech to an unfolding of his theory of conspiracy.⁶² But not when we look back at the progression of effects and sequence of masks or *personae* which are the underlying structure in this analysis of his political development. For proof of the conspiracy justifies the outrage which through a metastatic process transforms the *vir bonus* of Peoria into an Old Testament prophet publicly declaring, by manner and by content, that "God is with us."⁶³ This is the Lincoln which we hear in the central passages of the debates with Douglas in the summer of 1858:

> It is the eternal struggle between these two principles—right and wrong—throughout the world. They are two principles that have stood face to face from the beginning of time; and will ever continue to struggle.⁶⁴

And the Lincoln who writes in his "Fragment on Sectionalism" that accommodation such as made the Union, in the form of a few additional Southern senators, would now degrade it, and that moral considerations should obtain, whatever the cost.⁶⁵ The new Lincoln of the House-Divided address is, by the agreement of most authorities, the most "radical" and "Garrisonian" to have appeared thus far.⁶⁶ If we are to believe the accounts of reliable witnesses,

---

62   An interesting discussion of the divisions of the speech appears on 82-83 of Don E. Fehrenebacher's *Prelude to Greatness: Lincoln in the 1850's* (Stanford, CA: Stanford University Press, 1962).

63   *Collected Works*, II, 385.

64   *Collected Works*, III, 315. Lincoln's kind of "argument from definition" belongs properly only to the inception—the planning stage in the history of a regime. Its successful introduction into the political discourse of a people always means that a refounding is in prospect.

65   *Collected Works*, II, 349-353. He later backed away from this—when it was too late—and accepted the idea of the Indian territories as a slave state, plus a plan to admit New Mexico on the same terms. But these concessions were only modifications of a basic hostility to the South—part of his *pretense* of moderation, the mask which he never dropped entirely. See Oates, 124.

66   See Luthin, 193; also Fehrenebacher's *Prelude to Greatness*, 72; and 107-109 of Vol. I of James G. Randall's *Lincoln the President: Springfield to Gettysburg* (New York: Dodd, Mead and Company, Inc., 1945). Voegelin

the shift leftward embodied in these remarks was a matter of conscious choice. For in the weeks prior to the convention where it was delivered, Lincoln "warned friends ... he might fatally damage the Republican Party by making its existence synonymous with a destruction of the government .... But he was persistent.... He believed he could discern the scope and read the destiny of impending sectional controversy. He was sure he could see far beyond the present and hear the voice of the future."[67] Hence the word crisis in the lines which I have quoted, what he calls elsewhere the "tug."[68] A "destruction of the government" as it had been would indeed be necessary, perhaps a small war. But Lincoln as Man of Destiny could not scruple at such slight inconveniences. All that remained of his evolution was a claim to direct communication with the god of history, of which we hear a great deal once Lincoln got the crisis which he wanted.

---

describes the development of this species of persona on 135-136 of *The New Science of Politics*.

67 Quoted from 146 of Vol. I of James G. Blaine's *Twenty Years of Congress: From Lincoln to Garfield* (Norwich, CT: The Henry Bell Publishing Company, 1884). Benjamin P. Thomas quotes Orville H. Browning to the same effect on 61 of his *Portrait for Posterity: Lincoln and His Biographers* (New Brunswick, NJ: Rutgers University Press, 1947): "I know Mr. Lincoln was a firm believer in supernatural and overruling agencies and events. I know that he believed the destinies of men were, or at least, that his own destiny, was shaped and controlled by an intelligence greater than his own, and which he could neither control or thwart." Browning, however, can attribute no other religious beliefs to his friend.

68 See Benjamin P. Thomas, *Abraham Lincoln: A Biography* (New York: Modern Library, 1968), 230. Lincoln admonishes Senator Trumbull, "The tug has to come." A small rebellion, easily subdued, Lincoln may have expected as early as 1858. Or at least Southern misconduct of a sort that would ruin the Democrats for years to come. And make possible a "refounding." The question of Lincoln's part in bringing on Secession is central to the reading of his career. There is no evidence that he expected so large a struggle as the one that occurred. Which reflects to the credit of his character—and to the discredit of his judgment. For a criticism of the impact of Lincoln's Presidency on constitutional government in the nation's subsequent history, see 17-62 of Gottfried Dietze's *America's Political Dilemma* (Baltimore: Johns Hopkins University Press, 1968)

I will not dwell here on the overt and implicit blasphemy of portions of Lincoln's Presidential oratory. Though my remarks on this subject that are now a matter of record are not the complete treatment which I intend.[69] It is this occasion to observe that the affected Puritanism of the period after 1854 was quite likely to propel Lincoln as Lord Protector and Judge over a Northern Israel into believing his own prophecies—especially when we remember that the powers of calculation which had brought him to the highest office of the Republic did not seem to suffice once he was there and that his own image for his situation as war leader, summoned up from the depth of his dreams, was that of a man moving through darkness in a ship under another's control, heading toward a destination he could not foresee.[70] But one Puritan device remained in his arsenal: in the midst of his ordeal the technique of sorting out or discerning the providences after the fact. In the months preceding the Emancipation Proclamation, and again at the very end of the War Between the States, Lincoln's faith that he was able to perform this prophetic, teleological task took hold of his mind.[71]

Much of the evidence of Lincoln's direct attribution of the decision to free those slaves still in Southern possession to a sign or a leading from God appears in his correspondence of 1862-63.[72] Some of the rest is in private memoranda to himself and in records

---

69   I refer to the chapter "Lincoln, the Declaration and Secular Puritanism: A Rhetoric for Continuing Revolution" in my collection, *A Better Guide than Reason: Studies in the American Revolution* (La Salle, Illinois: Sherwood Sugden & Company, 1978). There I detail other elements of my objections to Lincoln's reading of the American Revolution. Plus certain observations on the irrational appeals of quasi-biblical, epideictic rhetoric—the attempt at Gettysburg to imitate the tone of Holy Scripture. On Lincoln and biblical rhetoric, see also Cushing Strout, *The New Heavens and New Earth: Political Religion in America* (New York: Harper and Row, 1974), 193-200; and 194 of William J. Wolf, *Lincoln's Religion* (Boston: Pilgrim Press, 1970).

70   Discussed by Oates, 316.

71   See my remarks on Lincoln and "scanning the providences" in 1865 "The Heresy of Equality: Bradford Replies to Jaffa," *Modern Age* XX (Winter 1976), 64-73.

72   See *Collected Works*, V, 478; VII, 282; 535; VIII, 356.

of conversations.⁷³ But though he also spoke of the Proclamation as a gambit in the games of war and international politics, we should take seriously the reports of members of his cabinet and leaders of the Republican Party in Congress that he saw in the Union victory at Antietam a direct communication from on high.⁷⁴ Prior to that event, his language echoes Cromwell's in the period leading up to the execution of Charles I. As did his prototype, the Emancipator declares that he has "preconsulted nothing" and that "whatever shall appear to be God's will, I will do."⁷⁵ And again, after the decision has been made, he sounds the Cromwellian note, echoing Old Noll's disclaimer, "I have not sought these things; truly, I have been called unto them by the Lord."⁷⁶ Long before Lincoln in his Second Inaugural discusses the providential meaning of the chapter of history completed at Appomattox and sets himself as

---

73   *Collected Works*, II, 403-404. "Mediation on the Divine Will": "... God wills this contest, and wills that it should not end yet." See 156 of William J. Wolf's *Lincoln's Religion* for a passage from L. E. Chittenden's *Recollections of a President and His Administration*. There Lincoln is quoted: "I am satisfied that, when the Almighty wants me to do or not to do, a particular thing, he finds a way of letting me know it."

74   *Collected Works*, V., p.343: letter of July 26, 1862, "To Reverdy Johnson"; also Oates, 318-323. Lincoln meant the Proclamation as a war measure; he framed it to be minimally pro-Negro, but profoundly anti-Southern; and he offered the freedman almost nothing to go with it, even in his plans for Reconstruction. Yet he still drew upon it for moral capital. On Lincoln's indifference to what would happen to the former slaves, see his remark at the Hampton Roads conference of 1865 as reported on 615, Vol. II, of Alexander H, Stephens, *A Constitutional View of the War Between the States; Its Causes, Character, Conduct and Results, Presented in a Series of Colloquies at Liberty Hall* (Philadelphia: National Publishing Company, 1870).

75   *Collected Works*, V. 425: "Reply to Emancipation Memorial Presented by the Chicago Christians of All Denominations," Sept. 13, 1862. There Lincoln asserts that God would tell him, if He told any American of His particular will (p. 420). See *The New Science of Politics*, 93. On the parallel of Lincoln and Cromwell, see my "Writ of Fire and Sword: The Politics of Oliver Cromwell," *Occasional Review*, Issue 3 (Summer, 1975), 61-80, especially 66, 69-71.

76   "A Writ of Fire and Sword," 66. I quote from 364 of Antonia Frazer's, *Cromwell: The Lord Protector* (New York: Knopf, 1974).

the "godded man," beyond most of the radical Republicans in his understanding of these events as part of "universal history," the direction of the United States toward whatever is meant by "finish the work" has fallen into the hands of "God's new Messiah," the "homemade Jesus" of the Lincoln myth.[77] Lincoln's apotheosis through martyrdom served only to put a divine seal of approval on his understanding of himself. Or so we should be persuaded by what his fellow Americans made of the assassination and funeral, coming as they did at the end of a civil war[78] and surrounded as they were in a language promising salvation through social and political change.[79]

What then are the final implications of the political example of Abraham Lincoln? And what the enduring consequences of his sanctification as our only Father and preceptor in times of national crisis? The preceding narrative of his development as rhetorician intends to suggest that his public career must be subdivided if we are to make a proper reply. The Lincoln of the Whig years is clearly the heir of Enlightenment intellectuality as described for us by Professor Voegelin and Professor Niemeyer.[80] While in this role he remained within the boundaries established in 1688 and 1776: a part of the Anglo-American tradition of "aristocratic

---

[77] On the "godded man," see 92-97 of *Science, Politics and Gnosticism*; also the earlier discussion in *The New Science of Politics*, 110-113. Lincoln is both prophet and leader of his "third age" of America. But he is serious about the "holiness" of his politics. "God's New Messiah" is another quote from James Russell Lowell—this time from "The Present Crisis," line 23.

[78] For a fine summary of this first stage in the evolution of the Lincoln legend, I recommend Lloyd Lewis' *Myths after Lincoln* (New York: Harcourt, Brace & Company, 1929).

[79] See Voegelin on Comte and Turgot in *From Enlightenment to Revolution* (Durham: Duke University Press, 1975), edited by John H. Hallowell. This promise of course leads to "continuous warfare," conducted by men who profess an "ardent desire for peace," described on 171-173 of *The New Science of Politics*.

[80] See in particular 44-75 of Niemeyer's *Between Nothingness and Being* (Baton Rouge: Louisiana State University Press, 1971)—on the "laws of history."

parliamentism."[81] For this Lincoln, law is law and scripture, with no conflation of the two.[82] It is possible to contend with him on the ordinary political grounds, within the forensic and deliberative modes. But there are two elements in this Lincoln which mark him as a dangerous man. The first is his faith in necessity, and his suspicion that he knows its disposition for the future. This pseudo-philosophical reduction of the old Calvinist doctrine surfaces at regular intervals throughout his life. The second ingredient is a streak of rhetorical dishonesty, located primarily in his use of an *ad hominem* mask.

The second Lincoln, the artificial Puritan of the period between 1854-1861, is altogether gnostic in his purchase on American politics. He has become the dreadful Caesar warned of in his Springfield Lyceum address, the man who writes and speaks "wholly for effect." His political idiom is drawn from the England of the 1640s, and no constitutional order could survive under its unremitting pressure. Here the manner of Lincoln's speaking becomes its matter. Social peace and gradual reform become impossible; and the core of policy which is hidden beneath the sense of destiny, the false dilemma, and the righteous mask is difficult to perceive. Yet, on reflection, we should recognise the operation of a formula which draws upon the mixture of Christian and democratic feeling in his audience. By implication, says this Lincoln, "I am an ordinary, humble man. And if this be so, my ideas are not the product of my own intellect or sensibility. Hence, they must come from some other source, either the common feeling of my peers or the leadings of a higher authority."[83]

But the final Lincoln is the worst. For by him the real is defined in terms of what is yet to come, and the meaning of the present lies only in its pointing thither. This posture, when linked

---

81 *The New Science of Politics*, 188. The language of its passage describes rather well Lincoln's political enemies—the antebellum conservative Democrats, who were the least gnostic of American political parties.

82 *Ibid.*, 143. Puritans always replace the common law by scriptural law.

83 Hofstadte*r*, p.111.

to one of the regnant abstractions of modem politics, can have no other result than a totalitarian order.[84] In its train it has left us, as a nation, with a series of almost insoluble problems in our social, economic, and political policy, to say nothing of our foreign affairs: with a series of promises impossible to keep. For approaching these dilemmas, Lincoln leaves us with nothing but deformations of experience, cut off forever from the real—and with an inability to call a political question by its proper name. It is a peculiar characteristic of Anglo-American politics since the beginning of the modern era that our leaders tend so often, when put to the test, to revert from the mild and materialist meliorism or gnosticism of the New Whigs to the activist and sectarian arrogance of their forefathers of that other Israel; though they rightly sense that in that role they are, for an electorate formed within a tradition of bibliolatry, difficult to resist.[85] Regrettably, whenever they succumb to this temptation, to take the easy way to power, they partake as heirs in the legacy of Abraham Lincoln and join with him in once again dividing the house.

---

[84] *The New Science of Politics*, 132: "Totalitarianism, defined as the existential rule of Gnostic activists, is the end and form of progressive civilization." The result of impose freedom or equality is always enslavement by the state.

[85] This entire essay is in obvious debt to Professor Voegelin's discussion of Richard Hooker's critique of the Puritan mind. *The New Science of Politics*, 135-152. For a contrary view of Lincoln's neo-Puritan civil theology, see Glen E. Thurlow, *Abraham Lincoln and American Political Religion* (Albany: State University of New York Press, 1976).

4.

The Lincoln Legacy: A Long View (1980)

With the time and manner of his death Abraham Lincoln, as leader of a Puritan people who had just won a great victory over "the forces of evil," was placed beyond the reach of ordinary historical inquiry and assessment. Through Booth's bullet he became the one who had "died to make men free," who had perished that his country's "new birth" might occur: a "second founder" who, in Ford's theater, had been transformed into an American version of the "dying God." Our common life, according to this construction, owes its continuation to the shedding of the sacred blood. Now after over a century of devotion to the myth of the "political Messiah," it is still impossible for most Americans to see through and beyond the magical events of April 1865. However, Lincoln's daily purchase upon the ongoing business of the nation requires that we devise a way of setting aside the martyrdom to look behind it at Lincoln's place in the total context of American history and discover in him a major source of our present confusion, our distance from the republicanism of the Fathers, the models of political conduct which we profess most to admire. The examination of Lincoln's career as divided into Whig, artificial Puritan, and serious Cromwellian phases should facilitate that recovery. And provide a proper word to break the silence that will not let us know any judge.[1]

Of course, nothing that we can identify as part of Lincoln's legacy belongs to him alone. In some respects, the Emancipator was carried along with the tides. Yet a measure of his importance is that he was at the heart of the major political events of his era. Therefore, what signifies in a final evaluation of this melancholy man is that many of these changes in the country would never have come to pass had Lincoln not pushed them forward. Or at least not come so quickly, or with such dreadful violence. I will emphasize only the events that he most certainly shaped according to his relentless will, alterations in the character of our country for which he was clearly responsible. For related developments touched by Lincoln's wand, I can have only a passing word. The major changes advanced here, if proved, are sufficient to impeach the most famous and respected of public men. More would only overdo.

The first and most obvious item in my bill of particulars for indictment concerns Lincoln's dishonesty and obfuscation with respect to the nation's future obligations to the Negro, slave and free. It was of course an essential ingredient of Lincoln's position that he make a success at being anti-southern or anti-slavery without at the same time appearing to be significantly impious about the beginnings of the Republic (which was neither anti-Southern nor antislavery)—or significantly pro-Negro. He was the first Northern politician of any rank to combine these attitudes into a viable platform persona, the first to make his moral position on slavery in the South into a part of his national politics. It was a posture that enabled him to unite elements of the Northern

---

[1] This essay is a draft of a conclusion to a larger study of Lincoln's career, other sections of which appeared in *Modern Age*. See, "The Heresy of Equality: Bradford Replies to Jaffa," *Modern Age* 20 (Winter 1976): 62-77; "Dividing the House: The Gnosticism of Lincoln's Political Rhetoric," *Modern Age* 23 (Winter 1979): 10-24. See also "Lincoln, the Declaration, and Secular Puritanism: A Rhetoric for Continuing the Revolution," in *A Better Guide than Reason: Studies in the American Revolution* (LaSalle, Ill.: Sherwood Sugden and Co., 1979), 185-203.

electorate not ordinarily willing to cooperate in any political undertaking. And thus, enabled him to destroy the old Democratic majority—a coalition necessary to preserving the union of the states. Then came the explosion. But this calculated posturing has had more durable consequences than secession and the federal confiscation of property in slaves. Even after the passage of over a century, with each new day they unfold with additional and ever-deepening iteration and threatened to produce divisions that make those explored on the battlefields of Virginia, Maryland, and Tennessee seem mild indeed: so, threaten most especially since it has become impossible to single out the South as the particular locus of "improper" attitudes on the subject of race.

In the nation as a whole what moves toward fruition is a train of events set in motion by the duplicitous rhetoric concerning the Negro that helped make Abraham Lincoln into our first "sectional" president. Central to this appeal is a claim to a kind of moral superiority that costs absolutely nothing in the way of conduct. Lincoln, in insisting that the Negro was included in the promise of the Declaration of Independence and that the Declaration bound his countrymen to fulfill a pledge hidden in that document, seemed clearly to point toward a radical transformation of American society. Carried within his rejection of Negro slavery as a continuing feature of the American regime, his assertion that the equality clause of the Declaration of Independence was "the father of all moral principle among us," were certain muted corollaries.[2] By promising that the peculiar institution would be made to disappear if candidates for national office adopted the proper "moral attitude" on that subject, Lincoln recited as a litany the general terms of his regard for universal human rights. But at the same time, he added certain modifications to this high doctrine: modifications required by those of his countrymen to whom he hoped to appeal, by the rigid racism of the Northern electorate, and by "what his own feelings would admit."[3] The most important of these reservations was that

---

2 See volume 2, page 449, of Roy Basler's edition of *The Collected Works of Abraham Lincoln* (New Brunswick: Rutgers University Press, 1953).

3 Lincoln, *Collected Works*, 3:79.

none of his doctrine should apply significantly to the Negro in the North. Or, after freedom, to what he could expect in the South. It was a very broad, very general, and very abstract principle to which he made reference. By it he could divide the sheep from the goats, the wheat from the chaff, the patriot from the conspirator. But for the Negro it provided nothing more than a technical freedom, best to be enjoyed far away. Or the valuable opportunity to "root, hog, or die."[4] For the sake of such vapid distinctions he urged his countrymen to wade through seas of blood.

To be sure, this position does not push the "feelings" of that moralist who was our sixteenth president too far from what was comfortable for him.[5] And it goes without saying that a commitment to "natural rights" which will not challenge the Black Codes of Illinois, which promises something like them for the freedman in the South, or else offers him as alternative the proverbial "one-way-ticket to nowhere" is a commitment of empty words. It is only an accident of political history that the final Reconstruction settlement provided a bit more for the former slave—principally, the chance to vote Republican; and even that "right" didn't last, once a better deal was made available to his erstwhile protectors. But the point is that Lincoln's commitment was precisely of the sort that the North was ready to make—while passing legislation to re-

---

[4] The choices available to the Negro, once free, according to Abraham Lincoln at the Hampton Roads conference of 1865, as reported (among other authorities) by Alexander H. Stephens, *A Constitutional View of the War Between the States* (Philadelphia: National Publishing Co., 1870) 2:615.

[5] See pages 363-38 of Harry V. Jaffa's *Crisis of a House Divided: An Interpretation of the Lincoln-Douglas Debates* (Seattle: University of Washington Press, 1973). Jaffa makes the best case possible for Lincoln's hard remarks concerning the Negro. But he turns the teaching upside down by contending that Lincoln was a racist only for political effect, did not really have those "feelings" he so emphasized, and meant what he said only when he spoke of equality. The prospect entertained by Lincoln of making Negroes who had been Federal soldiers into good Republican voters *down South* proves nothing about his plans for Illinois and Indiana. On this subject see also George M. Frederickson, "A Man but Not a Brother: Abraham Lincoln and Racial Equality," *Journal of Southern History* 41 (Feb. 1975): 39-58.

strict the flow of Negroes into its own territories, elaborating its own system of segregation by race, and exploiting black labor through its representatives in a conquered South. Lincoln's double talk left his part of the country with a durable heritage of pious self-congratulation, what Robert Penn Warren has well described as "The Treasury of Virtue."[6] Left it with the habit of concealing its larger objectives behind a facade of racial generosity, of using the Negro as a reason for policies and laws which make only minimal alterations in his condition; and also with the habit of seeming to offer a great deal more than it is truly willing to give. In the wake of the just concluded "Second Reconstruction" of 1955-1965, the Northern habit has become national, visible every time one of the respected polls examines our ostensible opinions on race relations. There we appear the soul of charity, though our conduct voting "with our feet" belies every statistic that we produce. Where such insubstantial sentiment will lead, we cannot say. It is enough to observe that mass hypocrisy is a contagious disease. Or to put matters another way, it would be well if we learn to say no more than we meant. For the alternative is to produce in the targets of our beneficence the kind of anger that comes with the receipt of a promissory note that contains, as one of its terms, the condition that it need never be paid. Better than this would be a little honest dealing, whatever its kind.

The second heading in this "case against Lincoln" involves no complicated pleading. Neither will it confuse any reader who examines his record with care. For it has to do with Lincoln's political economy, his management of the commercial and business life of the part of the Republic under his authority. This material is obvious, even though it is not always connected with the presidency of Abraham Lincoln. Nevertheless, it must be developed at this point for it leads directly into the more serious charges upon which this argument depends. It is customary to deplore the Gilded Age, the era of the Great Barbecue. It is true that many of the corruptions of the Republican Era came to a head

---

6 See pages 59-66 of Robert Penn Warren's, *The Legacy of the Civil War: Meditations on the Centennial* (New York; Random House, 1961).

after Lincoln lay at rest in Springfield. But it is a matter of fact that they began either under his direction or with his sponsorship. Military necessity, the "War for the Union," provided an excuse, an umbrella of sanction, under which the essential nature of the changes being made in the relation of government to commerce could be concealed. Of his total policy the Northern historian Robert Sharkey has written, "Human ingenuity would have had difficulty in contriving a more perfect engine for class and sectional exploration, creditors finally obtaining the upper hand as opposed to debtors, and the developed East holding the whip over the underdeveloped West and South."[7] Until the South left the Union, until a High Whig sat in the White House, none of this return to the "energetic government" of Hamilton's design was possible. Indeed, even in the heyday of the Federalists it had never been so simple a matter to translate power into wealth. Now Lincoln could try again the internal improvements of the early days in Illinois. The difference was that this time the funding would not be restrained by political reversal or a failure of credit. For if anything fell short, Mr. Salmon P. Chase, "the foreman" of his "green printing office," could be instructed "to give his paper mill another turn."[8] And the inflationary policy of rewarding the friends of the government sustained. The euphemism of our time calls this "income redistribution." But it was theft in 1864 and is theft today.

A great increase in the tariff and the formation of a national banking network were, of course, the cornerstones of this great alteration in the posture of the federal government toward the sponsorship of business. From the beginning of the Republican Party Lincoln warned his associates not to talk about their views on these subjects. Their alliance, he knew, was a negative thing: a league against the Slave Power and its Northern friends. But in private he made it clear that the hidden agenda of the Republicans

---

7 Quoted on page 115 of Ludwell H. Johnson's, *Division and Reunion: America, 1848-1877* (New York: John Wiley and Sons, 1978).

8 Quoted on pages 207 and 208 of G. S. Boritt's, *Lincoln and the Economics of the American Dream* (Memphis: Memphis State University Press, 1978).

would have its turn, once the stick was in their hand. In this he promised well. Between 1861 and 1865, the tariff rose from 18.84 percent to 47.56 percent. And it stayed above 40 percent in all, but two years of the period concluded with the election of Woodrow Wilson. Writes the Virginia historian Ludwell H. Johnson, it would "facilitate a massive transfer of wealth, satisfying the dreariest predictions of John C. Calhoun."[9] The new republican system of banking (for which we should note Lincoln was directly accountable) was part of the same large design of "refounding." The national banking acts of 1863 and 1864, with the earlier legal tender act, flooded the country with $480 million of fiat money that was soon depreciated by about two-thirds in relation to specie. Then all notes but the greenback dollar were taxed out of existence, excepting only United States Treasury bonds that all banks were required to purchase if they were to have a share in the war boom. The support for these special bonds was thus the debt itself—Hamilton's old standby. Specie disappeared. Moreover, the bank laws controlled the money supply, credit, and the balance of power. New banks and credit for farms, small businesses, or small town operations were discouraged. And the Federalist model, after four score and seven years, finally achieved.

As chief executive, Lincoln naturally supported heavy taxes. Plus, a scheme of tax graduation. The war was a legitimate explanation for these measures. Lincoln's participation in huge subsidies or bounties for railroads and in other legislation granting economic favors is not so readily linked to "saving the Union." All of his life Lincoln was a friend of the big corporations. He had no moral problem in signing a bill which gifted the Union Pacific Railway with a huge strip of land running across the West and an almost unsecured loan of $16,000 to $48,000 per mile of track. The final result of this bill was the Credit Mobilier scandal. With other laws favoring land speculation it helped to negate the seemingly noble promise of the Homestead Act of 1862—under which less than 19 percent of the open land settled between 1860 and 1900

---

9   Johnson, *Division and Reunion*, 10.

went to legitimate homesteaders. The Northern policy of importing immigrants with the promise of this land, only to force them into the ranks of General Grant's meatgrinder or into near slavery in the cities of the East, requires little comment. Nor need we belabor the rotten army contracts given to politically faithful crooks. Nor the massive thefts by law performed during the war in the South. More significant as Lincoln's openly disgraceful policy of allowing special cronies and favorites of his friends to trade in Southern cotton—even with "the enemy" across the line—and his calculated use of the patronage and the pork barrel.[10] Between 1860 and 1880, the Republicans spent almost $10 million breathing life into state and local Republican organizations. Lincoln pointed them down that road. There can be no doubt of his responsibility for the depressing spectacle of greed and peculation concerning which so many loyal Northern men of the day spoke with sorrow, disappointment, and outrage. Had they known in detail of Lincoln's career in the Illinois legislature, they would have been less surprised by the disparity between the lofty platform language of their leader and his domestic performance.

A large part of the complaint against Lincoln as a political precedent for later declensions from the example of the Fathers has to do with his expansion of the powers of the presidency and his alteration of the basis for the Federal Union. With reference to his role in changing the office of chief magistrate from what it had been under his predecessors, it is important to remember that he defined himself through the war powers that belonged to his post. In this way Lincoln could profess allegiance to the Whig ideal of the modest, self-effacing leader, the antitype of Andrew Jackson, and, in his capacity as commander-in-chief, do whatever he wished. That is, if he could do it in the name of preserving the Union. As Clinton Rossiter has stated, Lincoln believed there were "no limits" to his powers if he exercised them in that "holy cause."[11] Gottfried Dietze compares Lincoln in this role to the committee of

---

10 Ibid., 115-21.

11 See page 233 of Clinton Rossiter's *Constitutional Dictatorship* (Princeton: Princeton University Press, 1948).

public safety as it operated in the French Revolution. Except for the absence of mass executions, the results were similar.[12] War is of course the occasion for concentration of power and the limitation of liberties within any nation. But an internal war, a war between states in a union of states, is not like a war to repel invasion or to acquire territory. For it is an extension into violence of a domestic political difference. And it is thus subject to extraordinary abuses of authority—confusions or conflations of purpose which convert the effort to win the war into an effort to effect even larger, essentially political changes in the structure of government. War, in these terms, is not only an engine for preserving the Union; it is also an instrument for transforming its nature. But without overdeveloping this structure of theory, let us shore it up with specific instances of presidential misconduct by Lincoln: abuses that mark him as our first imperial president. Lincoln began his tenure as a dictator when between April 12 and July 4 of 1861, without interference from Congress, he summoned militia, spent millions, suspended law, authorized recruiting, decreed a blockade, defied the Supreme Court, and pledged the nation's credit. In the following months and years he created units of government not known to the Constitution and officers to rule over them in "conquered" sections of the South, seized property throughout both sections, arrested upwards of twenty thousand of his political enemies and confined them without trial in a Northern "Gulag," closed over three hundred newspapers critical of his policy, imported an army of foreign mercenaries (of perhaps five hundred thousand men), interrupted the assembly of duly elected legislatures and employed the Federal hosts to secure his own reelection—in a contest where about thirty-eight thousand votes, if shifted, might have produced an armistice and a negotiated peace under a President McClellan.[13] To the same end he created a state in West Virginia, arguing of this blatant violation of the explicit provisions of the constitution that

---

12   See page 40 of Gottfried Dietze's *America's Political Dilemma: From Lincoln to Unlimited Democracy* (Baltimore: Johns Hopkins University Press, 1968).

13   Johnson, *Division and Reunion*, 87.

it was "expedient."[14] But the worst of this bold and ruthless dealing (and I have given but a very selective list of Lincoln's "high crimes") has to do with his role as military leader per se: as the commander and selector of Northern generals, chief commissary of the Federal forces, and head of government in dealing with the leaders of an opposing power. In this role the image of Lincoln grows to be very dark—indeed, almost sinister.

The worst that we may say of Lincoln is that he led the North in war so as to put the domestic political priorities of his political machine ahead of the lives and the well-being of his soldiers in the field. The appointment of the venal Simon Cameron of Pennsylvania as his secretary of war, and of lesser hacks and rascals to direct the victualing of Federal armies, was part of this malfeasance. By breaking up their bodies, the locust hoard of contractors even found a profit in the Union dead. And better money still in the living. They made of Lincoln (who winked at their activities) an accessory to lost horses, rotten meat, and worthless guns. But all such mendacity was nothing in comparison to the price in blood paid for Lincoln's attempts to give the nation a genuine Republican hero. He had a problem with this project throughout the entire course of the war. That is, until Grant and Sherman "converted" to radicalism. Prior to their emergence all of Lincoln's "loyal" generals disapproved of either his politics or of his character. These, as with McClellan, he could use and discharge at will. Or demote to minor tasks. One thinks immediately of George G. Meade—who defeated Lee at Gettysburg, and yet made the mistake of defining himself as the defender of a separate Northern nation from whose soil he would drive a foreign Southern "invader."[15] Or of Fitz John Porter, William B. Franklin, and Don Carlos Buell—all scapegoats thrown by Lincoln to the radical wolves. In place of these heterodox professionals, Lincoln assigned such champions of the "new freedom" as Nathaniel P. ("Commissary") Banks, Benjamin

---

14   Lincoln, *Collected Works*, 6:26-28.

15   See a discussion of this episode on page 352 of Stephen B. Oates's *With Malice toward None: A Life of Abraham Lincoln* (New York: Harper and Row, 1977).

F. ("Beast") Butler, John C. Fremont, and John A. McClernand. Speaking in summary despair of these appointments (and adding to my list, Fritz Siegel and Lew Wallace), General Henry Halleck, Lincoln's chief-of-staff, declared that they were "little better than murder."[16] Yet in the East, with the Army of the Potomac, Lincoln made promotions even more difficult to defend, placing not special projects, divisions, and brigades but entire commands under the authority of such "right thinking" incompetents as John Pope (son of an old crony in Illinois) and "Fighting Joe" Hooker. Or with that "tame" Democrat and late favorite of the radicals, Ambrose E. Burnside. Thousands of Northern boys lost their lives in order that the Republican Party might experience rejuvenation, to serve its partisan goals. And those were "party supremacy within a Northern dominated Union."[17] A Democratic "man-on-horseback" could not serve those ends, however faithful to "the Constitution as it is, and the Union as it was" (the motto of the Democrats) they might be. For neither of these commitments promised a Republican hegemony. To provide for his faction both security and continuity in office, Lincoln sounded out his commanders in correspondence (much of which still survives), suborned their military integrity. And employed their focus in purely political operation. Writes Johnson:

> Although extreme measures were most common in the border states, they were often used elsewhere too. By extreme measures is meant the arrest of anti-Republican candidates and voters, driving anti-Republican voters from the polls or forcing them to vote the Republican ticket, preventing opposition parties from holding meetings, removing names from ballots, and so forth. These methods were employed in national, state and local elections. Not only did the army interfere by force, it was used to supply votes.

---

16   Quoted in Johnson, *Division and Reunion*, p.90.
17   *Ibid.*, 123.

Soldiers whose states did not allow absentee voting were sent home by order of the President to swell the Republican totals. When voting in the field was used, Democratic commissioners carrying ballots to soldiers from their state were ... unceremoniously thrown into prison, while Republican agents were offered every assistance. Votes of Democratic soldiers were sometimes discarded as defective, replaced by Republican ballots, or simply not counted.[18]

All Lincoln asked of the ordinary Billy Yank was that he be prepared to give himself up to no real purpose—at least until Father Abraham found a general with proper moral and political credentials to lead him on to Richmond. How this part of Lincoln's career can be reconciled to the myth of the "suffering savior" I cannot imagine.

We might dwell for some time on what injury Lincoln did to the dignity of his office through the methods he employed in prosecuting the war. It was no small thing to disavow the ancient Christian code of "limited war," as did his minions, acting in his name. However, it is enough in this connection to remember his policy of denying medicines to the South, even for the sake of Northern prisoners held behind the lines. We can imagine what a modern "war crimes" tribunal would do with that decision. There may have been practicality in such inhumane decisions. *Practicality* indeed! As Charles Francis Adams, Lincoln's ambassador to the Court of Saint James and the scion of the most notable family in the North, wrote in his diary of his leader, the "president and his chief advisers are not without the spirit of the serpent mixed in with their wisdom."[19] And he knew whereof he spoke. For

---

18 Ibid., 126.
19 Unpublished diary of Charles Francis Adams, May 18, 1864, quoted on page 19 of Harriet Chappell Owsley's "Peace and the Presidential Election of 1864," *Tennessee Historical Quarterly* 18 (March 1959): 3-19. This article gives an account of the embassy of Thomas Yeatman and is drawn from evidence long concealed among the Adams family papers.

practical politics, the necessities of the campaign of 1864, had led Lincoln and Seward to a decision far more serious than unethical practices against prisoners and civilians in the South. I speak of the rejection by the Lincoln administration of peace feelers authorized by the Confederate government in Richmond: feelers that met Lincoln's announced terms for an end to the federal invasion of the South. The emissary in this negotiation was sponsored by Charles Francis Adams. He was a Tennessean living in France, one Thomas Yeatman. After arriving in the United States, he was swiftly deported by direct order of the government before he could properly explore the possibility of an armistice on the conditions of reunion and an end to slavery. Lincoln sought these goals, but only on his terms. And in his own time. He wanted total victory. And he needed a still-resisting, impenitent Confederacy to justify his re-election. We can only speculate as to why President Davis allowed the Yeatman mission. We know that he expected little of such peace feelers. (There were many in the last stages of the conflict.) He knew his enemy too well to expect anything but subjection, however benign the rhetoric used to disguise its rigor. Adams's peace plan was perhaps impossible, even if his superiors in Washington had behaved in good faith. The point is that none of the peace moves of 1864 was given any chance of success. Over one hundred thousand Americans may have died because of the Rail-Splitter's rejection of an inexpedient peace. Yet we have still not touched upon the most serious of Lincoln's violations of the Presidential responsibility. I speak, finally, of his role in bringing on the War Between the States.

There is, we should recall, a great body of scholarly argument concerning Lincoln's intentions in 1860 and early 1861. A respectable portion of this work comes to the conclusion that the first Republican president expected a "tug," a "crisis," to follow his election. And then, once the secession had occurred, also expected to put it down swiftly with a combination of persuasion, force, and Southern loyalty to the Union. The last of these, it is agreed, he completely overestimated. In a similar fashion he exaggerated the force of Southern "realism," the region's capacity to act in its own pecuniary interest. The authority on Lincoln's political economy has remarked that the Illinois lawyer-politician and old line Whig always made the mistake of explaining in simple economic terms the South's hostile reaction to anti-slavery proposals.[20] To that blunder he added the related mistake of attempting to end the "rebellion" with the same sort of simplistic appeals to the prospect of riches. Or with fear of a servile insurrection brought on by his greatest "war measure," the emancipation of slaves behind Southern lines, beyond his control. A full-scale Southern revolution, a revolution of all classes of men against the way he and some of his supporters thought, was beyond his imagination. There was no "policy" in such extravagant behavior, no human nature as he perceived it. Therefore, on the basis of my understanding of his overall career, I am compelled to agree with Charles W. Ramsdell concerning Lincoln and his war.[21] Though he was no sadist and no warmonger, and though he got for his pains much more of a conflict than he had in mind, Lincoln hoped for an "insurrection" of some sort—an "uprising" he could use.

The "rational" transformation of our form of government which he had first predicted in the "Springfield Lyceum Speech" required some kind of passionate disorder to justify the enforcement of a new Federalism. And needed also for the voting representatives of the South to be out of their seats in Congress. It is out of keeping with his total performance as a public man and in contradiction of his campaigning after 1854 not to believe that Lincoln hoped for a Southern attack on Fort Sumter. As he told his old friend Senator Orville H. Browning of Illinois: "The plan succeeded. They attacked Sumter—it fell, and thus did more service than it

---

20 Boritt, *Lincoln and the Economics of the American Dream*, 163-65.

21 See Charles W. Ramsdell's "Lincoln and Fort Sumter," *Journal of Southern History* 3 (August 1937): 259-88. The best reply is by David Potter, developed in several of his essays. See his *Impending Crisis: 1848-1861* (New York: Harper and Row, 1976). Don E. Fehrenbacher completed the chapter on Fort Sumter, 553-83. See also Kenneth Stampp, *And the War Came* (Baton Rouge: Louisiana State University Press, 1950); and Potter's *Lincoln and His Party in the Secession Crisis* (New Haven: Yale University Press, 1971).

otherwise could."[22] And to others he wrote or spoke to the same effect. If the Confederacy's offer of money for federal property were made known in the North and business relations of the sections remained unaffected, if the Mississippi remained open to Northern shipping, there would be no support for "restoring" the Union on a basis of force. Americans were in the habit of thinking of the unity of the nation as a reflex of their agreement in the Constitution, of law as a limit on government and on the authority of temporary majorities, and of revisions in law as the product of the ordinary course of push and pull within a pluralistic society, not as a response to the extra legal authority of some admirable abstraction like equality. In other words, they thought of the country as being defined by the way in which we conducted our political business, not by where we were trying to go in a body. Though once a disciple of Henry Clay, Lincoln changed the basis of our common bond away from the doctrine of his mentor, away from the patterns of compromise and dialectic of interest and values under a limited, Federal sovereignty with which we as a people began our adventure with the Great Compromise of 1787-1788. The nature of the Union left us by Lincoln is thus always at stake in every major election, in every refinement in our civil theology; the Constitution is still to be defined by the latest wave of big ideas, the most recent mass emotion. Writes Dietz:

> Concentrations of power in the national and executive branches of government, brought about by Lincoln in the name of the people, were processes that conceivably complemented each other to the detriment of free government. Lincoln's administration thus opened the way for the development of an omnipotent national executive who as a spokesman for the people might consider himself entitled to do whatever he felt was good for the Nation, irrespective

---

22   Johnson, *Division and Reunion*, 79.

of the interest and rights of states, Congress, the judiciary, and the individual.[23]

If a President could behave in this way, so might Congress or the Supreme Court, interpreting something like Rousseau's General Will, as understood by those prophets who know what we need better than we, lacking their afflatus, can expect to understand it. It is a formula which makes the private morality of men a law, and of Union its instrument. Which is a long way from the government of laws with which we began.

But in my opinion the capstone of this case against Lincoln as an American model, this bill of particulars *contra* the Lincoln myth, is not the patricide (as one recent historian has called it) of his refounding, his conversion of the national government into our juggernaut with which we are all more familiar than we would like.[24] Rather, his overall worst is what he has done to the language of American political discourse that makes it so difficult for us to reverse the ill effects of trends he set in motion with his executive fiat. When I say that Lincoln was our first Puritan president, I am chiefly referring to a distinction of style, to his habit of wrapping up his policy in the idiom of Holy Scripture, concealing within the Trojan horse of his gasconade and moral superiority an agenda that would never have been approved if presented in any other form. It is this rhetoric in particular, a rhetoric confirmed in its authority by his martyrdom, that is enshrined in the iconography of the Lincoln myth preserved against examination by monuments such as the Lincoln Memorial, where his oversized likeness is elevated above us like that of a deified Roman emperor. Or in the form of a god-king, seated on his throne. The place is obviously a temple, fit for a divinity who suffered death and was transformed on Good Friday. It is both unpatriotic and irreligious to look

---

23 Dietze, *America's Political Dilemma*, 58.

24 See George B. Forgie, *Patricide in the House Divided: A Psychological Interpretation of Lincoln and His Age* (New York: W. W. Norton and Co., 1979). Forgie's book, which won the Allan Nevins Award, does, however, break much new ground and is valuable in correcting the myth.

behind the words of so august a presence and period and to imitate Lincoln's epideictic, quasi-liberal rhetoric employing his favorite normative terms is to draw upon the authority generated by Lincoln idolatry and the imagery that surrounds it. In this universe of discourse, this closed linguistic system, all questions are questions of ends, and means are beside the point. And every "good cause" is a reason for increasing the scope of government. All that counts is the *telos*, the general objective, and bullying is not merely allowed, but required. It would be simple enough to be ruled directly by messages from God. But an imitation of that arrangement most properly leaves us uneasy.

For over one hundred years we have been on the course charted out for us by the captain of the flying ship of Lincoln's recurrent wartime dreams. Though as we recall, even that captain was not sure of his destination, only of the velocity of the voyage, and of the necessity for holding on to the boat. As in Lincoln's dream, we sail in darkness. Under such circumstances the worry is that we are more likely to arrive at the final plain of desolation than to a happy port in the New Zion of the Puritan vision. Once we have become "all *one* thing or all *another*," we may understand better what it means to "loose the fearful lightning of that of the terrible swift sword."

5.

Lincoln and the Language of Hate and Fear: A View from the South (1984)

In 1854 we come to the central portion of Lincoln's career, and to the sequence of speeches which made of him a national figure and, finally, a President. To be specific, the watershed occurs after he had played a minor role in the campaign of Winfield Scott; after the deaths of Clay and Webster; after a brief (and maladroit) adventure as the Sucker Whig in Congress; and (more important) after Stephen Douglas had returned from Washington to Illinois to answer the objections made there among his neighbors to his part in passing the Kansas-Nebraska Act. To the Little Giant's role in the repeal of the Missouri Compromise and the opening of the new territories west of Missouri and Iowa to their organization as either free or slave states there had been a general remonstrance in the Northwest. And, in the fall of 1854, Douglas went home to face the electorate which had raised him to a seat of power in the Senate of the United States and to account for the decisions that he had made in order to facilitate the development of the West. Douglas began this campaign of persuasion upstate, and then worked his way south. Outside of Chicago he was well received. But when he reached the Springfield area, Lincoln rose to give him answer. A few days later he repeated his reply to Douglas's set speech in Peoria, Illinois. It is with this second version of Lincoln's rejoinder (known since as the "Peoria Speech"), given October 16, 1854, that he puts behind him his identity as a disciple of Henry Clay. Though he does not officially leave the party until 1856—after many of its members have located themselves, with varying degrees of discomfort, under a heterogeneous Republican tent.[1]

In considering what Lincoln now becomes it is *extremely* important to remember what he had been in all the years before, how he has conducted himself as a man and an Illinois politician, and what shifts have occurred in the intellectual atmosphere in which he moves. For it is a consensus of *all* the scholarship that the "Peoria Speech" brings before us a "second Lincoln," a figure greatly altered from the moderate opportunist of the early years. The usual explanation of this metamorphosis is that "devotion to a cause" has had a magic effect on the prairie lawyer.[2] Or that "the Kansas Nebraska Act transformed his thinking on the whole subject [of slavery]."[3] In the quiet years following his return from the single (and disastrous) term in the House of Representatives, Lincoln had probably thought of himself as a man with no political future.[4] Then, with the Kansas Nebraska Act, he got another chance, but not as an orthodox Whig. He was not about to let it pass.

With his 1854 reappearance in the political arena, we encounter suddenly (and without forewarning) an orator who suggests the character we have so often been encouraged to admire: encounter a foreshadowing of the man in the myth. And indeed, Lincoln's change in manner is remarkable, but it is only a change in strategy.

---

1 On the origins of the Republican Party, see Eric Foner, *Free Soil, Free labor, Free Men: The Ideology of the Republican Party* (New York: Oxford University Press, 1970). In 1856, Lincoln backed Fremont, not Milliard Fillmore.

2 Benjamin P. Thomas, *Abraham Lincoln* (New York: Modern Library, 1952), p.143.

3 Don E. Fehrenbacher, *Prelude to Greatness: Lincoln in the 1850s* (Stanford: Stanford University Press, 1962), 23.

4 See the comments of Albert Taylor Bledsoe quotes (p. 176) in Harry E. Pratt's "Albert Taylor Bledsoe: Critic of Lincoln," *Transactions of the Illinois Historical Society*, 1934, 153-83.

Knowing him as he was before Douglas left the opening on his flank, we find it difficult to believe that the human substance concealed within this altered persona is so very different from the clever, ruthless, and yet ordinary country politician who was a leader among Illinois Whigs, from what one of his biographers describes as "an essentially self-centered, small-town politician."[5] Such transformations, rot from such materials, belong only to hagiography, and even with God's grace, the saints rarely come so far.

There will always be, of course, a certain number who will believe Lincoln's statement that his only motive for returning to the campaign trail was a desire to assist Richard Yates of Jacksonville in his candidacy for re-election as representative of the Seventh District of Illinois; and that, at that time, he had "no thought of a new political career for himself."[6] These credulous souls who accept on its face Lincoln's every word may also be persuaded that his newfound anxiety at the expansion of slavery, and his new rhetoric for treating of that prospect, issued from nothing more complex than his disinterested concern for the common good. Or that he was just an overgrown country boy, the *vir bonus* of the classical description: a "warm hearted and simple minded man," as Herndon says in mocking summary of this view.[7] To convince these men of trust that the cause cannot interpret the man, that Lincoln should not be seen through the prism of his assassination, is to threaten something of themselves which is made specific in their

---

5   Thomas, *Lincoln*, 143; Albert J. Beveridge, *Abraham Lincoln, 1809-1858* (Boston: Houghton Mifflin Co., 1928), 2:244, observes that his speech does not seem to have been written by the same man who authored Lincoln's earlier addresses and is "wholly unlike any before made by him." He adds that the "Peoria Speech" also anticipates everything Lincoln wrote before the Emancipation Proclamation.

6   Thomas, *Lincoln*, 146; Fehrenbacher, *Prelude to Greatness*, p.37, notes that Lincoln spoke mostly outside of Yates's district. See also, Donald W. Riddle, *Congressman Abraham Lincoln* (Urbana, IL: University of Illinois Press, 1957), 248-49.

7   Quoted from William Herndon's 1866 speech, "Facts Illustrative of Mr. Lincoln's Patriotism and Statesmanship," *Abraham Lincoln Quarterly* 3 (December 1944): 188.

attachment to the Lincoln myth. But the reading of these middle years, and of the language by which they are defined, which we will test in the following discussion is of another kind, resting on the theory that we should explicate our Lincoln *seriatim,* from the beginning, forward; and that, as Herndon insisted, he was a "cool man," guided by "policy" in all things, by "profound calculation and logical precision."[8] It will be our argument that he proceeded and spoke as he did in order to get the way to the Senate opened for himself. With his good friend, Senator Lyman Trumbull, we will assume that it is "... a popular mistake to suppose Mr. Lincoln free from ambition. A more ardent seeker after office never existed. From the time when, at the age of twenty-three, he announced himself a candidate for the legislature from Sangamon County, till his death, he was constantly either in office or struggling to obtain one."[9] Let us see how well this perspective accounts for what Lincoln said and did.

While discussing Lincoln's earliest reactions to the Kansas-Nebraska Act and his effort to capture the Senate seat of his old adversary, James Shields, Donald W. Riddle has written, "Lincoln was not fighting for a cause. He was using the slavery issue, conveniently presented by the Kansas-Nebraska Act, to advance his own political standing. He was using the Act to run for office; ... [without it] there was not the slightest likelihood of his election." A bit later, the Illinois historian adds, "Never before had Lincoln run for office on the slavery issue, but never afterward would he run on any other."[10] Riddle's reading of Lincoln's conduct in this period is sound enough, so far as it goes. But it might easily lead us to ignore the fact that Lincoln's true target is never slavery or even the regime of the South, but rather certain public men in the North who are skilled in working with the established powers below the Old Surveyor's Line. Which is to say that his true target has not

---

8   *Ibid.*
9   Horace White, *The Life of Lyman Trumbull* (Boston: Houghton Mifflin Co.), 429, quotation from the senator's letter to his son.
10 Riddle, *Congressman Lincoln*, 249, 252.

really changed at all. It is the Democratic Party, and particularly the Illinois Democrats. The Whigs had ceased to be a national force when Tyler and Fillmore disappointed the reasonable expectations of their "Old Federalist" wing. That party had died with Webster and Clay. In its place was left a vacuum, partially filled by two or three almost viable new organizations. But these almost-parties were apparently too narrow to grow.[11] To win against the hated Locos, a candidate at the national level would have to combine strength from most of these with what remained of the Whigs, and with the disaffected Democrats. And the same situation obtained in many state and local races. Irregular Democrats were especially important in this formula. For the special synthesis achieved by Andrew Jackson was also on its way to disillusion and no equivalent catalyst was in sight. The year of 1854 was therefore a good time for a Midwestern politician to turn his coat—or at least re-tailor it with curious (and contradictory) additions. We must admit in fairness that Lincoln was not quick to change his political identity and did not invent the new persona which he adopted, though he finally got on with the new job of self-recreation and became the master of a new political style. All of which we can demonstrate from the text of his works. Lincoln's formula was simple: if the Whigs could lose their national following, so might the Democrats. The old spirit of sectional accommodation could be easily discredited, particularly in the Northwest, a territory filling rapidly with new citizens who did not understand it, or its importance to the possibility of Union: a region rapidly developing a proud identity of its own.[12] With

---

11 The Liberal Party, the Know-Nothing, the Anti-Mason Party, the Free Soil Party, and many more were almost-parties.

12 See David M. Potter, *The Impending Crisis, 1848-1861* (New York: Harper & row, 1976), 152, for Stephen A. Douglas's 1853 speech on the coming empire of the Northwest: "There is a power in the nation greater than either the North or the South—a growing, increasing, swelling power that will be able to speak the law to this nation .... that power is the country known as the Great West—the valley of the Mississippi, one and indivisible from the Gulf to the Great Lakes, and stretching ... from the Alleghenies to the Rocky Mountains. There, sir, is the hope of this nation—the resting place of the power that is not only to control, but to save, the Union." Naturally, he concluded that this new combination would be directed out of Illinois.

Illinois politicians who spoke another language Lincoln was now prepared to deal, attacking with a great host already at his back.

To understand how it came to be possible to divide the Democrats and create a Northern sectional party it is necessary for us to review what happened to change Illinois and the remainder of the Northwest between 1834, when Lincoln and Douglas first encountered one another in the old capital in Vandalia, and the time of their exchange in Peoria, some twenty years later. For as the line of settlement moved westward and the empty lands were filled, the spirit of comity left by the Revolution and early years within the Union was subjected to periodic strains. Almost always the unstated issue was whether an additional state would lend its political support to the South or the Northeast; to the agricultural or the commercial interest, to limited or energetic government. Yet often the idiom in which these possibilities were explored, the framework for the distribution of power, was a dispute over the advantage and disadvantage of holding Negro slaves. Or at least it was safe to predict that slavery would be brought into the discussion. At times it seemed that neither side would agree to increase the voting strength of the other, even when geography and the movements of population left them with little choice.[13] These problems of rightful distribution of power reached a climax after the conclusion of the Mexican War. The Compromise of 1850 and the Kansas-Nebraska Act follow in this train. Expansion of the national boundaries to the Pacific, with the Oregon Treaty of 1846 and the Treaty of Guadalupe-Hildago, had brought matters to a head. The South was reluctant to agree to any further admissions of new states unless it could expect its share. It spoke of the example of its own generosity in surrendering the region above the Ohio to the Northern states as their outlet for growth. Indeed, the 1787 Northwest Ordinance is the datum for much of this dispute—and also the circumstances surrounding its adoption. For they play a major role in Lincoln's years as an affected or pseudo-Puritan—are the centerpieces of his jeremiad against Democratic innovation, his ac-

---

13   Although curiously enough at other times everyone behaved well and states entered the Union or were organized as territories with no dispute.

cusation that there is a plan to nationalize the Peculiar Institution, a plan designed by Northern politicians, though he understood the Ordinance and its 1787 meaning not at all, or else distorted both with conscious intent. And as with Lincoln, so with many other "new breed" Northern politicians—spokesmen who practiced upon the paranoia of the Free States in speaking of a Slave Power and its dark designs,[14] when in fact nothing new to the operation of American politics was attempted in the West.

What Lincoln maintained with monotonous iteration throughout these middle years is that the nation's Fathers had specified their desire to put slavery "on the road to extinction" through the provisions which they had made, while we were yet governed under the Articles, to preclude its spread into the lands north of the Ohio ceded into their care by Virginia; and that, with and by this instrument of exclusion, they had established a fixed precedent for future restrictions. Which is to misconstrue the business altogether; and also, to deny certain self-evident truths concerning human nature. For it is not to be believed that any society would self-consciously arrange for the possibility of its own destruction. The proper reading for the almost total support given to the Northwest Ordinance by the representatives of the Southern states voting in the Continental Congress is that the antislavery clause was put into the text to certify that these lands were to be reserved for settlers from New England and the Middle Atlantic states: to provide these Americans, through a gesture both practical and symbolic, with a fresh incentive to loyalty toward a confederation of which many were afraid; and, incidentally, to prevent competition with established Southern agriculture.[15] It does not occur to Father Abraham that, in 1788, everyone expected the South to be the region of rapid

---

14   See David Brion Davis, *The Slave Power Conspiracy and the Paranoid Style* (Baton Rouge, LA: University of Louisiana State Press, 1969), 62-86.

15   See William Grayson, as quoted in a note to 198 of Hugh Blair Grigsby, *The History of the Virginia Federal Convention of 1788* (New York: D Carpo Press, 1969). Col. Grayson of Virginia presided over the Continental Congress when it voted on the Northwest Ordinance.

growth.[16] Or that the South, out of generosity, would provide for new states without slavery, hoping thereby to make many a Yankee a sound Union man, and still have absolutely no notion of giving up slavery itself. The spirit which perceived that a balance, half-slave, half-free, should be kept he did not comprehend, nor the truth that even the abolitionists recognised: that the South had, it believed, provided for its security against any external interference in the Constitution and Bill of Rights, and felt that it could afford a little generosity.

As to the Federal encouragement or regulation of the spread of slavery into the open territories, there is no consistent evidence that the Founders were of one mind concerning their legal authority and its limitation.[17] But Jefferson and Madison both counseled against such regulation, using arguments from law or precedent and arguments from definition.[18] As did James Monroe and Henry Clay. They encouraged the expansion of slavery into the West. John C. Miller in summarizing Jefferson's "diffusionist theory" condenses the great Democrat's advice to a new generation of bondsmen as follows: "Go West, young slave, go West. There you will find kind treatment more humane masters, a better chance

---

16 See *The Antislavery Vanguard: New Essays on the Abolitionists*, ed. Martin Duberman (Princeton: Princeton University Press, 1965), 321-22. The passage which I cite is from Staughton Lynd's essay, "The Abolitionist Critique of the United States Constitution." In it he observes that most of the Fathers expected the South to outgrow and outpopulate the North. On the same subject see also Donald L. Robinson, *Slavery in the Structure of American Politics, 1765-1820* (New York: Harcourt, Brace, Jovanovich, Inc., 1971), 445-46.

17 Of the Framers, only James Wilson of Pennsylvania actually read the Constitution as implying the right of the national government to restrict the movement of slaves inside the United States. And he did so only for effect in order to secure ratification in his state—in a context where no one had the authority to deny his construction. See Robert R. Russel, "Constitutional Doctrines With Regard to Slavery in the Territories, "*Journal of Southern History* 32 (Fall 1966): 466-86. Also useful is Glover Moore, *The Missouri Controversy, 1819–1821* (Lexington: University of Kentucky Press, 1953).

18 See Robinson, *Slavery in American Politics*, 141, 529. See also John Chester Miller, *The Wolf by The Ears: Thomas Jefferson and Slavery* (New York: The Free Press, 1977), 234-42, for the Jefferson theory of "diffusion."

at eventual emancipation."[19] And this irony could be applied just as well to statements concerning the "positive good" of such distribution made by a complete set of early American statesmen, champions of freedom and Founders, beginning in 1798 with those solid Jeffersonians, William Giles and George Nicholas of Virginia.

Lincoln, in treating of this question, of course always invokes his version of the Founders' intentions. But if Jefferson and Madison do not qualify as Founders, it is difficult to say who does. To the idea that section 9 of Article I in the federal compact even "hinted ... at a power ... to prohibit an interior migration of any sort," the latter spoke directly:

> But whatever may have been intended by the term "migration" or the term "persons," it is most certain, that they referred, exclusively to a migration or importation from other countries into the United States; and not to a removal, voluntary or involuntary, of Slaves or freemen, from one to another part of the United States. Nothing appears or is recollected that warrants the latter intention. Nothing in the proceedings of the State conventions indicates such construction there.

Wrote Mr. Madison in 1819, "it is easy to imagine the figure [such a construction] would have made among the numerous amendments to it proposed by state conventions, not one of which amendments refers to the clause in question...."[20] The rest of Lincoln's historical argument is as fragile as his comment on the Northwest Ordinance and his imagination of a 1787 Philadelphia plan to restrict the spread of slavery into the West. Centerpieces were a notion that criticism of a simplistic view of the Declaration was an ominous innovation, unheard of in the early years of the

---

19 Miller, *Wolf by the Ears*, 238.

20 For Madison's remarks, see *The Records of the Federal Convention of 1787*, ed. *Max* Farrand (New Haven: Yale University Press, 1966) 3:436-37.

Republic, and a highly selective narrative of various measures passed by Congress to interdict American participation in the international slave trade.

But contrary to Lincoln's claim, outrage at misunderstanding or misuse of the equality clause was as old as the Declaration itself: and, as early as 1804-1805, a commonplace, not heresy, when the youthful John C. Calhoun learned it from Lincoln's intellectual forebearers while reading law in the Federalist citadel at Litchfield, Connecticut. Even earlier, Henry Lee called the broad view of the Declaration "a splendid edifice built upon kegs of gunpowder."[21] In 1789 General James Jackson of Georgia developed the same theme in a speech before the House of Representatives.[22] By the time of the debates on Missouri, many legislators were calling the Declaration "a fanfaronade of metaphysical abstraction" with "No standing in American Law."[23] In a 1796 Independence Day oration, Congressman William L. Smith spoke in Charleston to the same effect.[24] As, at other times, spoke the younger John Tyler, William Pinkney, Josiah Quincy, Jr., John Randolph of Roanoke, John Taylor of Caroline, and Joseph Clay. The last of these, a representative from Pennsylvania, summarized moderate sentiment on the subject. In his opinion, "The Declaration of Independence is to be taken with great qualification."[25] Of this kind of evidence there is a plethora. Just as soon as American politicians began to read our instrument of separation as Lincoln was to read it in later years, other Americans said them nay; and, therefore, the interpretation of the document made by Douglas (and then by Chief Justice Taney) was nothing more than the forceful expression of a conventional view of the subject.

---

[21] George Fitzhugh, *Sociology for the South* (Richmond: A. Morris, 1854), 182,189.

[22] *Annals of Congress*, 1st Cong., 1st Sess., May 31, 1789, pp.336-37.

[23] Robinson, *Slavery in American Politics*, 244.

[24] William Sumner Jenkins, *Pro-Slavery Thought in the Old South* (Chapel Hill, NC: University of North Carolina Press, 1935), 61.

[25] *Ibid.*, 59.

Lincoln's explanation of laws passed to restrict the importation of slaves from overseas is equally artificial. He sees in the widely supported 1807 bill to end the trade from Africa and the West Indies a movement against the institution itself and supports this view with reference to earlier bills forbidding foreign importation into the territories. But the truth of things is very different. For many in the South saw in open importation a threat to the value of their property and also a threat of black overpopulation. Which is to say nothing of a general fear of difficult slaves, perhaps touched off by the spirit of the uprising in Santo Domingo—a fear which reached far beyond the boundaries of the slaveholding states.

Other elements of Lincoln's theory of the Fathers' "ancient faith" in a plan for eventual abolition deserve some mention. For, like most of the elements already examined, these last components tell us much about the widespread confusion concerning slavery and the birth of the nation current in the Midwest when Lincoln answered Douglas in 1854. One has to do with the refusal of the Framers to mention slavery by name. Some hostility to allowing the general government to speak of the institution in *any way* may be inferred from this silence, and also the desire of the authors, "so far as possible, to take [slavery] out of the national arena."[26] Another error concerns the meaning of the Mississippi Ordinance of 1798 and the policy of prohibiting slavery "except where it already existed," which is related to his ignorance of the Southwest Ordinance of 1790 and the Louisiana Ordinance of 1804. Each of these bills was subject to debate and in the case of the first, opponents of slavery made specifically the point that slavery had not yet taken root in the Mississippi Territory any more than it was established in Iowa and Illinois. Congress refused, by a clear majority vote, to prevent such introduction,[27] and likewise refused to interfere in Louisiana, even though it was a "national acquisition." The absence of debate on the Southwest Ordinance identifies it as either a quid pro quo or the product of intersectional

---

26   Robinson, *Slavery in American Politics*, 244.
27   Ibid., 389-91.

amity, in both cases reflecting a connection with its companion ordinance for the Old Northwest. Kentucky and Tennessee came into the Union under its terms, and not a word about slavery in either case.[28] In each and every instance to which Lincoln refers, the policy which he recommends for the entire West has been rejected by his predecessors. For they recognised in such total exclusion a violation of the principle first followed in the allocation of unsettled lands to various spheres of influence: the principle of compromise and rough equity in division.

Concerning the Northwest Ordinance, Donald L. Robinson has written, "Perhaps the most important reasons for Southern support for the ordinance was that its passage signaled the end of the attempt to prohibit slavery south of the Ohio River."[29] We must remember that there were no "federal lands" before the old states gave up their legitimate claims to Western lands. Virginia and North Carolina did not surrender Kentucky and Tennessee to federal control until they were certain that no question of slavery would be raised when they were ready for admission as states.[30] Indeed, they withdrew earlier offers of such cession during the sectional hostilities surrounding Jay's Treaty; and the same pattern holds true with later cessions by Georgia and South Carolina. Robinson's detailed narrative discussions of slavery in the early years of the Republic should be required reading with students of Lincoln and the years leading up to the War Between the States. But most particularly the pages dealing with the 1819 ordinance for the territory of Arkansas. This law, passed by the very Congress that broke apart over Missouri, came into being with the clear understanding of those who voted in its support that they were introducing "the smudge of slavery" upon a veritable "tabula rasa."[31] Taylor of New York moved to prohibit such an introduction

---

28 *Ibid.*, 385-86, 527.

29 *Ibid.*, 385.

30 *Ibid.*, 38. They entered in 1792 and 1796, after a few years under the Southwest Ordinance.

31 *Ibid.*, 413-14.

in precisely these terms. His motion was rejected. Which proves that many Northern legislators "saw the issue strictly in terms of political power within the Union and felt that Arkansas belonged to the South." Even in the time of the debate over Missouri, many Northerners continued to acknowledge the "Compromise of 1787." Missouri seemed to them a little far to the north but the idea of prohibiting slavery from all the new territories was not their plan. Usually, after push and pull, most Americans were drawn back to the original formula, *quid pro quo*—Maine for Missouri—though tilted a little in favor of the North not tilted all the way. Hence the line of the Missouri Compromise. Says Robinson elsewhere, "Northerners were far more concerned to halt the spread of slavery's influence than to wrestle with the institution itself."[32] In other words, concerned with the Slave Power. Upon the basis of such fears, Lincoln worked his will, invoking always his myth of "those old-time men" who "hedged and hemmed" the inherited evil "to the narrowest limits of necessity."[33] Preserving both the spirit and letter of the basic law that had first made us a country was not the task he had set for himself.

To grasp the implications of the early Liberty party or Free Soil movement (as opposed to the honest abolitionists, who simply desired to divide the country or change the Constitution), it is

---

32   *Ibid.*, 411, 430, 537. Rufus King of New York is Lincoln's predecessor in these debates and he concludes, "The premise of both arguments was that blacks had no permanent, stable place in equalitarian America except as slaves in regions where white men refused to work."

33   Abraham Lincoln, *The Collected Works of Abraham Lincoln*, ed. By Roy P. Basler, et al. 8 vols. (New Brunswick, N. J.: Rutgers University Press, 1953), 2: 267, 33. All subsequent citations are to this edition. (Citations to the Peoria speech are hereafter within the text.) We are reminded of the words that one of the Framers, Charles Pinckney of South Carolina, uttered during the debates over Missouri. It was his opinion that Northern opposition to slavery in the new states was unrelated to "the love of liberty, humanity, or religion" but sprang rather from "the love of power, and never ceasing wish to regain the honors and offices of the Government, which they know they can never be done but by increasing the number of non-slave holding States." (Charles S. Sydnor, *The Development of Southern Sectionalism, 1819-1848* [Baton Rouge, LA: University of Louisiana State press, 1948], 128.) Jefferson often spoke to the same effect.

necessary for us to learn the neglected truth about the attitude towards Negroes in the Old Northwest, plus the limited objectives of antislavery benevolence throughout the country. For this will tell us why the repeal of the Missouri Compromise so outraged the people who became Lincoln supporters and what the Slave Power signified to most of them. Antebellum Midwesterners were, to speak bluntly, more anti-Negro than the slaveholders themselves. Many of them opposed the spread of slavery simply because it meant the distribution of black men into places where whites, their kindred and friends, might come to live. Even those who could imagine a benefit to the country in the destruction of the Peculiar Institution included nothing in the way of additional liberties for the freedman to attach to the end of bondage per se. Lincoln, as I have argued frequently, was extremely careful not to offend against any of this sentiment—in part because he shared in much of it, and also because if he crossed the line it drew his political career would come to a sudden end. David Potter calls this kind of antislavery thinking empty and likely to engender an "'equality' ... somewhere between freedom and slavery."[34] Thereafter he adds that its "attenuated" commitment to a technical freedom was easily "embarrassed" when set over against fierce claims of a moral superiority over those whose position appeared to deny that the Negro was a man.[35] Lincoln spoke well for the movement he later came to lead when he called for the open lands to be reserved for "the settlement of free white labor" as an "outlet for *free white people, everywhere,* the world over."[36] The advanced views of Negro rights promised by the opponents of slavery's extension, in 1820,

---

34 David M. Potter, *The Impending Crisis, 1848-1861* (New York: Harper & Row, 1976), 345.

35 *Ibid.*, 346. On the Illinois Black Codes, see Beveridge, *Abraham Lincoln*, 1: 163-64. As he notes, *no* Illinois politician challenged their justice, even though for the Negro they offered nothing better than a choice of emigration, serfdom, or reenslavement.

36 Lincoln, Works, 2: 268, 498; 3: 312. The emphasis is Lincoln's own. See also Thomas, *Lincoln*, 142 where he reports the anger of German immigrants with Stephen Douglas for "Africanizing" their prospective "homeland."

1850, and 1854 are well summarized in the often analyzed Black Codes of Illinois—laws against which Lincoln never complained, or which he helped to enact.[37] And in the one-way boat trip to Liberia which was (since Jefferson) always a corollary of the design to acknowledge the humanity hidden behind a sable complexion. The meaning of extinction, as Lincoln used the word, thus becomes clear in the original constitutions of Kansas and Oregon—excluding slavery and excluding Negroes. Antislavery meant, among other things, white, or as close to white as circumstances allowed: with a provision in most cases for a kind of control over the freedman, should he be around, that was morally inferior to slavery itself.

But if the crusade to confine slavery was not really about the Negro himself, what was the impetus? The question takes us back to the explanation of Midwestern reaction to the Kansas-Nebraska Act. In Peoria, Lincoln could not hope to get the rhetorical effect to which he aspired from his support for the Wilmot Proviso or his efforts to forestall the spread of slavery into New Mexico or Utah or the other portions of the Mexican Cession. What gave him an edge was the general impression spreading across the North that Democratic politicians were going against the Compromise of 1787, the formula of quid pro quo, opening the way to Southern development and control of *all* the open lands under national jurisdiction. His best argument was against Democratic innovation, a cry of conspiracy. These are the central words of the Peoria Speech: "The declared indifference, but as I must think covert *real* zeal for the spread of slavery, I cannot but hate."[38] In years to come, this imaginative construct grows to include the charge that an eventual expansion of slavery into free states is contemplated in the enemy's long-range plan—and a further charge that both black and white are to be bound.[39] I will return to this bugbear as

---

37 According to Lincoln, one argument for emancipation was that it would foster racial purity. See Lincoln, *Works*, 2: 409.

38 Lincoln, *Works*, 2:255. The speech (247-283) is Lincoln's longest recorded address. References to its text are cited in the body of the rhetorical analysis of the structure of the speech.

39 Lincoln, *Works*, 2: 341, 385 553; 3:95.

it unfolds. But for the moment it is my point that Lincoln conflates opposition to the expansion of slavery into the New Northwest with opposition to slavery per se and both with opposition to Stephen Douglas and the Democrats—all the while swaddling around the innovations which *he* introduces as ostensible reverence for the established ways.

What Lincoln ignores throughout his discourse is the reason behind Douglas's support of a repeal of the Missouri Compromise—a reason well known. Douglas could not promote his favorite dream of a new empire reaching to the Pacific, of railroad building and land speculation, of farms for the immigrants pouring in from Europe, and of everlasting credit for the Democrats *without Southern votes*. He was the legislative leader of a party dominated by Southerners. To get a bill organizing new territories in Kansas and Nebraska (legislation necessary to his plan for a transcontinental railroad), he required the help of legislators who could gain nothing for their own constituents with his plan.[40] New senators from the free states were the only certain results, plus more immigration into the North and more Yankee votes. The Midwest had a genuine stake in these prospects. Lincoln is correct in asserting that "the public never demanded the repeal of the Missouri Compromise."[41] But they did demand the authorization that went with, and was tied to, that repeal. Professor Riddle is therefore correct in observing that Lincoln left out of his performance in Peoria "a fair estimate of the purpose of the Kansas-Nebraska Act," and that he was "shrewd" to do so.[42] It is a powerful speech, sometimes lacking in logic; but the confusion it fosters is not by accident.[43]

---

40   See Potter, *Impending Crisis*, 145-76. See also Robert W. Johannsen, *Stephen A. Douglas* (New York: Oxford University Press, 1973), 394-98.

41   Lincoln, *Works*, 2:261.

42   Riddle, *Congressman Lincoln*, 248.

43   Not even its apparent rambling from point to point is accidental. We are mistaken whenever we imagine that Lincoln is without purpose in what he does, for much of what Lincoln wrote for oral delivery he expected to be preserved in print.

The structure of this address is a close study in itself. In design, it pretends to be deliberative; in fact, it is forensic. Its ostensible objective is to recommend restoration of the Compromise of 1820; but its actual burden is the necessity to distrust Stephen Douglas, his friends, and all their works. In truth, the restoration of the Missouri Compromise in 1854 would have been to Lincoln like the peaceable conclusion of the Civil War in 1863: politically fatal! With a brief exordium (247-48), claiming a horror of everything that is "narrow, sectional, and dangerous to the Union" and a clear disclaimer of any threat to slavery as an "existing institution," Lincoln is ready to declare his good intentions and review the history of the Missouri Compromise. The historical blunders included in this argument from the record are indicated in my discussion just above; or rather, a representative selection of these blunders. Added to them is an account of events subsequent to the Missouri Compromise, running on through the Compromise of 1850, the general election of 1852, and Douglas's introduction of a new bill to give Nebraska territorial government (248-55). To this point, Lincoln has said little that is outrageous. We can be irritated with the invention by the future emancipator of a bit of Virginia history, made up to suit his purposes, and also by his feigned surprise at the Democrats' claim to see in certain kinds of federal legislation, touted to be benevolent, a threat to corporate liberty. But these errors are standard political fare and are couched in a tone consonant with Whig moderation. Not so the charge that follows.

Lincoln's initial public reference to a "Slave Power Conspiracy," noted above as the central passage of his speech, combines accusation with the word *hate*. It is an unusual term to appear in a Whig political discourse and marks an intensification in the tone of Lincoln's argument. True, it is covered up quickly with lofty references to the "republican example" of the United States in the world and by an invocation of the Declaration of Independence as the text of our political religion—both beside the point if one does not read the Declaration as Lincoln does. But he returns throughout the remainder of the speech to water the seed he has sown.

The crucial paragraph (255) is followed by a full-page (255-56) of rhetorical concession: a digression on Lincoln's good feeling toward the South and his ambivalence about blacks. That it contains matter in contradiction to the general principle which he announces in his subsequent remarks is typical of Lincoln during these middle years. But that such doubts about what may be done if the slaves are freed might conflict in logic with his assumption of a moral advantage through loyalty to the Declaration as including Negroes in its generalizations about "all men" Lincoln never stops to think. Or else denies. The conceding done; however, this rural Cicero returns to his prosecution.

Lincoln takes some time to answer these arguments used to justify the repeal of the Missouri Compromise: that Nebraska needed a territorial government; that the public had demanded repeal; and that "repeal establishes a principle which is intrinsically right." Lincoln's responses to his own set of questions take up a major portion in his dispute with Douglas. These responses are on the surface plausible. If the Congress could be persuaded to vote for it, it was legal for Nebraska to be organized as a free territory. Lincoln omits to mention, however, that no such votes were available. That many Northern states wanted to facilitate developments in the West, possible only if Nebraska were organized as a territory, Lincoln does not acknowledge. And though in this portion of his speech he praises the principle of "equivalents" as that of the Missouri Compromise, the 1850 Compromise, and the original Constitution of 1787 (272), he denies that he had violated that principle when he himself voted not to extend the line of separation westward to the Pacific (257). To violate the principle of mutual concession in behalf of the higher principle, that slavery is a wicked thing, all men are equal, and Negroes are men in their "natural rights," is the formula he achieves. Or else he offers no logic at all. He reinforces his construction with attendant arguments concerning the side effects of slavery—the three-fifths clause, the South's attitude toward slave dealers, the size of the Negro population, both free and bond, and rumors of continued slave importation. But he has not asked these questions just in order to respond to them.

Rather, he is concerned with other charges that those answers give him an opportunity to declare. For a moment he repeats the earlier concession, still insisting that his position does not necessitate "political and social equality" for the freedman, and that it rests upon his veneration for those "old-time men" who defined the original American "SPIRIT OF COMPROMISE" (272). Yet he withdraws these reservations elsewhere, contending that any extension of slavery is a threat to every American's liberties (270), and that the "ancient faith" of the Declaration is violated by Douglas's doctrine of "popular sovereignty." He then returns swiftly to his charge that the friends of the South have no interest in compromise and are bent upon the inculcation of a "NEW faith" (275).

After some additional historical misinformation, Lincoln perorates. I will return to the tone of this passage in a moment. But it is proper to note that his own peculiar gloss upon the Declaration of Independence is at its heart: the idea that it contains serious and critical allusions to Negro slavery, and that to say about it anything to the contrary is an astonishing impiety toward the Fathers. The remainder of Lincoln's address is rather anticlimactic (276-83). It amounts to a reply to what he expects Douglas to offer in rejoinder. But he makes it clear that what he means by "re-adopt the Declaration of Independence by restoring the Missouri Compromise" comes to something more than that. It is also a direct and personal reproach to Senator Douglas and his kind: a reproach which marks Douglas as an enemy to popular sentiment in the North, particularly with respect to his view of the black man's place in the future of America. This conclusion, however, is a more organic portion of the document than at first appears, for it enables Lincoln to leave his audience thinking about Stephen Douglas, and the charges brought against him.

The basic rhetorical strategy of Lincoln's "Peoria Speech" is familiar to us from his earlier work. In the effort to ruin Douglas with the Illinois electorate, he employs a version of the false dilemma. For though he pays lip service to the sacrosanct principle of the Founders, Webster and Clay, that principle of accommodation is finally denied by the rest of his appeal and replaced by the argument which we ordinarily connect with the "House Divided Speech" of 1858. The difference between these two orations consists of the aforementioned lip service to equivalence or compromise and a more tentative view of how slavery can be extinguished through containment: a difference in tone. He is content with only the implication of what he states openly in the speeches to come: that legal confinement with reprobation will produce emancipation of *some* sort, at *some* undetermined time. In 1854 Lincoln still wishes to keep one foot in the Whig camp. But only one. He still pretends civility and claims not "to question the patriotism or to assail the motives of any man, or class of men."[44] But there is no doubt that with "covert *real* zeal" he is on his way to a larger objective, to a neo-Puritan war on the powers of darkness: "Two universal armed camps, engaged in a death struggle against each other."[45] For the final burden of his remarks cannot be mistaken: either the Northwest Ordinance of 1787 will be applied throughout the West, and the balance of sections destroyed forever, or the bugbear of slavery expansion will be released to spread throughout the land, leaving, in the end, no free states—and few free men. We understand now what Lincoln meant when, later, he told his friends that his debating strategy would, finally, leave Stephen Douglas "a dead cock in the pit,"[46] and what combative, utterly partisan spirit—determined to "beat the Democrats," to "Fight the devil with fire; that is, with its own weapons ... whether

---

44 Lincoln, *Works*, 2:248. A disclaimer made "wholly for political effect," like the charges which follow it—recalling to us the 1842 difficulty with insults to James Shields. Yet he accuses Douglas of being party to a covert design and (by implication) of treason. Even though he elsewhere gives his own charge of collusion with the South the lie—admitting that Douglas "cares nothing for the South"and that the Little Giant's plan is to "hold on to his chances in Illinois." See Lincoln, *Works*, 2:530. So much for the Slave Power.

45 Lincoln, *Works*, 3:315. Lincoln's language here (in 1858) belongs to an order of millenarian rhetoric described by Eric Voegelin in *The New Science of Politics* (Chicago: University of Chicago Press, 1952), 151. I quote Voegelin's summary of the usual Puritan style of debate.

46 Herndon, "Facts Illustrative of Mr. Lincoln's Patriotism," 188.

true or false, fair or foul"—was hidden beneath the rambling informality and apparent righteous indignation of the surface of the speech,[47] or in the design of the seemingly artless oratory that followed—the oratory which made Lincoln the American Caesar of his age.

In the "Peoria Speech" Lincoln was doing precisely what his Whig mentors had taught that the patriotic statesman did not do. He congratulates the Free Soilers for lofty motives which he elsewhere admits were less noble than they claimed. For his talk of conspiracies and trends threatens the identity of Midwestern society—its sense of its own worth and hopes for its future. And this, in its turn, was calculated to drive a breach between it and the South, redounding to the disadvantage of the hated Northern Locos, who must be beaten "or the country will be ruined."[48] The reasoning went thus: with *the distinctive Southern institution* went other Southern modes and orders; and the exclusion from all roles of importance of those who were not, by birth and training, part of the Slaveocracy. Hatred of slavery was thus a logical corollary of Know-Nothing hatred of Roman Catholic and free black immigration. Both excited the fear of the Yankee and immigrant that a familiar, accepted, and soon-to-be beloved way of life would not expand and, perhaps, would not even survive. Which would explain the development in the North of an attitude well described by David Potter, holding that "slavery was objectionable not because it gave pain to slaves but because it gave pleasure [and power] to slaveowners."[49] Henry Clay had mocked such attitudes as contradictory and hypocritical in Congress and during a visit to

---

47 Albert Taylor Bledsoe, from his review of Ward H. Lamon's *The Life of Abraham Lincoln: From His Birth to His Inauguration, Southern Review*, no. 26 (April 1873): 360-61.

48 Pratt, "Albert Taylor Bledsoe," 178.

49 Potter, *Impending Crisis*, 37. See also Foner, *Free Soil*, 316: "Much of the messianic zeal which characterized political anti-slavery derived from his faith in the superiority of the political, social, and economic institutions of the North, and a desire to spread these to their ultimate limits."

Indiana.⁵⁰ Daniel Webster had warned that disunion would result in American politicians were moralistic for effect and failed "to treat each other with respect."⁵¹ But that was an older politics. It would not defeat the Democrats. It had not studied under William Seward and Salmon P. Chase and would not move the Midwest to accept the necessity of a "new founding," or of a "new founder," operating with the authority of an expurgated version of our collective past.

Here, in the already mentioned peroration, is Lincoln's summary of the case from precedent against the Kansas-Nebraska Act:

> Thus, we see, the plain unmistakable spirit of that age, towards slavery, was hostility to the PRINCIPLE, and toleration, ONLY BY NECESSITY.
>
> But NOW it is to be transformed into a "sacred right." Nebraska brings it forth, places it on the high road to extension and perpetuity; and, with a pat on its back, says to it, "Go, and God speed you." Henceforth it is to be the chief jewel of the nation—the very figurehead of the ship of State. Little by little, but steadily as man's march to the grave, we have been giving up the OLD for the NEW faith. Near eighty years ago we began by declaring that all men are created equal; but now from the beginning we have run down to the other declaration, that for SOME men to enslave OTHERS is the "sacred right of self-government." These principles cannot stand together. They are as opposite as God and mammon; and whoever holds

---

50   Robinson, *Slavery in American Politics*, 41, and Clement Eaton's *Henry Clay and the Art of American Politics* (Boston: Little, Brown, and Company, 1957), 129-31. Further evidence of Clay's contempt for hypocrites may be found in *Annals of Congress*, 15th Cong., 2nd sess., September 15, 1819, 1174-75.

51   Irving H. Bartlett, *Daniel Webster* (New York: W. W. Norton & Co., 1978), 252.

to the one, must despise the other. When Pettit, in connection with his support of the Nebraska bill, called the Declaration of Independence "a self-evident lie" he only did what consistency and candor require all other Nebraska men to do. Of the forty odd Nebraska Senators who sat present and heard him, no one rebuked him. Nor am I apprized that any Nebraska newspaper, or any Nebraska orator, in the whole nation, has ever yet rebuked him. If this had been said among Marion's men, Southerners though they were, what would have become of the man who said it? If this had been said to men who captured André, the man who said it, would probably have been hung sooner than André was. If it had been said in old Independence Hall, seventy-eight years ago, the very door-keeper would have throttled the man, and thrust him into the street.

Let no one be deceived. The spirit of seventy-six and the spirit of Nebraska, are utter antagonisms; and the former is being rapidly displaced by the latter.[52]

I have already examined the historical distortions behind these lines. From them Lincoln goes further to make of Douglas's refusal to read the Declaration as he does a threat to the liberties of white men, while neglecting to explain how the usual Midwestern view of the document came closer to conveying "a very vivid impression that the negro is a human."[53] But what distinguishes the passage is

---

52 Lincoln, *Works*, 2: 272.

53 *Ibid.*, 281. Nothing in the state laws of the Midwest indicates a view that Negroes had "natural rights" or that they had a full membership in the human family. Lincoln's claim that hostility to slavery in Illinois rested upon a higher regard for Negroes as men than the view expressed by Stephen Douglas cannot be supported by the evidence. It merely flatters his audience into a sense of moral superiority that costs them nothing in charity or social inconvenience—a kind of superiority that has caused the Republic much trouble throughout its history.

not its content but its tone, with its talk of hanging and throttling, and its allusion to André, the enemy spy, and his fate. We are, with such elements, drawn beyond debate and toward indictment. The appeal is to violent emotions, and in no way subtle. Despite its official piety toward the law, there is a violent edge to the new politics of this quondam Whig. Yet he follows it quickly with a reversion to his familiar claim of moral superiority. Echoes from the scripture are included. Suddenly, we are in the presence of Puritan rhetoric, with an unmistakable lineage going back to the Protector and the Holy Commonwealth. The new Lincoln is never without it. To that authority the South could not submit.

By 1854, the Midwest was rapidly filling with people who did not understand American history, politics, or constitutional law and with people who had fewer ties with the South than the earlier settlers "down in Egypt" or in the central counties.[54] Many of these could see in the South only an analogy to the European societies from which they had fled. In 1854, Lincoln recognised these changes and Stephen Douglas did not. The repeal of the Missouri Compromise, when coupled with renewed Southern truculence concerning new states, railroads, internal improvements, tariffs, and the rest of the familiar "Federalist model," gave a certain plausibility to charges that political innovation was underway. The difference between legal or political questions and moral questions in a nation in which basic law is sovereign and not a particular generation of men thus slipped from public perception while the role of slavery in the West was put in doubt. Lincoln rose in this inflamed atmosphere, keeping always one step behind the "higher law" spokesmen and two behind the abolitionists per se. His trick, learned basically from Salmon P. Chase and his "Appeal of the Independent Democrats," was to combine efforts looking toward federally sponsored abolition and reverence for an imaginary

---

54 We should recall that Illinois helped to get Missouri into the Union as a slave state. One of its senators in 1820 was Lincoln's brother-in-law.

American past: radicalism and anti-radicalism,⁵⁵ all of the time being very careful not to suggest that the Negro had any natural rights apart from the right to be free at some very remote date and to be then returned to an Africa that would be even more unfriendly to him than were the prairies and hamlets of Illinois.

That this kind of politics would destroy the Union did not worry Mr. Lincoln. Instead, he scrawled in envy little meditations on his own humble state (due doubtless to principle) and the Little Giant's fame.⁵⁶ He burned with ambition to have a "name" and found in vilification his *modus vivendi*. In Peoria he had only begun, was still in transition—offering "equivalents" (concessions to the South) at one point, and drawing the line at another.⁵⁷ But once he was finished in his career, he had left behind him a trail of blood, an emancipation under the worst possible circumstances, and a political example which continues to injure the Republic which he did so much to undermine. It is at our peril that we continue to reverence his name.

---

55 Foner, *Free Soil*, 73-102, traces the origins of Lincoln's favorite arguments in the speeches, or pamphlets of Chase, Seward, and Charles Sumner.

56 See untitled fragment comparing his career to that of Douglas in Lincoln, *Works*, 2: 382-83. It is a self-righteous performance, concealing Lincoln's envy in unctuous reflections on his own rectitude, which was what he had for his trouble when in 1855 another man won away James Shields's seat in the United States Senate. We are reminded of the "family of the lion" and the "tribe of the eagle" in his 1838 speculations on an American Caesar.

57 See Lincoln, *Works*, 2:259, 272. In this speech he had to be contradictory.

6.

Against Lincoln:
A Speech at Gettysburg
(1984)

To speak on this particular occasion, in this small Pennsylvania town and to this audience is, for a scholar whose opinions concerning Abraham Lincoln have been so widely discussed and systematically misrepresented, a matchless opportunity. For the papers delivered here and the books from which they derive provide a proper context in which to set the record straight, to clarify just what it is that I have maintained against the Emancipator, and what I've not said. And especially this is true of Professor Boritt's remarks on the Whig tradition in American social and economic theory.[1] Beginning with these, I may hope to situate myself in relation to both the best of modern Lincoln scholarship and the relentless gravity of the Lincoln myth, contribute to the larger conversation of this conference and still stand aside from its drift in the rigor of my criticism of the sixteenth President of the United States.

For the past three years the mere rumor of my complaints against the continuing influence of Father Abraham's example on the nation's public life has seemed to have a life of its own, surviving and even growing in inverse proportion to the number of

---

1 Evidence developed in Gabor S. Boritt's *Lincoln and the Economics of the American Dream* (Memphis, TN: Memphis State University Press, 1978) which I find to be generally persuasive.

times when some deflation or correction of it has been attempted in my own work or in the writings of my friends. What I think of Lincoln has therefore become an issue wholly apart from what I really think of Lincoln—an issue for editorials, front-page reports and passionate commentary—all to my general astonishment and painful instruction. In one sense it may thus be argued that the press caricature of my view of Lincoln is a confirmation of the case I make against the influence of the Lincoln myth operating to the contrary of thoughtful deliberation where the great questions of our era are concerned: pushing us instead, with diction and rhetoric, in the direction of mindless obedience and quasi-religious submission to the secular religion summarized by the greatest monument in Washington City, the Lincoln Memorial.

With respect to Lincoln I have been the subject of outraged reports issuing from Keene, New Hampshire to Los Angeles, California—and from such various sources as the *New York Times, Chicago Sun-Times, Washington Post, Wall Street Journal, Newsweek, New Republic, Chronicle of Higher Education, New York Review of Books*, and the CBS afternoon news. It would appear that my real function and all of these has been like that of Goldstein in George Orwell's *1984*, as rhetorical icon or symbolic adversary. I have found that I "favor slavery," consider it to be a "tenuous multiracial experiment" yet to receive the final verdict of history, and that I censure Lincoln because of "what he did for racial equality." My "destructive idea" is that due process of law was violated by the Emancipation Proclamation. My reservations concerning Lincoln's epideictic, quasi-Biblical rhetoric are described as "insulting to Lincoln's idea of liberty." And the very errors embodied in such wild charges, requiring (as they do) some rejoinder, "prove" that there is something wrong with my character, regardless of their implausibility. Furthermore, I have been described as "committed to the proposition that popular sovereignty defines the nature of democratic government," and of causing my erstwhile associate, George Will, to seethe and "smolder" by implying an admiration for the 1854 Kansas–Nebraska Act. I have "overturned the Declaration of Independence," called Lincoln a "villain" and argued that "there is no right principle of action but self-interest." None of which can be documented from anything I have written.

Even so, despite outrage at a gratuitous, partisan caricature, the misrepresentation of my views is proof of how careful Lincoln scholars must be in specifying just how much we mean to say— especially if the possibility of reflection on the motives of our political "new Messiah" is at stake: proof of the social problem of our research and analysis when it comes up against the force of an hieratic orthodoxy based on the logical fallacy of *post hoc, ergo propter hoc*. For according to the popular argument, the essential ingredients of the myth, since the Union was preserved and the bondsman set free by the momentous series of events which had as their climax the great battle fought out on this ground and the hero then martyred after the completion of his victory, any criticism of Lincoln is a criticism of those results and a desecration of that sacrifice. Thus if we fault Lincoln in anything it will be reported that we object to both the purposive and the incidental consequences of his career. Or that we reject even the best possible construction of these results. Or blaspheme. Moreover, goes the inference, that as Lincoln did, so should we, providing for freedom an endless series of "new births." In arranging for such a sequence, the United States may deserve to be described as "the last best, hope of earth."[2] Even now, Lincoln's place among us is no merely antiquarian concern. As current demonstration of his continuing (and irrational) influence I need only mention the habit of Paul Simon of Illinois in using his anger with my "terrible" Lincoln essays as ethical proof of his right to a seat in the United States Senate in 1984.[3] It is still important for any public figure or politician to "get right with Lincoln," even if he is confused about what the effort will cost him and where the example of Lincoln's total career will lead.

The focus of my work in Lincoln studies is upon the language and rhetorical strategy of what Lincoln wrote and said. This

---

2 See Vol. V, 357 of Roy Basler's edition of *The Collected Works of Abraham Lincoln* (New Brunswick, NJ: Rutgers University Press, 1953).

3 Demonstrated on 34 of the *Wall Street Journal* of March 6, 1984.

emphasis brings me to examine directly Lincoln's invocation of the American dream of personal success, his announced devotion to certain "propositional" truths and his dependence upon the authority of "those old-time men" who had accomplished the American Revolution and established the Republic where "the original idea" of our national enterprise might unfold and prosper. In the pattern of his utterance and the relation of his words to his life I have found reason to consider Lincoln as primarily a *rhetor* and to treat his speeches and other writings, in all of their opportunistic variety, not as expressions of a political philosophy, but as exercises in management and manipulation, an artful music played to lift and lower the passions and, in behalf of a "policy" never fully stated (in fact, altered as he went along), to persuade.[4] It is in the context of an essentially rhetorical identity that Lincoln invokes a version of the American dream—Professor Boritt's "right-to-rise economics." But Lincoln is no more consistent about that doctrine than he is about other questions of principle. Or any more straightforward and inclining, as he does from the beginning of his political life, toward packaging up a "black cockade" Federalist substance inside a democratic, Jacksonian wrapper:

> ... I presume you all know who I am. I am humble Abraham Lincoln. I have been solicited by many friends to become a candidate for the Legislature. My politics are short and sweet, like the old woman's dance. I am in favor of a national bank ... in favor of the internal improvement system and a high protective tariff.[5]

---

4 My comments on Lincoln's rhetoric appear in *A Better Guide than Reason: Studies in the American Revolution* (La Salle, IL: Sherwood Sugden & Co., 1979) 29-57 and 185-203; in "Dividing the House: The Gnosticism of Lincoln's Rhetoric," *Modern Age*, 23 (1979), 10-24; and in "The Lincoln Legacy: The Long View," *Modern Age* 24 (1980), 355-63.

5 Quoted on 65-66 of Lord Charnwood's *Abraham Lincoln* (New York: Henry Holt & Co., 1917).

Add to this oxymoronic posturing related commitments to protection of the interests of property, land policies which served the advantage of speculators and general sympathy with the business and professional classes (as opposed, for instance, to farmers, Negro freedmen, or immigrant laborers)—to the idea that wealth, political order and personal liberty "down from the top"—and you have the image of an orthodox Whig covered up by a Democratic persona—a potent and calculated brew, with an egalitarian touch of "poor mouth" tossed in for a soupcon. But nothing any conservative Republican of our time could endure, even from a distance.

By his remark that government should "do for a community of people, [that] which they need to have done, but cannot do, *at all*, or cannot, *so well do*, for themselves," Lincoln drew a blank check on the bank of political necessity.[6] His devotion to liberal economics was like his devotion to "... Mind, all conquering mind" and to "cold, calculating unimpassioned reason."[7] and like his attachment to the moderate rhetoric of Washington, Webster, and Clay.[8] He stuck by them so long as convenient, so long as they fed fuel into that little "engine" which knew no rest, his political ambition, whose hopes for building a political party and with it, reconstituting the government of the United States—as Solon had "remade" Athens and like Lycurgus Sparta in olden times—depended on a certain flexibility: a policy "to have no policy." None of which is to say that Lincoln did not, other things being equal, prefer free states to slaveholding states, honest elections to stolen votes, the letter of the Constitution (read in a Hamiltonian way) to usurpation and tyranny, and the fruits of a free economy to fiat money, graft, peculation, and wealth created by the sponsorship

---

6   *Works,* II, 220.

7   *Works,* I, 279.

8   On the Whig disposition to favor a moderate rhetoric on divisive questions, see Irving H. Bartlett, *Daniel Webster* (New York: W. W. Norton, 1978), 252; Clement Eaton, *Henry Clay and the Art of Politics* (Boston: Little, Brown, 1957), 129-130; and *Annals,* 15th Cong. 2nd Sess., 9/15/1819, 1174-75.

of the state. And also peace to war. But not enough to put these preferences ahead of his political advantage. Lincoln perceived as primarily a rhetorician is more or less the mixed figure of Ludwell Johnson's recent analysis of the War Between the States, a man political in most public things, but transformed into something very different by the bullet of John Wilkes Booth.[9]

The rhetorical analysis of Lincoln's work, of course, depends in great measure on insights and information developed by other kinds of Lincoln scholarship—some of it the handiwork of my associates in this conference. For rhetorical criticism derives some of its authority from a well developed sense of the context in which a specific effort at persuasion must occur. Where the Framers of the Constitution are concerned, I have drawn up my own measure of the distance between "the old policy of the Fathers" and Lincoln's distortion of their teachings.[10] With respect to other facets of Lincoln's career, I have learned much from such commentators as Donald W. Riddle, John S. Wright, Edmund Wilson, Gottfried Dietze, V. Jacques Voegeli, Eugene H. Berwanger, Leon Litwack, Harry Jaffa, Willmoore Kendall, and James A. Rawley.[11] But the reason I understand Lincoln as I do is what I find in the text of

---

9   I refer to Ludwell Johnson's *Division and Reunion: America, 1848-1877* (New York: John Wiley and Sons, 1978).

10   *Works,* III, 538.

11   Donald W. Riddle, *Congressman Abraham Lincoln* (Urbana, IL: University of Illinois Press, 1957); John S. Wright, *Lincoln and the Politics of Slavery* (Reno, NV: University of Nevada Press, 1970); Edmund Wilson, *Patriotic Gore: Studies in the Literature of the American Civil War* (New York: Oxford University Press, 1962); 99-130; Gottfried Dietze, *America's Political Dilemma: From Limited to Unlimited Democracy* (Baltimore: Johns Hopkins University Press, 1968); V. Jaque Voegeli, *Free But Not Equal: The Midwest and the Negro During the Civil War* (Chicago: University of Chicago Press, 1967); Eugene Berwanger, *The Frontier Against Slavery: Western Anti-Negro Prejudice and the Slavery Extension Controversy* (Urbana, IL: University of Illinois Press, 1967); Leon F. Litwack, *North of Slavery: The Negro in the Free States, 1790-1860* (Chicago: University of Chicago Press, 1961); Harry Jaffa, *Crisis of the House Divided* (Seattle, WA: University of Washington Press, 1973); Willmoore Kendall,"Equality: Commitment or Ideal," *Phalanx* I (1967); and (with George Carey) *Basic Symbols of the American Political Tradition*

Roy Basler's edition: the trope of affected modesty; the *oraculum* (speaking, in the epideictic vein, the language of the gods); the *diabole* (slandering, predicting the worst); the *argumentum ad populum* (flattering the people); the false dilemma (*crocodilities*—unacceptable choices); and, especially, the argument *ad verecundiam* (an appeal to traditional values, to the prescription of the Revolution). Only the last of these strategies involves a serious pretense of rationality; and even in appealing to an imaginary history, Lincoln is being duplicitous. Contrary to the ethics of rhetoric, he is employing all of these techniques to essentially self-serving ends: to inspire fear and anger in other men that they might act as they otherwise would not, if he were a less skillful rhetorician. In his mastery of the arts of persuasion, Lincoln leads all the other Presidents of the United States. Even when he is talking about economics; or slaves; or when he affirms the value and authority of the Union.

My favorite proofs of Lincoln's astonishing flexibility come from his statements about slavery and the Negro because, as I have learned from his thoughtless admirers, the devotees of the myth are made most uncomfortable by seeing them combined in a certain way. It is probable that Lincoln disliked Negro slavery during most of his life, just as it is obvious that most Southerners recognise slaves as human beings in that they hope to see them accept Christianity.[12] But the evidence is clear that Lincoln was engaged in moralistic posturing when he spoke of his "hatred" for the "peculiar institution." Otherwise we have a lot of trouble

---

(Baton Rouge, LA: Louisiana State University Press, 1970); and James A. Rawley, *Race and Politics: "Bleeding Kansas"and the Coming of the Civil War* (Philadelphia: J. B. Lippincott, 1969).

12 My answer to Harry Jaffa's claim (in "Equality, Justice, and the American Revolution: In Reply to Bradford's "The Heresy of Equality," *Modern Age* 21 [1977], 114-26) that the "authentic representation of the Old South appears in Alexander Stephens's Corner Stone speech of March, 1861, an appeal to racial theory. There is no purpose in extending the Divine Grace made available to men through the death of God's Son to creatures less than human. Differences in race pale into insignificance in the context of such connections.

explaining his actions in the 1847 Matson case, in which he attempted to enforce the Fugitive Slave Law and recover runaways. And even more trouble (in view of what he said about living off the "sweat of other men's faces") in explaining the case he filed in Lexington, Kentucky, October 2, 1849, to recover Todd slaves from Robert Wickliff, who had married into the family of Robert Todd.[13] Lincoln handled the interests of the older Todd children and the dispersal of their father's estate between 1849 and 1851.[14] This dispersal involved the sale of Negroes—as is clear from the Fayette County Court papers. The Lincolns did not scruple to take money from these sales—as Abraham Lincoln's public rectitude about such profits after 1854 would lead us to expect. When the Railsplitter got too intense about this question, he verged toward the hypocritical. Hence the measuring of distance between Lincoln's words and deeds.

The record of his rhetoric does indeed turn on October 16, 1854 with his speech against Senator Stephen Douglas and the Kansas-Nebraska Act in Peoria, Illinois, and then intensifies further in the June 16, 1858 speech at Springfield, Illinois, "A House Divided."[15] For in his August 1852 speeches to the Springfield Scott Club, Lincoln praised the Whigs for pacifying Southern fears of abolitionist excesses, for refusing to claim a special understanding of the divine will, and for avoiding all arguments from definition or original uses of the presidential power. His villain in these remarks is that "wicked free-soiler," Franklin Pierce of New Hampshire, who is satirized as "darker" than the mulatto girl of an old song. This is the Lincoln who told racial jokes and who had attacked Martin Van Buren for entertaining too advanced a view of Negro rights, not the Lincoln who spoke of "two universal armed camps engaged in a death struggle against each other."[16] This is the Lincoln who urged his friends to be quiet about "white only"

---

13   *Works,* IX, 333. See Kentucky *Reports,* 51, 289.
14   See Fayette County Papers File, 1849-1851.
15   *Works,* II, 247-283; 461-69.
16   *Works,* II, 248.

clauses in Western state constitutions; who allowed for serfdom on "loyal" plantations and spoke of emancipation as a "root, hog, or die" opportunity; and who, in his First Inaugural, agreed to accept a thirteenth amendment to the Constitution which would have precluded any effort at the Federal level (including any later constitutional amendment) to make this country "*all* one thing, or *all* the other" in the matter of slavery. We may set over against this Lincoln all of the familiar passages which more recent Lincoln scholars (who are determined to save him from his record) delight in quoting, and then add to them recent arguments on how he was about to transcend his "own feelings," as described in Illinois in 1858, and move toward the radical Republican camp on the question of the rights of the freed men. This is the Lincoln who, had he lived, would have come out for fair housing in Chicago and the 1964 Civil Rights Act—a product of wishful thinking. That is, unless Republican politics had required that he move in such a direction—*in both North and South*, which even Professor Oates is not likely to argue.[17]

I have here briefly emphasized the contradictions of Lincoln on slavery and race. But the focus could be turned as well to many other elements in Lincoln's career—his relations to persons, his view of power, his religion—or his attachment to the dreams of economic opportunity for all. In the latter instance we need think only of his suggestion that "the foreman" of his "green printing office," Salmon P. Chase, "give his paper mill another turn" and create a little money whenever funds ran short. Even on the subjects of millenarian hope and chiliastic rhetoric he "teaches it both ways," complaining quickly when someone uses the *ipse dixit* on him.

But, all of his arguments *ad hominem* in behalf of his own moral refinement aside, the case against a generous enthusiasm for the political prescription left to us by Abraham Lincoln turns

---

17 I refer specifically to Stephen B. Oates's *Abraham Lincoln: The Man Behind the Myths* (New York: Harper & Row, 1984), which exaggerates outrageously the connection between Lincoln and the cause of Civil Rights in our day.

on whether or not his was the *best* way to save the Union and free the slaves. Yet Lincoln did not save "the Union as it was." Rather as the scholarship tends to agree he played the central role in transforming it forever into a unitary structure based on a claim to power in its own right, a teleocratic instrument which, in the name of any cause that attracts a following, might easily threaten the liberties of those for whose sake it existed. By his success in getting elected on the basis of his rectitude concerning slavery, limited as that morality was by its anti-Negro base of support, Lincoln was the central agent in precipitating war. And his way of freeing the slaves—at bayonet point, in the midst of war, confined in a South angry and without means, with no Federal plan for an intermediate period of apprenticeship in freedom—in some respects is to blame for the nation's continuing problem with the Negro, which even today has not been resolved. Therefore, I refuse on principle to share in that enthusiasm, because I honor those original "political institutions" praised by Lincoln in his first important speech, to the Springfield Young Men's Lyceum in January of 1838.

There is another view of Lincoln's career and the events which surround it not suggested by the fallacy of *post hoc, ergo propter hoc,* a reading which carries a very different political lesson.[18] Our labor is to assure that the sacrifice made here and on other ground hallowed since shall not be dishonored by the apostate vanity and intellectual arrogance of those beneficiaries of remembered courage who would, even now, distort its meaning to serve lesser causes of their own and would use Lincoln to accomplish their distortion. In all of his protean complexity, the sad man from Illinois deserves a better fate.

---

18   To find it we should apply to Lincoln's career the machinery of modern political theory as it applies to the English Puritans—especially 110-13 and 124-32 of Eric Voegelin's *The New Science of Politics* (Chicago: University of Chicago Press, 1952).

7.

Lincoln's Republican Rhetoric: The Development of a Political Idiom (1988)

REGROUPING AND REASSESSMENT

In 1854, working outward from Illinois anger at Democratic mistakes, Abraham Lincoln made his first run at a national office. But when the new Illinois legislature convened in January of 1855, it did not give to Mr. Lincoln the United States Senate seat held previously by General James Shields. Democrats who disapproved of the course followed by Stephen A. Douglas in leading their party or of the Kansas-Nebraska Act were still unwilling to replace a Douglas Democrat with so partisan and narrow a Whig as the leader of the Sangamon County "junta." Some saw in the Springfield lawyer's newfound concern with the "moral evil" of slavery more of Lincoln's familiar political craftiness. They knew their man well, from the political wars of earlier years. In consequence Lincoln, though he started with a lead, was finally forced to release his votes to a Free Soil Democrat, Lyman Trumbull. Thereafter, Lincoln went home to nurse his wounds. Yet he had made a good effort. In addition, the cooperation with Trumbull undermined the suspicion of some Anti-Nebraska men that the entire effort to unseat Shields by "transcending" an "old politics" had been nothing more than a Whig plot to elect a senator without winning the requisite number of local elections: without a Whig majority in the Illinois House and Senate; and without any purpose larger than the old, familiar purposes of their party. Furthermore, Stephen Douglas, as Lincoln had come to realize in 1854, was still the proper target. Whoever could beard the Little Giant in his lair, man to man, would be the coming public figure on the national stage, as well as in Illinois. Four years should be enough to complete a "fusion" and to organize the elements of a more-than-Whig political machine that could finish the revolution in Illinois politics begun with the "Peoria Speech" of 16 October 1854. But the new arrangements would have to be "official," with no one floating between revised and bygone allegiances. It appears that these agreements were concluded in a caucus of Anti-Nebraska lawyers held in Springfield in December of 1855.[1] Part of the package was that Abraham Lincoln was to be their candidate against Douglas in 1858.

But many of the circumstances affecting Lincoln's rhetorical posture in facing Douglas changed between 1854 and the next senate race. To begin with, the charge that the Kansas-Nebraska Act would result in the spread of slavery lost much of its force. Douglas himself had a major role in defeating the imposition of the so-called Lecompton Constitution of Kansas. In consequence, many antislavery men in the East called in their counterparts in the Northwest to consider that Douglas, following his break with Buchanan and the South, might be a political leader for their "holy crusade," even their Presidential candidate, and certainly their spokesman from Illinois in the Senate of the United States. If the new party was not to die before it was born, Lincoln and his friends had to position themselves as more radically opposed to slavery than they had appeared to be in simply opposing its

---

1 This essay continues an analysis of the emergence of Lincoln's mature, post-Whig political rhetoric which begins with my "Lincoln and the Language of Hate and Fear: A View from the South," *Continuity* No. 9 (Fall 1984): 87-108. The "Peoria Speech" appears in Roy P. Blaser, ed., *The Collected Works of Abraham Lincoln* (New Brunswick, NJ: Rutgers University Press, 1953) 2: 247-83. All of my citations to *Works* are to this edition. See John S. Wright, *Lincoln and the Politics of Slavery* (Reno: University of Nevada Press, 1970), 92-97; See also *Works*, 3: 306, where Lincoln says that he elected Trumbull.

extension into the new territories in the West. They had to do this without offending the constitutional scruples of the old line Whigs, or exciting the fears of the Free Soil Democrats—fears that Abolitionist doctrine (or political combination with Abolitionists) would have disruptive implications for race relations in the North. Lincoln accomplished this masterful bit of positioning through tireless repetition of his charge that Stephen Douglas was the tool of a proslavery conspiracy and by further repetition of his complaint against his adversary's lack of moral sensitivity where the rights of the Negro under the Declaration were concerned. Once it was available to him, Lincoln added to this set of negations what play he was able to get out of Northern outrage over the United States Supreme Court decision in the case of Dred Scott. But the most important quality in his performance between the two senate races is his perseverance. He remained on the attack and focused his fire on the one target of opportunity always within his range, Stephen A. Douglas.

The volume of Lincoln's reiterations that there was a "covert design" to nationalize slavery dating from the time of the "Peoria Speech" through the months just preceding his nomination for the Presidency in 1860 is literally astonishing. According to Basler's edition of his *Collected Works*, on at least 50 occasions during this period Lincoln made this charge.[2] There were probably many more. Without a doubt, these charges are the lynch pins of his rhetoric in this central portion of his career. In most of these speeches, the rest of his argument seems to organize around a core of personal accusation. When called upon to summarize and defend the teaching of his "House-Divided Speech," the address which finally propelled him into the White House, Lincoln emphasized only Stephen Douglas and his important role in a "plan ... leading

---

2   See *Works*, 2: 355-56, 375, 379, 391, 409, 452-54, 465, 514-15, 515, 520-21, 525-26, 538-39, 545, 548-53; 3: 20-21, 23-24, 38, 48, 80, 95, 117, 121, 180-81, 223-24, 245, 250, 254, 282, 304, 308, 349, 368-69, 375, 379, 388, 391, 394-95, 398, 404-405, 407, 421, 423-26, 429, 431, 441-53, 484, 488, 501, 504, 548, 551, 553; 4: 13, 21, 28-29. And there was certainly more that is not preserved.

directly to the nationalization of slavery."[3] Not the wisdom and virtues of his own associates, not the Kingdom Coming or the Day of Jubilo. Only the evil incarnate in his stumpy nemesis, the Illinois Giant. This charge he called "the main argument of my speech before the Republican state convention in June." In these many orations Lincoln made heavy use of argument from character, *ad hominem*, against the Democrats and the man likely to be their leader in the years to come. "Stephen, Franklin, Roger and James," so ran Lincoln's list of rogues: a Senator, a President, a Chief Justice, and another President.[4] One was either against these four prominent Democrats or against the Illinois most of Lincoln's audience had come to love. Any public man, if he were not for the spread of slavery nationwide, must be committed by means of moral pressure and legal confinement to driving it from the land. Indeed, one was either opposed to the hated Locos, determined that "the public mind shall rest in the belief that [slavery] is in [the] course of ultimate extinction" or a party to the conspiracy to impose it upon a reluctant North.[5] Never mind the evidence that his charge of Democratic collusion and secret motives was a classic illustration of the ancient fallacy of *post hoc, ergo propter hoc*: a false reasoning from effect to cause. Never mind the deep divisions that precluded any cooperation among the various members of his nefarious quartet. That his theory of conspiracy was, in the language of one Lincoln scholar, "an absurd bogey" is beside the point.[6] Or rather, unimportant so long as it worked. And work it did. The seed of suspicion was planted in the fruitful soil of intersectional dispute. All that was required to bring the thorny harvest of political revolution was a constant repetition of the idea

---

3   *Works*, 2: 539.

4   *Works*, 2:465; the four "carpenters" of conspiracy are Stephen Douglas, Franklin Pierce, Roger B. Taney, and James Buchanan.

5   *Works*, 3: 461.

6   See Allen Nevins, *The Emergence of Lincoln: Douglas, Buchanan and Party Chaos, 1857-1859* (New York: Charles Scribner's Sons, 1950) 362. See also James G. Randall, *Lincoln the President: Springfield to Gettysburg* (New York: Dodd, Mead and Company, Inc. 1945) 1: 108-09.

that Northern Democrats were traitors against their own. Charges and more charges, with no end of them in sight.

Crossing Over: The Kalamazoo Speech

For a few months after the defeat in January 1855, Lincoln licked his wounds and kept quiet. As he wrote his abolitionist friend, Owen Lovejoy, "just now, ... I fear to do anything, lest I do wrong."[7] But once the December bargain was struck, Lincoln stuck by his pledge. A call was issued for a state convention, with Lincoln's name attached. And when it met at Bloomington, Illinois, Abraham Lincoln gave the principal speech—the famous "lost speech." From that day forward, Lincoln was the accepted leader of the Republican Party in Illinois. He opposed the nomination of John C. Fremont because he feared that the Pathfinder would not run well among old line Whigs. His prediction was sound. Nevertheless he made close to 50 speeches for Fremont. Yet though Buchanan carried Illinois with ease, the Republicans did well otherwise, electing a governor, many congressmen, and a large portion of the state legislature. Lincoln offered the Republican faithful an analysis of their prospects in a post-election Chicago address.[8] His prophecy was hopeful. "God is with us," he declared. And his advice was simple. Republicans must "continue to do the same things they have been doing so well." Lincoln advised them to stick to the target, with a steady eye on the one "real issue." He also encouraged them to forget all the past differences; to counter the charge that existing institutions have been threatened in existing states; to ring the changes on the promise of the Declaration of Independence as they had chosen to read its second paragraph; and to remember always that the other popular view of that passage had as its champion the diminutive leader of the Illinois Democracy, Stephen A. Douglas.

---

7   *Works,* 2: 361.

8   *Works,* 2: 383-85. He ended the campaign just as he had begun it with the speech at the Bloomington convention.

But the most important Lincoln speech of 1856 was not given in Illinois. It was part of a campaign trip into Michigan and offered to a fiercely antislavery audience unlike the electorate Lincoln had come to know around Springfield. In August of that year the future President addressed a huge audience at Kalamazoo, Michigan.[9] There he emphasized that the Republicans were of necessity a "one issue" party, or else were thus single-minded until that issue should be resolved. He warned in these remarks that discussion of subjects other than slavery played into the Democrats' hands and lost for the new alliance he represented the moral advantage which was to be its stock in trade. The Michigan trip had, it appears, a great effect on Lincoln's political rhetoric. For it persuaded him that the upper sections of the North were secure for the Republicans and ready to hear an advanced teaching. To combine them with areas closer to the South would be the problem. The regions settled by immigrants and Yankees (Americans from New England, New York, and Pennsylvania) had little experience of freedmen, and no patience with the special problems (and special influence) of the South. Nor did they have understanding of other more conservative Republicans influenced by such considerations. Party spokesmen in Ohio, Iowa, Pennsylvania, Missouri, and the lower half of Illinois would have to offer something new to these aggressive folk—something toward an eventual dissolution of the Slave Power, something to answer the image of Charles Sumner bleeding on the Senate floor—while still retaining their own constituencies and avoiding the obvious vulnerability that would come with any suggestion of real equality for black men. What Lincoln offers them is a new promise wrapped up in a new tone: the message that "the Government of the United States [shall] prohibit slavery in the United States" [by, we suppose, restricting its spread] and the influential message of his language that they have a right to a righteous anger because that government has not already done as they wish—all the while edging closer to the ultimate challenge to

---

9   *Works*, 2: 361-63. Reinhard H. Luthin, on 185 of his *The Real Abraham Lincoln* (Englewood Cliffs, NJ: Prentice-Hall, Inc., 1960), finds it to be curious that Lincoln accepted so radical a platform as that of the Republicans in 1856. But, as we can see, he had no other way to go.

national stability that came with his acceptance of the Republican nomination in 1858.

The gravamen of Lincoln's speech in Kalamazoo is a pleading to the group pride of his audience, a xenophobic *argumentum ad populum*, and an attendant appeal to the feelings of anger, envy, and hatred certain to be spawned by the dark spectre, the "black demon" of a threat to that identity.[10] In this address there is little of the argument from definition against slavery sometimes identified as a dominant characteristic of Lincoln's rhetoric.[11] And though the authority of the Declaration of Independence (one read into the Constitution) is invoked in his peroration, it serves here chiefly as a way of complimenting the Old Northwest—his America—where "wealthy" slaveowners do not corrupt the probity of their neighbors, where ballots of all citizens are weighed equally, and where economic progress reigns supreme. The kind of opportunities taken for granted by the men and women in his audience, Lincoln argues, will soon be in danger: the circumstances in which "every man can make himself." Yet the Free States, they are reminded, have done well in following their own ways. They can be proud of themselves, even though the slaves owned by the South are worth over one billion dollars; even though the politically privileged Southerners say that their system is the real success; and even though James Buchanan (with Stephen A. Douglas working behind him) means to spread that Southern system throughout the land, thus diminishing the opportunity and dignity of white men who own no slaves. A less philosophical argument is hard to imagine.

Once more we are confronted with Lincoln's rhetorical use of an extreme variety of the false dilemma—called appropriately

---

10 The *argumentum ad populum* flatters the audience and plays upon their collective vanity.

11 See for instance remarks on Lincoln's argument from definition on 94-95 and 105-107 of Richard M. Weaver's *The Ethics of Rhetoric* (Chicago: Henry Regnery, 1953).

by the ancients *crocodilities*.[12] Either way, the choice will be disruptive. Either "slavery is to be made the ruling element in our government" (reading, for slavery, the Slave Power), or else we must "prohibit slavery in the United States" (i.e., destroy that adversary). Lincoln is not yet so plain as he becomes in the "House-Divided Speech." As usual, he muffles these alternatives with the assurance that Fremont and his fellow Republicans are not really Abolitionists. He further moderates their impact by insisting that his interest is in preserving the West "for the homes of free white people," not in Negroes *per se*. He makes pious Whig noises about compliance with all that is promised "in the Constitution" and a few other conservative sounds about his devotion to the Union and his faith in its security, regardless of who wins the Presidential election. But no doubt is left concerning his desire to see the culture represented by the Michigan audience listening to his words given hegemony over the nation's future development: given "an outlet through which it may pass out [of its present boundaries] to enrich our country." This Lincoln enjoys the role of defender of established things. If in Illinois and Indiana and Iowa that posture (but only that posture) could persuade peaceful division, certainly it could be expected to energize those portions of the North with no historical or cultural links with the South even as the Republic began: energize them to lead their more timid, less Yankee compatriots into an intersectional test of wills, particularly if their other choice is to be abolished themselves. Far better to "strike, and strike again!"

DOUGLAS AND DRED SCOTT

Lincoln spoke, with real confidence, of the future of his party at the post-election Chicago banquet of December 1856. Yet another year of relative silence and political inactivity followed upon that celebration, a year for regrouping and reorganization. Only one

---

12   See Quintilian, *Institution Oratoria*, I, x, 5n.2: "A crocodile, having seized a woman's son, said that he would restore him, if she would tell him the truth. She replied, '"you will not restore him.' Was it the crocodile's duty to give him up?"

important Lincoln speech belongs to 1857. Yet, in comparison with what followed that performance, it deserves close attention as a more thoughtful, discursive preliminary to the campaign orations of 1858. Moreover, it provides an occasion for treating in detail the importance of Lincoln's special reading of the Declaration of Independence—a work that must be done before moving on to the great debates. The circumstance of this performance was topical if not directly political. And, as we would expect, it involved a challenge from Stephen Douglas. For on 12 June the Little Giant had, at the request of the Federal Grand Jury for Illinois, delivered a discussion of the Dred Scott decision in the Hall of Representatives at Springfield. Though without the auspices of a similar invitation, Lincoln replied to him on 26 June.[13]

Douglas in his speech had developed three themes: the progress of the Territory of Kansas toward the achievement of statehood, the misconduct of the Mormons in Utah, and the Dred Scott decision of the previous March.[14] Lincoln answered what the leader of the Illinois Democracy had to say in each connection, though he emphasized what he saw as an anomaly in Douglas's defense of the High Court. For the Little Giant's address gave Lincoln a fresh opportunity to assail what he perceived as the ingenuousness of his adversary's doctrine of Popular Sovereignty and to assert once more that Douglas's interest was not in allowing the will of the people, as determined at a local level, to decide how they should live, and with what values, but rather in accommodating his clients in the Slaveocracy and thus perpetuating and increasing the political power of his party. The other significant component of this 1857 speech was another argument *ad verecundiam*, Lincoln's

---

13 *Works*, 2: 398-410. It was Lincoln's first important speech outside of Illinois.

14 Douglas's speech was very well reviewed. Twenty thousand copies were printed and distributed throughout the country. The New York *Herald* thought it the opening of Douglas's campaign for the Presidency in 1860. Particularly influential was Douglas's definition of the limits of racial benevolence in the American Republicans in the years to come. Lincoln accepted the definition as a given but reinterpreted its theoretical underpinnings.

quarrel with the history employed as prescript by Chief Justice Roger B. Taney in rejecting Scott's plea for judicial relief.[15]

As regards to Kansas, Douglas was optimistic. The people there, he predicted, would soon resolve their problems: that is, if Kansas Republicans decided to participate in the Kansas election as they should.[16] Utah, in contrast, offered grounds for legitimate concern. The Mormons appeared to be in rebellion. Americans from other states were not always safe when in their midst. Many Mormon immigrants had refused to become naturalized citizens of their adopted country. Douglas proposed that Utah's organic act be repealed and the Mormon settlement placed under direct Federal authority. Lincoln, with amusement, agreed—but observed correctly that "it would be a considerable backing down by Judge Douglas from his much vaunted doctrine of self-government for the territories." Yet he is not surprised by such a palpable contradiction since, from its first announcement, Popular Sovereignty "was a mere deceitful pretense for the benefit of slavery." As for Kansas, there were no "free state Democrats" there to be abandoned by the Republicans. After certain irregularities in Kansas' system of registration, the Republicans had reason to fear that their participation in a rigged election could be used to legitimize a pro-slavery constitution.[17] Again the

---

15   The *argumentum ad verecundiam* is an appeal to historical identity, to traditional values, to a *respect* for tradition.

16   In this prediction Douglas was of course quite previous. Kansas had a proslavery territorial legislature, and an antislavery population. Douglas hoped that his friends in the territory would persuade the proslavery settlers from Missouri to accept the inevitable and submit to the people a constitution for a free state, a state that would come into the Union under the Democratic banner, with no hostility to the South. Instead the Lecompton Constitution was prepared and sent to Washington with no provision for a Kansas referendum on its features. These events split the Democratic Party: Douglas stayed with Popular Sovereignty, and President Buchanan went along with the proslavery Lecompton Constitution. Kansas was not admitted!

17   Part of the difficulty in Kansas was that the various factions sometimes refused to participate in elections held under the appointed territorial authorities. The legal legislature in Lecompton therefore did not represent

spectre of conspiracy is invoked. But all such is prologue. Most of this Lincoln speech concerns Dred Scott.

The thrust of the Senator's remarks on the new Court decision concerning slavery and the Declaration is borrowed from the old rhetoric of the Whigs and Federalists. The High Court was distinctly their institution. Douglas reasoned that men honoring that tradition must submit to the "highest judicial tribunal on earth." By its authority his part in repealing the Missouri Compromise had received vindication. The role of slavery in the territories had finally been resolved. And despite appearances to the contrary, no harm had been done to the operations of Popular Sovereignty. For even though the High Court had forbidden Congressional or local prohibitions of slavery in the territories, a refusal to pass domestic protective legislation for the peculiar institution would allow each new state to decide its status in their midst. No protective legislation, under the police power, and no slavery: so went the Douglas formula. And as for Taney's comment on the meaning of the Declaration as it originally applied to black men and women, it was altogether right and proper. Moreover, it should have a good effect on the popular response in the North to the nostrums of antislavery operators. "All men" in 1776 meant clearly the white citizens of the various colonies, particularly with reference to other Englishmen living under the inherited umbrella of English law. Or else "all civilized men," when faced by a government that threatened their lives, their property, and their hope of a future. To believe otherwise was to deny history and human nature. The apparent generality of the great instrument of separation was only hyperbole to introduce a specific appeal to a given law, with just a little invocation of the "higher imperatives" of self-preservation—always an important part of the apology for any revolution, and particularly of Anglo-Saxon revolutions modeled

---

the Kansas electorate. The same pattern prevailed with the constitutional convention. Only the statewide election held under the terms of the Lecompton Constitution drew out a cross section of the voters. The Republicans carried in that contest, giving rise to the possibility of a new slave state with an antislavery government. No wonder the early history of Kansas often puzzles those unfamiliar with its checkered course.

on 1688, framing their appeals on the models of the Great Charter, the Petition of Right, and the Bill of Rights. The Declaration of Independence was not meant to threaten Negro slavery, either at the time of its adoption or at some future date, but rather to threaten King George III and his minions. Indeed, in bringing about our separation from an authority which might attempt to regulate local American institutions, it might be called an indirect guarantee that slaves could be kept among us, if we so wished. It was thus rightly called "a white man's charter of freedom." Said Stephen Douglas, "No one can vindicate the character, motive and conduct of the signers of the Declaration of Independence, except upon the hypothesis that they referred to the white race alone, and not to the African, when they declared men to have been created free and equal!"[18] They were speaking only "of British subjects on the continent being equal to British subjects born and residing in Great Britain." To say otherwise was to ignore the fullness of the text. Or so he maintained.

Lincoln's answer to this reading is at the heart of his democratic rhetoric for a Whig policy.[19] For one thing, it enabled him to create

---

18   Quoted on 570 of Robert W. Johannsen's *Stephen A. Douglas* (New York: Oxford University Press, 1973). We should, however, remember before we oversimplify the meaning of these words that Douglas himself was mildly antislavery and for protecting free Negroes "in the exercise of all the rights they were capable of enjoying consistent with the good and safety of society" (571). Senator Douglas was never a devotee of the pure "natural rights" doctrine, for men of any color. He tended instead to think of legal and political rights and to derive his teaching on the subject from a notion of the priority of society to all forms of government and the inseparability of individual man from the social matrix. For support of Douglas's view of the Declaration see Jack P. Greene, *All Men Are Created Equal: Some Reflections on the Character of the American Revolution* (Oxford: The Clarendon Press, 1976). See also David M. Potter, *The Impending Crisis, 1848-1861* (New York: Harper & Row, 1976), 340; Douglas did not believe the intrinsic natural rights should be spoken of as support to or apart from political rights, as "carrying their own to fulfillment."

19   Whig/Federalist rhetoric was ordinarily an appeal to authority. It emphasized the paternal superiority of a political elect, in whose hands the chartered rights, property, and common good of the people might safely be entrusted. Virtue and prudence were the characteristics of this elite. Whig

a fellow feeling with his audience in the Midwest and later, in 1860, with an electorate throughout the North. Yet he accomplished this change in *persona* without compromising his status as a faithful communicant of the "political religion" of the United States Constitution, without any danger of disobedience to orders of the courts, or offenses against the majesty of the law.[20] While refusing to "acquiesce in it as precedent," Lincoln could accept the partisan ruling of a divided Supreme Court in the confidence that it would some day be reversed. Once new judges were appointed, all Americans might learn to construe the Declaration as did most sensible men north of the Ohio, with the cultural integrity of the "Free States" left secure and no slaves *or* free Negroes coming into Illinois. In other words, the practice of Republican politics would rectify Dred Scott, with the help of the voters for whom such politics were designed.

Equality for these people signified, as in the speech at Kalamazoo, a kind of equal liberty: a potential for upward mobility in the economic, political, or social sense of that term. There was no danger of condescension, only a manifest affection for a life they already knew—the individualism of the frontier, minus the violence and the kind of pre-Puritan English social inheritance that had so affected the South. And minus also the Negro. To say to his typical audience that "all men are created equal" was, for Lincoln, to assure them that they were as good as anyone with inherited wealth or social standing, that they would not be pressed down into a mudsill layer such as some of them had known in Europe and in the older states, and that the Declaration of Independence was their security against anything to the contrary. Once remade as a Republican, Lincoln argued repeatedly that there was no way of separating their kind of equality from a nominal acknowledgement of the right of the Negro not to be a slave. He was careful, however, to distinguish this small, natural, unalienable right from all the

---

rhetoric deplores all divisive talk of slavery, either for or against.

20   Lincoln is rightfully amused at the irony of such piety about the Supreme Court from so regular a disciple of Andrew Jackson as the Little Giant of Illinois, for Jacksonians regularly despised the Court.

social and political rights we ordinarily associate with language of this sort.[21] It was pleasant to think of the Negro as being free—at least so long as it were certain that he would enjoy that freedom somewhere else far away, in Africa or in the South. Thus Lincoln played upon the desire of a large portion of his audience, influenced by their religious heritage, to feel a certain moral advantage over those incapable of making such careful discriminations, to enjoy a cheap Puritan thrill. To confine the power of the South and think well of themselves, to focus the energies of the Northwest and combine them with the reformist fervor of New England and the practical desires of the new industrial and commercial interests, all the while producing no inconvenience for Illinois: these things Lincoln's doctrine could accomplish.[22] It was an antislavery position of value to white men, once paraphrased as follows by a strong Lincoln supporter in Ohio:

> The negro question, as we understand it is a white man's question, the question of the right of free white laborers to the soil of the territories. It is not to be crushed or retarded by shouting "Sambo" at us. We have no Sambo in our platform.... We object to Sambo. We don't want him about. We insist that he shall not be forced upon us.[23]

---

21 See Jacque Voegeli, *Free But Not Equal: The Midwest and the Negro During the Civil War* (Chicago: University of Chicago Press, 1967) 4: "In the Middle West, political and social rights were seldom, if ever, included in this category [with natural rights such as freedom and the security of property] ...."

22 Wright, 147.

23 See Leon F. Litwack, *North of Slavery: The Negro in the Free States, 1790-1860* (Chicago: University of Chicago Press, 1961) 270; also Eugene Berwanger, *The Frontier Against Slavery: Western Anti-Negro Prejudice and the Slavery Extension Controversy* (Urbana: University of Illinois Press, 1967) 133. Lyman Trumbull of Illinois in 1859 spoke to the same effect: "We, the Republican Party, are the white man's party. We are for the free white man, and for making white labor acceptable and honorable,

Or, to quote a more obvious authority, Senator Augustus Caesar Dodge of Iowa declared that he "could not remember anyone who had ever demanded the nonextension of slavery for the benefit of the Negro."[24] Though by reason of circumstance the Republican position did indeed eventually result in a politically motivated, conditional abolition of slavery, its true objectives, where the Negro was concerned, were his complete and final expulsion from the continent of North America. Or, failing that, a circumscribed freedom within the South or in some Latin colony. Like the equality of Jefferson in his most sanguine moments, Lincoln's is an advantage to be enjoyed in Liberia, where the onetime bondsman will be a worry to someone else, not to "statesmen" from Ohio, Iowa, and Illinois. Such doctrine does not connect him with the sort of "natural rights" theory as is presupposed in the most familiar expressions of modern political thought. Lincoln's feeling for blacks in this portion of his career (a sentiment which, most significantly, almost never erupted into the *argumentum ad misericordium* of the Abolitionists) was like that of the Ohio Congressman who in 1854 announced: "I sympathize with them deeply, but I have no sympathy for them in a common residence with the white race."[25] To speak plainly in the language of contemporary ethnic demagogy of Lincoln's "Dred Scott Speech," we can say that he was careful not to be "outniggered." Finally, says Father Abraham, the great trouble with Negro slavery is that it tends "horribly to amalgamation." "The separation of the races, it is clear, if ever effected at all, must be effected by colonization." Toward this conclusion all true patriots should urge the policy of their government through the election of right thinking, separationist representatives. With that

---

which it can never be when Negro labor is brought into competition with it." Senator Dodge of Iowa called the idea of racial equality "wicked and disgraceful."

24   Berwanger, 126.

25   Litwack 49. It is an impression reinforced by Lincoln's refusal to touch the Black Codes of Illinois, or even to criticize them, and by a reading from a selection of "nigger jokes," which were more likely cruel than kind. See, for an instance David C. Means, ed., *The Lincoln Papers* (New York: Doubleday & Company, 1948) 1: 169.

racist peroration Lincoln concluded his most interesting speech on equality. And thus leaves us with a puzzle.

For if Stephen Douglas and the other Democratic recreants do not promise to restrain and reproach the peculiar institution through the instruments of law and legislation, they are, in the moral calculus of the future Emancipator, unaware of the humanity of black people. Moreover, if students of the early Republic who share in that politics declare that the national prescription carries with it no mandate to recognise such humanity, they are identified as having a design upon the freedom of white men and are marked for public opprobrium. Yet, on the other hand, the same calculus allows for a political cooperation with men who burn copies of the Constitution and call it "a covenant with death," or to easy association because it will leave the free Negro, once on his own, to "die out" like the dodo bird.[26] To say nothing of the wholesome assistance of those Republicans who are, where the freedmen are concerned, convinced that "it would be better to kill them off at once, if there is no other way."[27] No wonder that many contemporary observers and certain scholars in our time come to conclude that in the 1850s hatred of the Negro was greater "at the North" than among slaveholders or those who in 1860 voted for Bell or Breckinridge.[28] But if the opportunism of Republican antislavery (the small number of sincere Abolitionists aside) was concerned "less over the future of the Negro than over the future of opposing [white] groups as their interests were affected by the Negroes in slavery," if the suspicion of Illinois Negro leaders

---

26   Berwanger, 138-39; Litwack 271: William H. Seward described the American Negro as a "foreign and feeble element like the Indians, incapable of assimilation ... a pitiful exotic unwisely and unnecessarily transplanted into our fields and which it is unprofitable to cultivate at the cost of the desolation of the native vineyard."

27   Litwack, 69.

28   Voegeli, 65; also James A. Rawley, *Race and Politics: Bleeding Kansas and the Coming of the Civil War* (Philadelphia: J. B. Lippincott Company, 1969) 14. He quotes the English journalist Charles Mackay that "white antipathy toward blacks was stronger in the North than in the South." And concludes that the agitation in the North concerning slavery was a mask for other concerns.

about Lincoln's candidacy had a substantial basis in fact, then why does he appear in the Lincoln myth as a simple friend of the slave?[29] The answer is of course the Emancipation Proclamation—the accidental result of Lincoln's divisive politics which we read after the fact as the product of conscious design. Reading all of the "Dred Scott Speech," *seriatim*, should remind us of how unpredictable these consequences were. By this speech we are forced to realize that Lincoln's objective was not to be consistent, but to defeat the Democrats by whatever means he could find; to appear in the role of protector for the past and future of the Old Northwest even though, as a result, he came to aggravate the very deterioration of public sympathy for the Negro of which he loudly complains in replying to Justice Taney; a deterioration which would leave the Negro with "all the powers of earth ... rapidly combining against him." (Including, on certain occasions, the power of Abraham Lincoln.)

Taney (perhaps mindful of the strength of antislavery agitation in the 1850s) had held, to the contrary, that the Negro was better thought of in his day than at any other moment in the nation's history. As we forget, there was no true Abolitionist movement in 1776. But it was always Lincoln's position that the bad times were "now," that there had been, in the generation of the Fathers, an interval of enlightened disinterest and high Charity, of "virtue" where race and slavery were concerned.[30] This was for him a rhetorically useful myth—one that, to this day, has its adherents in the scholarship of progressive historians, and in the oratory of our liberal politicians. But, as Professor C. Vann Woodward has told us, it was and is, however useful as a rhetorical past, a myth

---

29   Rawley, 274.

30   See my "The Heresy of Equality: Bradford Replies to Jaffa," *Modern Age*, XX (Winter, 1976): 62-77. For a discussion of how to read the Declaration of Independence. See also Don E. Fehrenbacher, *The Dred Scott Case: Its Significance in American Politics and Law* (New York: Oxford University Press, 1978). The difficulty with the Dred Scott case is, of course, not Taney's historiography but his judicial activism in speaking to more questions than were before the High Court.

and nothing more.[31] The truth about the high-sounding "left," the "radical Whigs" of the American Revolution, is that they were very like their nineteenth century Illinois disciple: full of "double talk"; ready to generalize their own complaints against the crown in order to enlist sympathy and recruits; but not about to allow this universalizing of a group grievance to embarrass them, once the dispute was over; not about to extend the implications of their arguments to sanction the demands of other groups, particularly if these demands worked to their expense. Said another way, it is usually the case with modern revolutionaries that their references to the generality of men, when they mean by them only themselves, are the political equivalents of the slick advertisers' "bait and switch." What comes to pass after the struggle is over is concluded for the benefit of a very small component of the human race—specifically, of the salesman of change—even though the interest of mankind has been invoked to implement their special (and unmentioned) designs.

Lincoln objects to most of the history behind Taney's decision in the case in question. But it is in his central criticism of the High Court's opinion (and of Douglas's support of that ruling) that the peculiarity of his position is most clearly revealed. And with it the progress of his political thought towards the definition it achieved in the campaign of 1858. In terms of its design, this material stands at the heart of the "Dred Scott Speech": immediately after his quibble over the distinction between obedience to a court decision and the acceptance of it as precedent, following his *concessio* and his dispute with Taney's reading of popular sentiment in 1776; and just before his peroration, with its core of racist nightmare. It is the climax of the address. And it is certainly of note that in these most important paragraphs Lincoln represents himself as prosecutor, with Stephen Douglas as the villain in his dock.

The distinctive element in Lincoln's reading of the Declaration, as I have suggested before, is his insistence that it was composed

---

31 I quote from C. Vann Woodward, "White Racism and Black `Emancipation'," *New York Review of Books* 27 February 1969: 11.

more with the future than with the present of American politics in mind. In his gloss what signifies about this document is that it "contemplated the progressive improvement in the condition of all men everywhere" and, in its reference to equality, "was of no practical use in effecting our separation from Great Britain." He deals with the obvious distance between the kind of America preserved and secured by the adoption of this instrument, and the kind of promise which, in his view, it embodies. Circumstances, he observes, will explain the gap. "They meant simply to declare the *right*, so the *enforcement* might follow as fast as circumstances should permit"—an explanation which makes of the authors of our independence the most unusual statesmen in the record of human experience. For Lincoln's Declaration of Independence is a kind of political time bomb, planted in the midst of the commonwealth by those responsible for its defense. The America preserved and protected in Philadelphia was, also, at the same time, marked for destruction. Or for radical transformation, once *enforcement* was possible. Only the beginning of paragraph two in the Declaration, the "abstract truth," means anything to Lincoln. The rest is, in his own words, a "merely revolutionary document."[32] And therefore he need not consider the meaning of equality of 1776, in the context where it appears: need not explain the racist complaints about "servile insurrection" and red "savages" or the appeals to a "common blood" which mark the various drafts of Jefferson's composition; or thus, once reinforced by the plural identity which speaks therein, connect the works to the long tradition of English legal theory, the "Old Whig" tradition which is the durable basis of our great experiment in republican self-government. That the anachronism of Lincoln's reading ever achieved widespread acceptance is astonishing: that is, if we take it on its merits, and ignore the vested interests of his admirers in the growth of Federal power. Which is a truth that would be called "abstract" by only a special few.

---

32   *Works*, 3: 375.

When in the year of the Declaration, the Continental Congress wished to define the corporate entity to which they would belong once independent of British authority, they asked Benjamin Franklin, John Adams, and Thomas Jefferson to devise for its representation a new national seal. On it these worthies put symbols of "England, Scotland, Ireland, France, Germany and Holland." But of the Latin, the Indian, or the African nothing.[33] So much for the inclusive definitions of the American "we," of the "all men" who are equal on that hot July day, regardless of how much slavery there is in the land. As to Lincoln's evidence about a few Negroes voting in a few colonies on the decision to secede from the larger British commonwealth, or on the later decision to form a "more perfect union," it is clearly an anomaly in the thought of one who derived some of his favorite theorems from "we the people" in the Preamble to the Constitution. For there can be no doubt that, as Justice Taney maintained, most Americans in the era of the Revolution and ratification of the Constitution thought of the Negro as anything but a citizen or potential citizen. A national plebiscite held at that time would have returned an overwhelming majority in favor of the Maryland Chief Justice and against the Illinois office seeker. Or separate plebiscites in a majority of the states. For the most part, free Negroes had the vote, in eighteenth-century America, in places where they did not reside. Or else they had an apparent right to vote only because the law did not explicitly exclude them from the polls. It is difficult to prove that they voted in the 1770s. And to argue that anything in the Constitution is a definitive comment on some part of the Declaration is not a convincing procedure. Everything that Taney contends concerning the legal definition of the Negro as man under the Constitution we cannot accept. The Fathers chose not to address such questions. But Lincoln's construction of the evidence is even more impossible. It is enough that we remember that the Old Constitution allowed states to exclude certain varieties of immigrants altogether and to define citizenship as narrowly as they pleased. When one of

---

33   See Donald L. Robinson, *Slavery in the Structure of American Politics, 1776-1820* (New York: Harcourt Brace Jovanovich, Inc. 1971) 135.

Lincoln's friends criticized the "no blacks" provision of the Oregon Constitution, Abraham Lincoln contended that he had made a mistake.[34]

> In those days, by common consent, the spread of the black man's bondage to new countries was prohibited; but now, Congress decides that it *will* not continue the prohibition, and the Supreme Court decides that it *could* not if it would. In those days, our Declaration of Independence was held sacred by all, and thought to include all; but now, to aid in making the bondage of the negro universal and eternal, it is assailed and sneered at and construed, and hawked at, and torn, till, if its framers could rise from their graves, they could not at all recognise it.

The distance traveled had been great. For all this evil and declension someone was clearly responsible: for the widespread assumption that "all men" originally meant "any men" and was precisely designed to effect the separation between two people living under a single law; for the theory that the generality of this appeal had more to do with the ends and limits of government than with the "rights of man": for the translation of such evidence into a politics coming down through Jefferson and Jackson from Patrick Henry and into the crucial arena of the Midwest. It is both a conspiracy against the Negro and against the people who "don't want him around": the people who will allow poor "Sambo" only the freedom to die at liberty, without a place where he can work or live; or, as an alternative, the freedom to leave their land. With the image of that malefactor functioning at his worst, and image of Stephen Douglas as enthusiastic slavemongering panderer and formal cause of the mixed blood in thousands of mulatto children, Lincoln organizes his inflammatory peroration. And gives the Giant a warning of the kind of campaign that will soon begin.

---

34   *Works,* 3: 351.

THE OPENING GUN OF THE GREAT CAMPAIGN

As was suggested above, Lincoln, in 1858, had not only a new advantage in selling his theory of Democratic conspiracy (after Dred Scott) but also a new problem in appearing to be *the* antislavery candidate (after Douglas's success in blocking the admission of Kansas to statehood under the proslavery Lecompton Constitution). Both influences help us to explain the new tone of his "House-Divided Speech." But he had been working toward the central phrases of this performance for years before he gathered them in their final form. For proof of this evolution, there is, for one thing, a letter to George Robertson of Kentucky, written on 15 August 1855, about the ability of the nation to survive its divisions over slavery unless it comes to have one policy on that subject.[35] And then the notes for his 18 May 1858 speech at Edwardsville, Illinois—a speech in which he refers to previous uses of the biblical formula, "a house divided against itself cannot stand."[36] But though Lincoln had to outbid the Giant for an antislavery vote newly respectful of Douglas's position, the choices left for that audience by Lincoln's new appeal were the choices he had offered them at Peoria: they would either support the Republicans or else give their vote to the expansion of the Slave Power, the movement of Negroes into their neighborhood, and (perhaps) the eventual enslavement of their own kind—or at least the devaluation of the liberty of Northern whites. No less an authority than Professor Jaffa has told us that "the rhetorical heart of the speech with which Lincoln began the memorable campaign of 1858 and which gave an intensely personal tone to the joint debates is the charge of a conspiracy to nationalize slavery."[37] That a "sly" Stephen Douglas

---

35   *Works*, 2: 318.

36   *Works,* 2: 452. The language is from Mark 3:25 and comes from Christ as he describes the divided house of Satan—a curious borrowing for an address to Christian people.

37   I quote from Harry V. Jaffa, *Crisis of the House Divided: An Interpretation of the Issues in the Lincoln-Douglas Debates* (New York: Doubleday & Company, 1959) 277. My general objections to Jaffa's interpretation of Lincoln's career appear in my "Against Lincoln: An Address

was a party to such a design, regardless of Lecompton, is the burden of seventy per cent of the "House-Divided Speech."[38] As usual, Lincoln expected the argument from character to carry him through and resolve his many rhetorical problems with attempting to "up the ante" but not up it too far. Ignorance of the Lecompton document and take seriously Dred Scott: so goes his counsel. For the former proves nothing about Douglas's long range plans and the latter is both proof that the Slave Power is on the move and that Douglas (in view of his attitude toward the case) will be the man to finish its work.

Though the gist of the "House-Divided Speech" is forensic, it is here that Lincoln begins to convert himself into a secular scripture and to sound the epideictic note.[39] The proposition with which this address begins, the *exordium* of rhetorical question and answer, is an instance of what is called *oraculum* in the classical texts; a conflation of the words of men with the words of the gods, using the holy texts for less than holy ends. It is this quality which made of the speech the watershed of Lincoln's career and identified him in the public mind with the "active wing" of the antislavery cause.

> If we could first know where we are, and *whither* we are tending, we could then better judge *what* to do, and *how* to do it.
>
> We are now far into the *fifth* year, since a policy was initiated, with the *avowed* object, and *confident* promise, of putting an end to slavery agitation.

---

at Gettysburg," *The Historian's Lincoln: Pseudohistory, Psychohistory*, Gabor S. Boritt, ed. (Urbana and Chicago: University of Illinois, Peru 1988) 107-15.

38   See Don E. Fehrenbacher, *Prelude to Greatness: Lincoln in the 1850s* (Stanford: Stanford University Press, 1962) 82-83, for a good discussion of the structure of the speech.

39   *Works*, 2: 461-469. Epideictic oratory occurs when all questions are closed or settled, nothing is to be decided or judged after the fact.

> Under the operation of that policy, that agitation has not only, *not ceased*, but has *constantly augmented*.
>
> In *my* opinion, it *will* not cease, until a *crisis* shall have been reached, and passed.
>
> "A house divided against itself cannot stand."
>
> I believe this government cannot endure, permanently half *slave* and half *free*.
>
> I do not expect the Union to be *dissolved*—I do not expect the house to *fall*—but I *do* expect it will cease to be divided.
>
> It will become *all* one thing, or *all* the other.
>
> Either the *opponents* of slavery, will arrest the further spread of it, and place it where the public mind shall rest in the belief that it is in course of ultimate extinction; or its *advocates* will push it forward, till it shall become alike lawful in *all* the States, *old* as well as *new*—*North* as well as South.
>
> Have we no *tendency* to the latter condition?

The generic statement from which Lincoln derives his particular conclusion is, to be sure, not linked to it by logical necessity. Moreover, it is especially out of place in the context of American politics. For houses are always divided. Or else ruled despotically. And these United States are, on many normative questions, only in part a unity by definition. The division which exercises the Republican candidate for the United States Senate seat of Stephen Douglas is a division over slavery. But is the division over religion any less important? Yet on that subject we read the "Congress shall make no law." Nor any law to create a uniform franchise. Or about all taxes. Or to effect a complete and equal distribution of wealth. Or to erase the effect of various national origins. Do not these large concerns divide the house? To say nothing of many, many more.

Lincoln formed his speech around a biblical quotation because, as he told Herndon, he wanted a phrase that would stick in the mind: a phrase that would rouse the audience to a sense of urgency and with which no one would wish to argue.[40] When Douglas complained of this strategy and cried that the Bible was being misused, Lincoln's reply showed how carefully, consciously he had framed his text and calculated its effects. Said he to Douglas's denial that division would destroy the house, it "is a question of veracity, not between him and me, but between the Judge and an authority of a somewhat higher character."[41]

To understand what has been added to the rhetorical arsenal employed by Lincoln in 1854-1857, we must examine closely the elements of his new appeal and their relationship with each other. The antislavery of "save the territories" was a nice position. It would serve to hide many other objectives while giving its adherents a sense of moral advantage: tariff, banking, and railroad interests, and speculation, commercial expansion and patronage.[42] Writes one of the neoabolitionist historians of the present generation:

> The institution of slavery did lie at the root of the economic and social schism between the sections. However, it was not the antihuman, immoral aspect of the institution which brought all the weight of

---

40 See William H. Herndon, "Facts Illustrative of Mr. Lincoln's Patriotism and Statesmanship," *Abraham Lincoln Quarterly*, III, Dec. 1944: 184, 186.

41 *Works*, 3: 17. There is, of course, a difference between a house peacefully divided, on the basis of internal agreement, and a house whose division "against itself" pits one of its components against another in a struggle for control within its walls. The original division within the American polity was of the first variety; Lincoln's formula converts it into a conflict of the second sort.

42 Wright, 147; see also Ludwell H. Johnson, *Splendid Division and Reunion: America, 1848-1877* (New York: John Wiley & Sons, 1978) 107-121. Johnson summarizes evidence from Charles A. Beard and Barrington Moore, Raimondo Luraghi has offered some related insights in "The Civil War and the Modernization of American Society: Social Structure and Industrial Revolution in the Old South before and during the War," *Civil War History*, XVII (Summer, 1972): 230-50.

the national power against it; it was the antitariff, antibank, anticapitalist, antinational aspect of slavery which aroused the united opposition of the only groups in the country with the power to make war: the national political leaders and controllers of the national economy.[43]

Or, to put the matter briefly, slavery "gave Lincoln and the North a moral issue to sanctify and ennoble what was ... a struggle for national power and economic control."[44] Lincoln was being more than usually dishonest when he had argued earlier that it could "not be demonstrated that the North will gain a dollar" by reducing the power of the South.[45] But after Douglas joined with the antislavery senators to block the Lecompton Constitution, and after slavery did not, as the result of the Kansas-Nebraska Act, spread into the territories, the old technique of conflation lost some of its force. It appeared that it might be difficult to keep alive the still infant fusion, the party of one issue. To revive the antislavery momentum and to move Illinois beyond the posture of being simply against expansion, it was necessary to convince the electorate of the Sucker State that it was still in danger and that only by taking the offensive against the conspiracy could it defend its place in the Union. With the false dilemma and the paranoid analysis of the "House-Divided Speech" Lincoln could give moral status to subverting the Constitution, the principles of multiplicity and variety, balance and compromise on which its foundation rests. Moreover, by announcing that the Republicans expected to put slavery on the road to extinction and to do so by way of electing candidates to national office, to Congress and the White House,

---

[43] See Howard Zinn, "Abolitionists, Freedom–Riders and the Tactics of Agitation," in *The Antislavery Vangard: New Essays on the Abolitionists*, ed. By Martin Duberman (Princeton: Princeton University Press, 1965), 445; Zinn quotes (with approval) Jefferson Davis on how the war was abut power, even though discussed in other terms.

[44] Zinn, 445.

[45] *Works*, 2: 352; also Johnson 109-15 on Lincoln as a model of sanctimonious effrontery.

Lincoln's representative argument, as his importance grew, drove the South to ask for new and unprecedented guarantees of its future: weapons of law with which to defend itself from the dangers implicit in Yankee expectations; securities against being reduced to the status of economic colony and arena for social experiment. No wonder this Lincoln speech was a chief cause of Southern alarm once he began to rise toward the leadership of his party. For the promise of his opening proposition would, eventually, have forced him to drop his mask of moderation, his commitment to "leave it where it stood," and compelled his party to "seek ways to secure the placing of slavery on the road to ultimate extinction within or without the framework of the Constitution."[46] Otherwise, the Republicans would disperse to their natural (and separate) post within the American political spectrum.

Lincoln's new position in 1858 is clearly in the tradition of New England High Federalism. Government is, by it, conceived as an instrument of moral regeneration, and "virtue" expected to flow from the top, downward.[47] Or such is the rhetorical coloring of his position. By using a generic proposition he treats the country as if the "founding" had been incomplete, with nothing given except for the Declaration of Independence and a few pieties concerning majority rule. But Illinois was not really so Puritan. It did not seriously wish to reform Virginia and Tennessee. And Lincoln knew that very well. He needed the energy and enthusiasm of the serious Abolitionists—hoped to prevent them from impatience with combination, from wandering away into impotent purity. Illinois would agree to nothing more than a general statement that slavery should end at some indefinite date. Or rather, to a statement that, in its probity, it expected everyone to agree to such a proposition. It would vote to effect that agreement. But it would reject every plan

---

46 Wright, 172.

47 See William H. Herndon, "Analysis of the Character of Abraham Lincoln," *Abraham Lincoln Quarterly*, I (Dec. 1941): 423. Fisher Ames in Jonathon Eliot, *The Debates of Several State Conventions on the Adoption of the Federal Constitution as Recommended by the General Convention at Philadelphia in 1787* (New York: Burt Franklin, n.d.) 158-9.

for abolition that the mind of man could devise. For they would either cost money or bring blacks into the Free States. Therefore the Abolitionists would have (for the moment) to be content with a statement about what men should believe—even if insulted while urged to conversion—and a target for their anger over long delays and small rewards. For the *exordium* of the "House-Divided Speech" leads not to the policy for antislavery, which is its opening promise, but the negation of the antithetical policy of proslavery (i.e., the Democrats), and of course, the condemnation of its chief men and anointed instrument. Toward this safe harbor Lincoln's discourse was headed from the first.

The way in which the focus in the body of his text, the long *narratio* of events connected with the controversy over slavery following the proposal of the Kansas-Nebraska Act, comes down upon the isolated character of Stephen Douglas is, as I said earlier, by reasoning from effect to cause. And by his very choice of a starting point for the account—as if there had been no Democrats and no threat of slavery expansion before the Missouri Compromise was repealed. The capstone of his denunciation, his claim of Douglas's complicity in the building of a new "house," is not however the Dred Scott case but the "decision [that] is probably coming, and will soon be upon us, unless the power of the present political dynasty shall be met and overthrown." Once more the real issue is identified with the freedom of white men—or the limits of the value of their freedom that the introduction of slavery will bring.[48] In a word, a bugbear. To substantiate his prediction Lincoln picks at a bit of language in the Kansas-Nebraska Act and construes with energy one portion of Taney's ruling against the Negro Scott. From this slight evidence, ignoring all indications to the contrary, he extrapolates. Stephen and Franklin and Roger and James have finished all but one part of an ominous structure with "all the tenons and mortices exactly fitting." That part will be the ruling that slavery shall be "lawful in all the states." Following all this *diabole* is the usual Lincolnian concession to unctuous

---

48 For the predictions of the enslavement of white men, see *Works*, 2: 341, 385, and 553; 3: 95.

civility, a disclaimer that no personal malice is intended and a mild acknowledgement of small areas of agreement between the senator and his Republican adversaries: on unimportant things like the Lecompton Constitution.[49] It is granted that Douglas has great ability, and that he sometimes cooperates with other Northerners. But why should Douglas be spared when so many dangers, including revival of the slave trade, are contained in his re-election; and when the Republicans are so close to victory?[50] And why should the prospects of that self-proclaimed "living dog," Abraham Lincoln, be sacrificed to keep around a "dead lion," even though he be a "very *great man*"? For no one can trust the Giant to make certain that the local freedom of choice (which is his "principle") will have the moral results that it should. The conspiracy charge, it turns out, is still not the main thing. The sin of Stephen Douglas is the wickedness of his theory of American politics. Which is precisely what Douglas said of Lincoln—when not complaining about how much he lied.[51]

A Rhetoric for War

The radicalism of Lincoln's "House-Divided Speech" was recognised by all who heard it almost as soon as its delivery was complete. And even before that moment by those on whom the orator had tried it out.[52] Senator Douglas spoke for a consensus of contemporary critical opinion when, in his 9 July reply in Chicago, he declared of the Republican choice for his replacement, "He goes for uniformity in our domestic institutions, for a war of the

---

49   *Diabole* is defined as a "slanderous denunciation of things that are able to take place in the future."

50   Speech of 9 December 1857, before the United States Senate, quoted in Johannsen's *Stephen A. Douglas*, 59.

51   The technique of "the Big Lie" was perfected in the German propaganda of World War II. The rhetoric of the Republicans in the 1850's was a prototype of this modern strategy. It invoked the simple repetition of a distortion continued until mere familiarity made it seem true.

52   William H. Herndon, *Herndon's Lincoln: A True Story of a Great Life*, ed. David F. Hawke, (Indianapolis: Bobbs-Merrill, 1970) 168-69.

sections, until one or the other shall be subdued. I go for the great principle of the Kansas-Nebraska Bill, the right of the people to decide for themselves." And to this he added, "I deny their right to force a good thing upon a people who are unwilling to receive it .... It is no answer ... to say that slavery is an evil and hence should not be tolerated. You must allow the people to decide for themselves whether it is a good or an evil."[53] When speaking to his associates, preparing them before the convention for what he would say, Lincoln gave a curiously similar description and "warned friends ... he might fatally damage the Republican Party by making its existence synonymous with a destruction of the government." But he was persistent. He believed he could discern the scope and read the destiny of impending sectional controversy. He was sure he could "see far beyond the present and hear the voice of the future."[54] The crisis-bringing elements of the speech, the properties that make of it a Puritan jeremiad, are therefore the results of conscious choice. If slavery was a way of marking boundaries between cultures, if all varieties of antislavery had more to do with attitudes toward the Negro, then Lincoln's position would naturally be translated "down there" to mean the danger of government by a permanently hostile majority: a threat to bind the strong man discussed in the rest of the passage in Mark from which the central formula was borrowed, and thus a threat to "spoil his house." Even admirers of Lincoln call the speech "Garrisonian" and marvel at its extreme doctrine.[55] Others emphasize the necessary distance between himself and Douglas which it helped create.[56] John S. Wright emphasizes the art of "frightening" the electorate into voting for an "uncompromising antislavery party on a defensive basis."[57] To the same effect George Fort Milton has observed that the propositional teaching of the address is "the shrewdest political formula ever construct-

---

53 Johannsen, 642-43.
54 Quoted in James G. Blaine, *Twenty Years of Congress: From Lincoln to Garfield* (Norwich, CT: The Henry Bell Publishing Company, 1884) 1:146.
55 See Fehrenbacher, *Prelude to Greatness* 72; also Luthin 194.
56 Potter, *The Impending Crisis* 348-49.
57 Wright, 168.

ed in America" because it gave release to the "emotional fixation of hundreds of thousands of Northern people." It allowed them to promise aggression against the source of their anxiety, to utter a "hidden threat" while disclaiming any such intent.[58] The Lincoln of this speech, and not the Lincoln of the Whig years, not the conservative lawyer of Springfield, is the Lincoln known to the country when nominated for the Presidency.[59] In delivering it he had acted out the principle of his party as stated clearly in a letter of advice by Judge John D. Caton to Lyman Trumbull. Said Caton, of the candidate in Lincoln's place, "he must keep up the agony and lay on the passion."[60] Such was Lincoln's course in the campaign that followed and throughout the next two years. The rhetorical pressure was compounded many times over. Woe be it, said Lincoln, to any Midwestern politician who plays it up to a solid South waiting to hear the highest bid.[61] The consequences of his stance are well described by an authority on these troubled years.

> The operation of the doctrine quickened and made final just such a shift from federal Union to a consolidated republic, just such an imposition of uniformity on American institutions and customs as Douglas had warned would come. In their interchanges on the House Divided doctrine it was Douglas, not Lincoln, who read the future right.[62]

The rail splitter promised that the Union would survive the challenge. But without a doubt a "refounding" had been on Lincoln's mind since the beginning of his public life. With that task

---

58 George Fort Milton, *The Eve of Conflict: Stephen A. Douglas and the Needless War* (Boston: Houghton Mifflin Company, 1934) 456-57.
59 Wright, 169.
60 Wright, 170.
61 *Works*, 2, 352.
62 Milton, 319.

he continued during the great debates, on through the election of 1860, and as the President of the United States.

8.

With the Lion and the Eagle
(1985)

Review of Gore Vidal, *Lincoln* (New York: Random House, 1984)

Throughout his long and stormy career Gore Vidal has enjoyed a well-deserved reputation for irreverence. He has held in contempt and treated as mere hypocrisy most of the values officially embraced by the majority of his countrymen. He has preferred Aaron Burr to Hamilton or Jefferson and Julian the Apostate to the Christians. It is therefore more than a little surprising when we observe that Vidal has now accepted at face value the Lincoln legend of the benign political alchemist and has honored the Emancipator with an essentially favorable treatment of his Presidency. That is, surprising until we remember that the mythology surrounding Father Abraham has been *the* public face of our times, replacing in the terrestrial sphere what religion once promised in another life—and until we notice what version of the Lincoln myth Vidal has adopted as his own.

Vidal's Lincoln is the fulfilled promise of the youthful lawyer who, in the 1838 "Address Before the Young Men's Lyceum of Springfield, Illinois," prophesised his own career in speaking of the difference between the ambitions of ordinary men (who wish only a "gubernatorial or presidential chair") and the dreams of distinction which drive forward those who belong to "the family of lion, or the tribe of eagle." His Lincoln has as counterparts not only Caesar and Alexander but also Otto von Bismarck and Oliver Cromwell—men of the "godly, thorough reformation," who bring their people to unity through the application of force. Each of these "reformers" transformed a commonwealth under his authority into what Vidal's John Hay describes as a "single, centralized nation." Moreover, what is true of the rest of these figures of "towering genius" is true also of Lincoln—that in their public lives they acted from the beginning out of conscious purpose, intending to "make all things new" even as they represented themselves as the slaves of circumstance.

Though inclined to underplay the influence of radical Republicans on the life and political atmosphere of the city, Vidal's book contains an interesting and otherwise persuasive account of the feel and pattern of what it would have been like to reside in Washington, with a place close to the administrative center of Federal power during the War Between the States.

Vidal does not tell about the South, or causes of Secession. He and his Yankee characters are ignorant on the subject—including Lincoln himself. His urban underworld is banal and unimpressive. And though his portraits of Lincoln's secretaries, family, and close associates are convincing, he does not offer to us a Lincoln who directly reveals the mainsprings of his policy. Indeed, he is more confident in his image of Salmon P. Chase, Edwin Stanton, and William Seward than he is in producing the tall man from Illinois. It is enough that he sticks close to the record, organized (with the advice of Professor David Donald) in a particular way, with only an occasional supplemental invention or misinterpretation—as when he has Lincoln to be moved by anxiety for Southerners who, in 1865, may be forced to live among numerous freedmen; or when he adds a moderating explanation to Lincoln's remark about leaving the Negro to the mercy of natural selection. The mystery of Lincoln he leaves to the speculation of others, even though he indicates which views of that puzzle he thinks plausible, and which unlikely, by his assignment of these opinions to particular characters.

But it is nonetheless the protagonist of the novel who holds our interest in Vidal's Lincoln—a man who knew that (again in Hay's language) "the Southern states had every constitutional right to go out of the Union" and still told them no; who dreamt of being swept along in the darkness in a frail vessel he cannot control, toward a shore he cannot perceive; who willed (or expected) his own death as an atonement "for having given so bloody and absolute a rebirth to his nation"; and who poured into the empty vessel of his idea of a sacrosanct Union whatever he thought the country needed in the way of goals and purposes suited to "finish the work." Though they profess to honor his name (and at their worst often follow his example), this is not a Lincoln which the radical politicians and our opinion-makers of our time can employ to serve their dark purposes.

It is therefore to be hoped that Vidal's *Lincoln* will be widely read. For it gives us most of the "new Messiah" that we need to know—the man who spoke at Springfield of the proud spirit who will, by any means that are available, win everlasting distinction and replace Washington as our "great man," whether "at the expense of emancipating slaves, or enslaving free men."

9.

From the Family of the Lion
(1991)

James McPherson, *Abraham Lincoln and the Second American Revolution* (New York: Oxford University Press, 1991)

There is a popular myth of Abraham Lincoln, our 16th president, that is known to most Americans. According to the orthodox version of this highly sympathetic construct, Lincoln was a plain and honest fellow, called by other plain, uncalculating men to preserve the handiwork of the Fathers, the Old Republic, perfecting that inheritance in the process of keeping it together. This Lincoln is no illustration of frenzied ambition, but rather a simple soul who had stumbled first into the practice of law and then into Illinois politics. He hated war but was determined to honor a trust put into his hands, even if that commitment meant more killing than in all other American wars put together. A reluctant and gentle conqueror, he stood ready, once secession had ended, to welcome the South back into the national family: like the father in the parable, rejoicing at the return of foolish children. Such is the Lincoln who grew melancholy in thinking of what blacks endured and who "died to make them free." This Father Abraham, the sad man of Illinois, the Prairie republican/Republican, in his spirit still hovers over this nation, giving direction and encouragement to successive generations of his countrymen. Of his early life we know that he identified with the poor, that he read by firelight, lost his sweetheart, deplored the

Mexican War, and served a frontier community as a member of the state legislature and the U.S. Congress. As a spokesman for wholesome, local ways, he debated Stephen Douglas. And he truly suffered in presiding over his country at war, spending blood only with agonized reluctance—certainly with no idea of reshaping its social and political order so as to make of it a vehicle for his private dreams of what power in the state might accomplish. So goes the myth.

In making, over a period of two decades, a series of scholarly objections to the distortion and oversimplification embodied in this myth, I had the pleasure of being treated briefly as the object of national puzzlement and irritation. For about five weeks I was cast as the leading villain in a political melodrama of what a public servant is allowed to believe, anathema because of what I said about the American past. Obviously, what I thought of Lincoln was not the real issue behind this affected and rhetorical outrage at my political heresy. But to my surprise, it is now evident that in most fashionable academic neighborhoods my understanding of Lincoln as transforming agent (which is, in essence, Willmoore Kendall's view of the evidence) has come all the way around to seem not at all farfetched. Or at least that is true of the descriptive component of my analysis.

James M. McPherson's *Abraham Lincoln and the Second American Revolution* summarizes the current trend in interpretive historiography on this subject. His Lincoln is a radical refounder of the "old Republic of the fathers," like the "lion" and "eagle" of which Lincoln had first spoken in his 1838 "Springfield Lyceum Speech": an American Caesar who, in McPherson's phrase, through "his own superb leadership, strategy, and sense of timing ... determined the pace of the revolution [of 1860] and endured its success." Arguing more or less to the same effect, Carl N. Degler in the *New York Times* last February 12 maintained that Lincoln was the American Bismarck and that "what the [civil] war represented, in the end, was the forceful incorporation of the South into a newly created nation." Which in both cases is what I have argued all the time.

However, there is one big difference between McPherson's Lincoln and what the record should lead us to conclude. For McPherson believes that all of this refounding by policy, construction, demagogy, and force of arms was wonderful to behold, pointing toward a "more perfect Union" than even James Madison could have imagined. In other words, he likes what the United States, as a political construct, has become better than he likes what it was. Those who do not, on balance, share in his enthusiasm for the present configuration of our political system in omnicompetent government obviously will not agree with McPherson's evaluation of Lincoln's handiwork; those who differ with him about a "new birth of freedom" brought about by violation of contract will see a rejection of the terms of that contract in the accomplishments at Gettysburg, at Atlanta, and at Appomattox Court House. McPherson's Lincoln "as he seems to us now" is a summary figure in one of the great American political traditions, that heritage which affirms the growing power of Leviathan to achieve ends and purposes it thinks proper, to apply its rhetoric and its energy to reshape the recalcitrant material of the body politic. In this system what seems to fit according to some extrinsic philosophical or moral standard is also lawful, regardless of what Constitution and statute leave to the irregular operations of free choice among constituent members. McPherson clearly belongs to that tradition. Those who measure the history of American politics against the paradigm of the old Constitution, or who affirm in public life no more regulation than what that document, as amended, permits will not, however, be at ease with McPherson on Lincoln's version of liberty, of unconditional surrender, implied powers, and revolutionary transformation *cum* preservation of the Union. Such Americans as are put off by this intrusive paradigm will not have so sanguine a view of Mr. Lincoln. For they come out of another American political tradition, the one which gave us our original Constitution and Bill of Rights. For them the Emancipator will always seem to be a crafty manipulator of men's emotions, a great incendiary, and almost a tyrant. Nothing in McPherson's evidence dislodges me from membership in this second company.

McPherson's arguments for Lincoln as a second founder is based on an analysis of the "scope and meaning of revolutionary transformations in both substance and process wrought by the Civil War" and "Lincoln's leadership in accomplishing these changes." McPherson doesn't dwell on the formal characteristics of the original Republic, what defined it before Mr. Lincoln came along. But he is serious about the word "revolution." Of what happened when the South was defeated and how Lincoln shaped that victory, he writes, "Abraham Lincoln was not Maximilien de Robespierre. No Confederate leaders went to the guillotine. Yet the Civil War changed the United States as thoroughly as the French Revolution changed that country." Lincoln accomplished this legerdemain by making liberty a gift of government—and by assigning to the federal power a general responsibility for the well-being of American citizens. This much it accomplished by freeing the slaves and preserving the Union by military means— not by persuasion and politics—thus putting the civil bond which makes a nation on a new basis. Of the origin of the old Republic in resistance to a power remote, unresponsive, and potentially hostile McPherson has little to say.

He praises Abraham Lincoln for his use of metaphor (Lincoln was the greatest master of the language among all our presidents) and for his ability to stick to one large objective. He treats the modern theory of total war leading to unconditional surrender as if it could conceivably enjoy moral standing. And he invents a doctrine of liberty with which most men might be enslaved, "for their own good." But these exercises are merely conventional and adjunctive. For McPherson is really about his business only in discoursing on his favorite American revolution and its objectives: to free the slaves; to end Southern domination of national politics; to change, internally, the social order of the South; and to commit the entire nation to a new politics, derivative of the second sentence of the Declaration of Independence, not the Constitution. After 1865 almost everyone in the South was poor. But McPherson is simplistic with reference to the essentially familial order of life in the region: politicization of private things did not come until after 1918. And for the meliorist, the progressive, destruction of slavery by war was a far more complicated business than this book or McPherson's earlier studies of abolitionists would allow. Concerning Southern domination of national politics he hits the mark. In retrospect, that shift in control was clearly the central meaning of this conflict. But as Charles Fairman, Philip Paludan, and Earl M. Maltz have taught us, the United States Supreme Court in the Reconstruction Era, with assistance from Congress and various Northern states, prevented the remaking of the Constitution: prevented even a radical reading of the Reconstruction amendments. Therefore, we have to conclude that McPherson's "revolution" is a product of the imagination; and his Lincoln less the practical politician (who at one point supported the *original* 13th Amendment that would have protected slavery forever) and more the American demigod of the Lincoln Memorial.

Thus, I cannot rejoice at the extent to which Professor McPherson would seem to agree with me. For McPherson on Lincoln the revolutionary constitutes a study in inversion of terms and ingenuity in argument—an abuse of the evidence—and is less impressive than Herndon in his narrative of the strong country lad who could wrestle and pin his enemy, who learned to play his cards as they came, and who could summon eloquence when he needed it—especially when he imitated the country preachers and the language of the Authorized Version.

In early August, I turned in this review to the literary editor of *National Review*, who had commissioned it. Although he indicated in a telephone conversation that he liked it well enough, later he informed me that the editors of *National Review* had decided not to run the piece because it might be taken as an expression of the magazine's editorial philosophy. As a result, I sent a letter to the editor-in-chief, terminating my association of 25 years with that publication.

Thomas H. Landess
on Lincoln and Bradford

10.

Abraham Lincoln and the Rhetoric of Love

*R*ecently I left the academic community and moved to an island off the coast of South Carolina, where I am running a business under an assumed name, known only to me and the state and federal tax services. My house is paid for, and I have enough money left to send my children through school and to pay my health insurance. As for surviving in the event that my business fails, the waters of the Atlantic Ocean are still full of crabs, fish, and shrimp, and there are kindly farmers living nearby who will supply us with vegetables and fruit.

It is only in the light of this newfound independence that I am publishing the following essay on Abraham Lincoln. I confess that it is only a small part of a study which I have been writing over the past few years-mostly late at night with the shades drawn and the doors locked. There are, after all, Lincoln lovers everywhere; and as my friend and former colleague M.E. Bradford found out, they are full of fierce, vindictive hatred for anyone who speaks ill of the Great Emancipator. As you will soon see, I have given up all hope of federal preferment. My will is written.

I need only add that the following is an excerpt and does no more than foreshadow a more explicitly political analysis of Lincoln's rhetoric, though the reader might be able to deduce the direction in which I am moving.

As Richard Weaver has demonstrated in *The Ethics of Rhetoric*, the lover and the rhetor have much in common. Indeed, when a young man calls on a young woman he is customarily both; for tradition requires that the language of love be artful as well as ardent, imaginative as well as earnest, free of trickery and deceit and designed to move the beloved to respond to the soul in addition to the body. Furthermore, in the best times the false rhetorician is deplored as much in matters of the heart as he is in matters of state, for integrity is the quality most sought after in both.

Lincoln clearly believed, as did his age, that the manner in which he conducted himself as a suitor had communal as well as private implications. Neither he nor the public he so frequently courted would have recognised a moral climate in which a politician's romantic or sexual indiscretions were ignored as irrelevant to his candidacy for office. His language in correspondence with women indicates, as we will soon see, a fervent desire to be understood as behaving within the boundaries of a very strict code of honor, one that clearly derives from a tradition which was already complicated and well formed in the time of Chaucer.

What also seems clear in examining these letters is the degree to which some historians have exaggerated the "natural" and "democratic" character of manners on the Illinois frontier. It is probably more accurate to suggest that manners in our own time are far less formal and aristocratic in their implications than they were in Lincoln's Sangamon County. To be sure there were wild spirits in 19th-century Illinois who lived as if they dwelt among the animals, but we must remember that the frontier was always striving to become a civilized community; and if the first priority of the men was the establishment of businesses and trade routes, the priority of the women was the reestablishment of all the social amenities that they had left behind. Chief among these, of course, were the rituals and niceties surrounding courtship, for women in 19th-century America still found themselves defined in terms of marriage and motherhood. If they had to shoot Indians, chop firewood, hoe beans, and jump over a broom as a prelude to cohabitation, it was not by choice that they did so but out of cruel necessity. There are few records of women who, like Daniel Boone, moved westward as soon as the space around the cabin was cleared to the length of a large tree.

There might be greater evidence to support the argument that at times the newer communities were nervously punctilious about affairs of the heart; because, without the protection of a stabler social order, women were more vulnerable to the triflings of men. Not that they could afford to be too punctilious, for life was hard, opportunities were few, and social lines were blurred. Yet Lincoln's own words indicate that he knew he was involved in an ancient game; that the rules were strict; that women, by and large, served as the referees; and that if he played falsely or left himself open to such a charge, his fierce ambition might be irremediably compromised.

In evaluating Lincoln's role as the rhetor of love, we are to some degree hampered by legend and by the well-meaning apologists who have fostered it, for we must first come to terms with the bittersweet image of Ann Rutledge, about whom such figures as Carl Sandburg and Edgar Lee Masters have written with lyric intensity. No American love story is more cherished and none more connotative of the Edenic myth of the old frontier where life was pristine and perilous. And no one ever rendered it with greater cunning than Carl Sandburg, who found Lincoln a subject matter more suited to his robust talents than even the slaughterhouses of Chicago.

Back to New Salem he came in the spring of 1835, and there was refuge for Ann Rutledge, with her hand in a long-fingered hand whose bones told of understanding and a quiet security .... In the fall she was to go to a young ladies' academy in Jacksonville; and Abraham Lincoln, poor in goods and deep in debts, was to get from under his poverty; and they were to marry. They would believe in the days to come; for the present time they had understanding and security.

The cry and answer of one yellowhammer to another, the wing flash of one bluejay on a home flight to another, the drowsy dreaming of grass and grain coming up with its early green over the moist rolling prairie, these were to be felt that spring together, with the whisper, "Always together!"

He was twenty-six, she was twenty-two; the earth was their footstool; the sky was a sheaf of blue dreams; the rise of the blood-gold rim of a full moon in the evening was almost too much to live, see, and remember ....

August of that summer came. Corn and grass, fed by rich rains in May and June, stood up stunted of growth, for want of more rain. The red berries on the honeysuckles refused to be glad. The swallows and martins came fewer.

To the homes of the settlers came chills and fever of malaria. Lincoln had been down and up, down again with aching bones, taking large spoons of Peruvian bark, boneset tea, jalap, and calomel. One and another of his friends had died; for some he had helped nail together the burial boxes.

> Ann Rutledge lay fever-burned. Days passed; help arrived and was helpless. Moans came from her for the one man of her thoughts. They sent for him. He rode out from New Salem to the Sand Ridge farm. They let him in; they left the two together and alone a last hour in the log house, with the slants of light on her face from an open clapboard door. It was two days later that death came.

This passage deserves momentary attention, if only as an example of the manner in which Sandburg assembled his monumental study of Lincoln, a work which is too often admired for the wrong reasons. A close examination of the episode reveals that the poet says more about the birds than about Lincoln and Ann Rutledge. The bare outline of their story is hardly a lean paragraph's worth of news: They knew one another; they were engaged; she caught the fever and died. As a matter of fact, Herndon's original account of this "love affair" is a little more complicated, involving a rival suitor and some hint of consequent difficulties; but Sandburg is not interested in complexities but in the poetic evocation of bittersweet memories, not only of his great epic hero but of the American frontier in all its simple glory, where love as well as politics was pure and untainted by the rise of an industrial class system.

All of the same images might be conjured up in rendering the love life of John Wilkes Booth, for whom the sky might also have been a sheaf of blue dreams; but any reader would have spotted and resented such a sentimental ploy. Not so with the reader of a Lincoln biography. Sandburg had license from a whole generation of Americans to "sweeten the image," to make of this spare tale a romance as fat and fleshy as anything written by Fanny Hurst or Frances Parkinson Keyes. Had he written such an account of George Washington's early loves he might well have been hooted off the front page of the *Times Literary Supplement*. After all, can we permit him that image of "the slants of light on her face from an open clapboard door?" Is there such a thing as a "clapboard door?"

How do we know Ann Rutledge lived in a clap board house? How do we know her bed was directly in the path of the door? But there is no need to go on with such nitpicking. Sandburg's purposes and techniques are all too clear.

Besides, a more important point needs to be made: There is no contemporary evidence that such a tender relationship ever existed. As Benjamin Thomas notes, "In the face of affirmative reminiscences, Lincoln students can scarcely declare with certainty that no such romance took place. But most of them regard it as improbable, and reject utterly its supposed enduring influence upon Lincoln."

The history of the Ann Rutledge legend is interesting, though a little too complex to detail. David Donald attributes its magnification to William Herndon's perennial quarrel with Mrs. Lincoln and his desire to inflict as much pain as possible on that already unhappy woman. Donald suggests that the creation of this tragic romance also helped Herndon to explain those long periods of melancholy that fell upon Lincoln from time to time. For Sandburg, it is an occasion for poeticisms and also coloration for the portrait of "Lincoln, the Man of Sorrows."

Unfortunately for 20th-century readers, the long shadow of Ann Rutledge obscures the details of a courtship that can be documented by letters and by written accounts of those people directly involved. Herndon's story of Ann Rutledge was based on a reminiscence of a man speaking almost 30 years after the death of Ann Rutledge, whom he does not name in his published version, though he does say that all the facts are available to any would-be investigator. The details of young Abe's relationship with Mary Owens are recorded in surviving letters, many of which are signed "Lincoln."

Though interpreters may disagree on their implications, the facts surrounding Lincoln's relationship with Mary Owens are fairly well documented in letters, in contemporary accounts, and in Herndon's correspondence with the lady herself after Lincoln's death. Like Lincoln, Mary was from Kentucky, but from a family of some means and gentility. The young Lincoln met her first when she was in New Salem visiting Mrs. Bennett Abell, her sister; and three years later when Mrs. Abell was in Kentucky, she persuaded Mary to return to New Salem, where she and Lincoln became involved in a relationship that eventually proved painful to both of them. From his letters and from her later recollections we can deduce that they had at least talked about marriage. Indeed, Lincoln apparently told Mrs. Abell that if she would bring her sister back from Kentucky he would marry her, though authorities disagree as to how serious his remark was intended or received. Perhaps Lincoln spoke in jest. Probably so. Whatever: The question of marriage was broached; the "lovers" entered into a period of courtship; the relationship was terminated on a discordant note; and both went on to marry others and to lead separate lives.

Not an unusual story, to be sure. Almost everyone experiences an early abortive romance—a near triumph or a narrow escape. What is important, however, is the manner in which one behaves under such circumstances. It is satisfying and provocative for historians to moon romantically over the possibly apocryphal story of Ann Rutledge, but Mary Owens did exist and was in fact courted by Abraham Lincoln. We have several accounts of the affair (including his own), and we can make some significant assessment of the man's character during this period of his life by examining this relationship, which was important to him at precisely the time he was beginning his political career.

Herndon, whose later life was devoted to research concerning the exploits of his old partner, wrote Mary Owens first for the letters, and later for her own explanation of what they meant. Her recollections of the relationship are obviously colored, and her words shed uncertain light on the portrait of two lovers:

> You say you have heard why our acquaintance terminated as it did. I too have heard the same bit of gossip; but I never used the remarks that Dame Rumor says I did to Mr. Lincoln. I think I did on one occasion say to my sister, who was very anxious

for us to be married, that I thought Mr. Lincoln was deficient in those little links which make up the chain of a woman's happiness—at least it was so in my case. Not that I believed that it proceeded from a lack of goodness at heart; but his training had been different from mine; hence there was not that congeniality which would otherwise have existed. From his own showing you perceive that his heart and hand were at my disposal; and I suppose that my feelings were sufficiently enlisted to have the matter consummated. At the beginning of the year 1838 I left Illinois, at which time our acquaintance and correspondence ceased, without ever again being renewed. My father, who resided in Green County, Kentucky, was a gentleman of considerable means; and I am persuaded that few persons placed a higher estimate on education than he did.

Edgar Lee Masters sees this account as corroborating Lincoln's own narrative in his April Fool's letter to Mrs. Browning. Masters's version of the affair, though unflattering to Lincoln, presents him as a thwarted lover whose egotism "killed any chances he ever had with her." But the relationship was surely subtler than Masters is willing to grant, as even this brief passage reveals. Had Mary simply rejected a suitor she thought unworthy, her remarks might have been gentler and more complimentary. But there is in them a keen edge that reveals her long-cherished resentment. She was made of finer clay than he. Her father, she will have Herndon know, was a "gentleman" and "of considerable means." A believer in education. How could anyone think that such a one as Lincoln could have aspired to so great a prize?

Yet she saved his three letters all of the years, during the time when he was no more than a country lawyer, through his many defeats in the political arena, finally producing them only after he had been elected president, served a term, and been assassinated.

In regarding them one cannot find the slightest trace of literary merit. There are no imaginative turns of phrase, no poetry, not even some extravagant praise for her charms that might have inspired a less than beautiful woman of some gentility to preserve just these crude words against the oncoming of age and forgetfulness. Surely she kept the letters because of the deep feelings she harbored for their writer, feelings not without their darker aspect.

And in her third exchange of correspondence with Herndon she reveals even more of her rancor. She recalls the time when Lincoln failed to assist her in crossing a stream, an event which she juxtaposes against his gallant rescue of a hog mired in mud. And then, with her bitterness showing, she recalls the jocular message that Lincoln sent her by way of Mrs. Abell years later: "Tell your sister that I think she was a great fool because she did not stay here and marry me." Her comment to Herndon was terse and revealing—"Characteristic of the man!"

Masters believes that she refers here to the "egotistical manner" which so offended her that she rejected Lincoln's proposal. All of the evidence together suggests that it was a subtler insult to which she refers. In order to define the nature of that insult, let us examine Lincoln's own letters relating to the subject.

The first of these is dated December 13, 1836, and suggests that the relationship between the two has progressed to the point where he can express some dissatisfaction at being apart from her, but most of his commentary is not personal but political, a report on doings at the state capital, full of references to specific issues and punctuated with comments on his own poor health and low spirits. In closing he apologizes for the letter, which he calls "so dry and stupid that I am ashamed to send it," suggesting, perhaps, that he is acutely aware of his ineptitude in the writing of *billets doux*.

Apparently by May 7, 1837 (the date of the next surviving letter), the relationship had progressed to the point where the two have talked of marriage, for Lincoln writes:

> I am often thinking about what we said of your coming to live at Springfield. I am afraid you would not be satisfied. There is a great deal of flourishing about in carriages here, which would be your doom to see without sharing in it. You would have to be poor without the means of hiding your poverty. Do you believe you could bear that patiently? Whatever woman may cast her lot with mine, should any ever do so, it is my intention to do all in my power to make her happy and contented: and there is nothing I can imagine, that would make me more unhappy than to fail in that effort. I know I should be much happier with you than the way I am, provided I saw no signs of discontent in you. What you have said to me may have been in jest, or I may have misunderstood it. If so, then let it be forgotten; if otherwise, I much wish you would think seriously before you decide. For my part I have already decided. What I have said I will most positively abide by, provided you wish it. My opinion is that you had better not do it. You have not been accustomed to hardship, and it may be more severe than you now imagine. I know you are capable of thinking correctly on any subject; and if you deliberate maturely upon this, before you decide, then I am willing to abide by your decision.

In this letter Lincoln is at best curiously ambivalent toward the woman whom he addresses "Friend Mary," wanting her to share his life but warning her over and over that if she chooses to do so she will probably be miserable. Since we do not know the precise nature of their conversation about her "coming to live at Springfield;' we cannot say with any certitude how Lincoln intended his letter to be received, though Mary's response to Lincoln's initial overtures seems to have been a good deal more positive than either she or Herndon would indicate some 30 years later.

It is possible, of course, that he was, as he suggested, so overcome by a desire to see her happy that he felt constrained to discourage her from "casting her lot with his." Such unselfish sentiments occasionally surface in romantic attachments, though we must suspect something less than complete altruism in one who constantly reminds his beloved that he is willing to make such a sacrifice. In the better fictional examples the hero will not allow his beloved to know he is "doing what is best for her:" Having been so informed, no woman could help but consider the possibility that she was being jilted.

Then again, we could place the most cynical construction on Lincoln's letter and argue that he wished to disengage himself from a sexual alliance which, once consummated, was no longer attractive to him, and from which he wished to extricate himself while at the same time enjoying the lady's continued affection. In short, we might contend that he wanted to string her along without having to marry her, as he had told her he would.

However, a third interpretation seems more likely. Beginning to weary of a half-hearted courtship from which he had hoped to derive more in the way of romantic satisfaction, he was looking for a way out—and one which would not only leave him with his honor intact but also divest him of any legal risk. For in the 19th century, breach of promise suits were more of a threat to the treacherous lover than they are in the latter half of the 20th century.

Notice that nowhere does he mention the word "marriage"; instead he writes of "your coming to live at Springfield." A cagey phrase, particularly when juxtaposed with his later "whatever woman may cast her lot with mine, should any ever do so ..."

Ambiguous though this letter may seem, however, it is the soul of clarity and directness when compared with the following, which we reproduce in toto, lest the full impact of its subtlety be lost in mere paraphrase.

Springfield Aug. 16th 1837 Friend Mary,

You will, no doubt, think it rather strange, that I should write you a letter on the same day on which we parted; and I can only account for it by supposing, that seeing you lately makes me think of you more than usual, while at our late meeting we had but few expressions of thoughts. You must know that I cannot see you, or think of you, with entire indifference; and yet it may be, that you, are mistaken in regards to what my real feelings towards you are. If I knew you were not, I should not trouble you with this letter. Perhaps any other man would know enough without further information; but I consider it my particular right to plead ignorance, and your bounden duty to allow the plea. I want in all cases to do right, and most particularly so, in all cases with women. I want, at this particular time, more than anything else, to do right with you, and if I knew it would be doing right, as I rather suspect it would, to let you alone, I would do it. And for the purpose of making the matter as plain as possible, I now say, that you can now drop the subject, dismiss your thoughts (if you ever had any) from me forever, and leave this letter unanswered, without calling forth one accusing murmur from me. And I will even go further, and say, that if it will add anything to your comfort, or peace of mind, to do so, it is my sincere wish that you should. Do not understand by this I wish to cut your acquaintance. I mean no such thing. What I do wish is, that our further acquaintance shall depend upon yourself. If such further acquaintance would contribute nothing to your happiness, I am sure it would not to mine. If you feel yourself in any degree bound to me, I am now willing to release you, provided you wish it; while, on the other hand, I am willing, and even anxious to bind you faster, if I can be convinced that it will, in any considerable degree, add to your happiness. This, indeed, is the whole question with me. Nothing would make me more miserable than to make you miserable—nothing more happy, than to know you were so.

In what I have said, I think I cannot be misunderstood; and to make myself understood, is the only object of this letter.

If it suits you best to not answer this—farewell—a long life and a merry one attend you. But if you conclude to write back, speak as plainly as I do. There can be neither harm nor danger, in saying to me, any thing you think, just in the manner you think it.

My respects to your sister.

Your friend

LINCOLN

Benjamin Thomas, who is among the fairest and most objective interpreters of Lincoln's life, writes of this extraordinary document: "Evidently Lincoln wished to escape gracefully from a romance now gone stale. If so, the lady obliged him. She ignored his letter, and they never met again."

And small wonder!

Undoubtedly Mary must have concluded at this point—if not earlier—that she was not only weary of indifference but also of a man who could not bring himself to speak honestly and openly of his feelings. Yet again we find more than merely the confused country swain in Lincoln's tortuous rhetoric. The legal mind is at work here, weighing every phrase against statute and precedents, careful lest any statement, however bland, be open to misconstruction by a third party. "You must know that I cannot see you, or think of you, with entire indifference."

One would hope that every human being could make that statement of every other human being. Indeed the sentiment must have seemed disagreeably fatuous from a man who was to write only a few sentences later: "Nothing would make me more miserable than to believe you miserable—nothing more happy, than to know you were so."

And yet: "I cannot see you, or think of you, with entire indifference." This limpid denial of disinterest is not the poetic understatement of an ardent swain paying an old compliment in a new way. Instead it suggests the tiptoeing of a wary bachelor who has, while groping down the dark boardinghouse corridor, inadvertently blundered into the old maid's bedroom.

Indeed he follows this disavowal with a qualification: Even though he does not feel "entire indifference;" "yet [YET!] it may be, that you, are mistaken in regard to what my real feelings towards you are." How could she possibly have any doubts after the earlier letters, the months of devoted attention to her (as well as to the mired hog), the moments of manly forthrightness that one would expect from the Lincoln of myth, whose blunt words on the stump so impressed the likes of the rough-hewn Clary's Grove boys? Yet if she were at this point still in doubt about his feelings—why, he would immediately clarify them for her. Or so he would seem to suggest. But, except for insisting his happiness is dependent on hers, he makes no further mention of his feelings. Instead he lapses into a rhetoric which is manifestly legalistic: "but I consider it my particular right to plead ignorance, and your bounden duty to allow the plea. I want in all cases to do right, and most particularly so, in all cases with women."

Did the lawyer take over unawares here, or did Lincoln write while holding a candle first over his letter and then over a well-thumbed copy of Blackstone? Either way the passage is a tricky transition in which the lawyer-lover neatly brushes aside his own feelings, still undefined, and focuses instead on the lady's sentiments, which he cautiously circles, advances on, pokes, and then jumps back from as if they were a dying rattlesnake.

"I'm just an ol' country boy," he says, "so you've got to spell it out for me. Because, shucks, if I only knew what would make you happy I would do it. It's all up to you. If you don't want to answer this letter (in effect, if you want to end our relationship), then I'll understand. In fact, if such a course of action will make you happy, then by golly I hope you do it. But wait a minute! Don't try to blame me for the breakup, because I'm not suggesting that at all. No ma'am! But I am willing to release you from any promise you might feel you've made, provided you want to be released, though I'm willing to make the relationship even more binding if such a bond would make you happy (which it probably wouldn't)."

And after his circumlocutious flirtation with meaning, Lincoln writes, "In what I have said, I think I cannot be misunderstood; and to make myself understood, is the only object of this letter."

Can anyone doubt the sly truth of this statement? Surely no one could have made his intentions clearer to a woman who was both educated and of refined sensibilities, while at the same time protecting himself from the literalist who, missing an outright disavowal of his earlier pledge, would conclude that such a pledge had never been offered. But Mary got the message, and saving what pride she still retained, she did what he hoped she would do—she never replied to his letter.

The latter-day reader can see in this well-honed document the incipient politician flexing his rhetorical muscles, and it might be profitable to pursue this line of thought to hint at its full ramifications. Let us regard Lincoln not as the lover but as political rhetor and Friend Mary not as some poor fat girl about to be jilted but as the public, struggling to understand the principles that motivate the public man speaking to them. Let us assume that he wants their good will, at the very least that they not be active in opposing him; but he realizes, even as he is about to speak, that should he completely reveal himself he would be vulnerable to attack, would be despised for his self-serving infidelity. Yet he must move his audience in a certain direction in order to satisfy these very passions that he dare not expose.

So the first thing that he establishes is the mask of that virtue in which he is most deficient. If he is greedy, he will begin by asserting that he has no desire for gain. If he lusts for power, he will pretend he has no designs on public office. If he is secretly bellicose, he will protest that he hates war. "I come to bury Caesar, not to praise him." says Antony, and then launches into an encomium that turns the crowd into his deadly instrument of revenge.

Politicians and lovers have always accomplished their desired ends through the heightened use of rhetoric—sometimes honestly, sometimes dishonestly—and if Lincoln the lover deliberately puts on a mask of candor while at the same time practicing the fine art of malicious pussyfooting, then what about the lofty language of his later speeches? Can we not see in his letter to Friend Mary an early example of rhetoric used to urge an audience toward one course of action while protesting that he is doing nothing of the sort?

"But, my God!" one might exclaim. "You can't use a young man's early amatory misadventures to discredit him in his later public life!" And to be sure there are obvious limitations to the use of the above analogy. For one thing, no political constituency could bear to be told so equivocally that it was held in high esteem. The politician who addressed the voters as Lincoln addressed Mary S. Owens would be rejected just as Lincoln had hoped to be rejected, despite his assurances to the contrary.

But the art of saying one thing when you mean its opposite informs this private document; and that same art is practiced again and again in Lincoln's important public utterances, as could be demonstrated, for example, in his speeches on the prospects of war immediately after his election.

11.

With Malice Toward Many: Washington, Lincoln, and God

Most Americans in the 18th, 19th, and early 20th centuries believed in the public expression of religious sentiments as surely as they believed in publicly proclaiming their patriotism. Such expression wasn't merely their right. It was their duty. Indeed, religious faith was part of the "given" of any political debate, the common ground upon which all candidates stood when they rose to disagree with one another. Even in the late 19th century—when great oratory had given way to high-flown platitudes—politicians could still, in all sincerity, invoke the Almighty at the slightest provocation.

Among the most common acknowledgments of religious faith were those delivered at ceremonial occasions where there were no votes on the table, no veterans or preachers to enlist, no pragmatic reason to haul out the colors of rhetoric. One such occasion was the inauguration of a president. At that moment, with the election over, the nation's new chief executive and head of state speaks to the people for the first time. It was probably a much more significant occasion in earlier times than it is today, after so many televised debates, so many interviews, so many 60-second spots. But even in the 21st century the significance of the moment remains.

George Washington set the precedent in his First Inaugural Address by expressing his own submission to God and then the submission of the nation as a whole. He understood the special significance of this occasion. It was the first inauguration of an American president—first in what he expected to be an unbroken chain stretching into the future as far as the eye of imagination could see. He therefore had a special obligation to establish a precedent for succeeding presidents to recognise and follow. Note the wording and length of the following statement:

> Such being the impressions under which I have, in obedience to the public summons, repaired to the present station, it would be peculiarly improper to omit in this first official act my fervent supplications to that Almighty Being who rules over the universe, who presides in the councils of nations, and whose providential aids can supply every human defect, that His benediction may consecrate to the liberties and happiness of the people of the United States a Government instituted by themselves for these essential purposes, and may enable every instrument employed in its administration to execute with success the functions allotted to his charge. In tendering this homage to the Great Author of every public and private good, I assure myself that it expresses your sentiments not less than my own, nor those of my fellow citizens at large less than either. No people can be bound to acknowledge and adore the Invisible Hand which conducts the affairs of men more than those of the United States. Every step by which they have advanced to the character of an independent nation seems to have been distinguished by some token of providential agency; and in the important revolution just accomplished in the system of their united government the tranquil deliberations and voluntary consent of so many distinct communities from which the event has resulted can not be compared with the

means by which most governments have been established without some return of pious gratitude, along with an humble anticipation of the future blessings which the past seem to presage. These reflections, arising out of the present crisis, have forced themselves too strongly on my mind to be suppressed. You will join with me, I trust, in thinking that there are none under the influence of which the proceedings of a new and free government can more auspiciously commence.

This statement occupied a substantial and preemptive place in his text, preceding his discussion of more pragmatic matters of state. Indeed, the passage was longer than his entire Second Inaugural Address. Here he said in so many words that, on such an occasion, propriety required the acknowledgment of God's role in the destiny of the United States. For the first time a president of the United States affirmed the belief that this nation had been especially blessed by God, Who looked with favor on its history and people. Succeeding presidents would echo these sentiments.

Washington, a faithful communicant of the Episcopal Church, specifically referred to the piety that all Americans shared at that moment when he said: "In tendering this homage to the Great Author of every public and private good, I assure myself that it expresses your sentiments not less than my own." "This is something about which we all agree," he was telling the new nation, "but it needs to be said all the same at public occasions such as this one."

He even closed this paradigmatic inaugural address by again invoking God's blessing:

Having thus imparted to you my sentiments as they have been awakened by the occasion which brings us together, I shall take my present leave; but not without resorting once more to the benign Parent of the Human Race in humble supplication that, since He has been pleased to favor the American people with opportunities for deliberating in perfect tranquility, and dispositions for deciding with unparalleled unanimity on a form of government for the security of their union and the advancement of their happiness, so His divine blessing may be equally conspicuous in the enlarged views, the temperate consultations, and the wise measures on which the success of this Government must depend.

Succeeding presidents followed Washington's example. Thus Thomas Jefferson, poster boy of People for the American Way, paid homage to the God of the Holy Bible: "I shall need, too, the favor of that Being in whose hands we are, who led our forefathers, as Israel of old, from their native land, and planted them in a country flowing with all the necessaries and comforts of life."

Following Washington's example, every president, including George W. Bush, has mentioned God in his inaugural address (or addresses) to the nation, a fact highly significant, since even in our own time—with the ACLU poised to pounce on every scurrying, squealing mention of the "G" word—newly elected presidents have invariably chosen to reaffirm the nation's belief that the United States remains a nation under God.

To be sure, many of these allusions to the Almighty were postponed until the final paragraph and in their brevity said little if anything about God's specific role in the nation's affairs. However, with one exception they clearly appealed to a benign and gracious Creator and Preserver. In that one address, He is presented as the angry scourge of the nation, a God who rained death and destruction on the American people as punishment for sin. Such a God is described in the Second Inaugural Address of our 16th president.

At his first inauguration, Abraham Lincoln's position as president was the very opposite of George Washington's. Washington had won a war that had united his people and established a new nation.

He was known to virtually every American and wildly popular, certainly the inevitable choice to be the nation's first president. By contrast, Lincoln, relatively unknown and supported by a minority of the voters, was a polarizing figure, whose very election triggered secession. He was facing the prospect of a war that threatened to undo the nation Washington's victories had established.

So how could Lincoln hope to avoid what later generations would call "the irrepressible conflict?" On what common ground could the two sides stand to engage in civil discourse? Lincoln knew that politicians North and South, as well as the people they served, were overwhelmingly Christian and that he was expected to appeal to the same God that Washington confidently invoked at the beginning of the nation. But Lincoln's own belief—or unbelief—placed him outside the Christian community.

The best evidence shows that Lincoln didn't believe Christ died to take away the sins of the world or that He was the Son of God. On rare occasions, he accompanied Mrs. Lincoln to the Presbyterian church; but, in an era where membership in a Christian denomination was *de rigeur* for politicians, he never joined. The people who knew him best said he was a free thinker, a scoffer, a man who looked on the New Testament as a crazy collection of stories and homilies that at best bewildered him.

Whether sincere or insincere, Lincoln, in his First Inaugural Address, said merely: "Intelligence, patriotism, Christianity, and a firm reliance on Him who has never yet forsaken this favored land are still competent to adjust in the best way all our present difficulty."

Note that Lincoln first cited "intelligence," then "patriotism," both of which he addressed in the body of his speech. As for "Christianity," he allowed the word to lie in its crib—unfed, unloved. It carried almost no rhetorical weight in this single sentence, which itself is no more than 30 words pasted near the end of a 3,633-word text. Like other presidents, he was following Washington's prescription for an inaugural address, but he didn't waste more than a single word on a religion for which he had little use, either as a practicing politician or as a man.

He spent most of the other 3,603 words appealing to "intelligence"—reasoning with those Southerners who had left the Union and those who were poised to do so. In these passages, he mustered his evidence like the good lawyer he was. First, he stated in clear, unambiguous language his position on the future of slavery, by quoting from one of his earlier speeches: "I have no purpose, directly or indirectly, to interfere with the institution of slavery in the States where it exists. I believe I have no lawful right to do so, and I have no inclination to do so."

As for the so-called "fugitive-slave" controversy, he quoted the very passage in the Constitution that mandated return of escaped slaves, said the Constitution must be obeyed, and pointed out that "all members of Congress swear their support to the whole Constitution—to this provision as much as to any other."

Having attempted to reassure Southerners that he was not to be confused with New England abolitionists, he told them in lawyerly language that the Union was a contract entered into by all parties and could not be rescinded unilaterally: "No State upon its own mere motion can lawfully get out of the Union; that resolves and ordinances to that effect are legally void, and that acts of violence within any State or States against the authority of the United States are insurrectionary or revolutionary, according to circumstances."

In his two-paragraph peroration, he appealed, not to God or to the Southerners' Christian beliefs, but to their patriotism.

> I am loath to close. We are not enemies, but friends. We must not be enemies. Though passion may have strained it must not break our bonds of affection. The mystic chords of memory, stretching from every battlefield and patriot grave to every living heart and hearthstone all over this broad land, will yet swell the

chorus of the Union, when again touched, as surely they will be, by the better angels of our nature.

It is an eloquent conclusion to a well-reasoned argument obviously crafted to persuade Southerners rather than to inflame Northerners. One has to understand the highly complicated circumstances surrounding secession not to wonder why it didn't motivate at least some Southern politicians to patch up the quarrel and remain in the Union.

Four years later—after hundreds of thousands of men had been killed on both sides (more Northern troops than Southern troops), Lincoln had won another election without gaining a majority, and antiwar sentiment had boiled over in New York City and elsewhere. When Lincoln composed his Second Inaugural Address, he had seen his hope of a quick victory turn to ashes and his tenuous popularity turn to widespread animosity.

Unlike his perfunctory nod to Christianity and the "Him" in his First Inaugural, Lincoln relied heavily on biblical language in his Second Inaugural, quoting from the Bible, rhetorically clenching his teeth and pounding the pulpit like an Old Testament prophet, wagging a reproving finger at the sins of an entire nation, while specifically directing his fury (and God's) at the people of the South.

He begins this sermonic address by reminding his audience of an ironic fact: Both sides in the War worshiped the same God, with each asking for help to prevail against the other. But he left no doubt as to which side had earned God's wrath. The slaveholding South was unworthy to ask *anything* from God: "It may seem strange that any men should dare to ask a just God's assistance in wringing their bread from the sweat of other men's faces …"

Was he talking about Northern factory owners as well as Southern slaveholders? And about those who were living off dividends from industrial stocks? They too profited from the product of other people's manual labor. However, as he developed his jeremiad, he made it clear: He was talking only about slavery. The ensuing paraphrase of words spoken by Jesus (Matthew

7:1) "but let us judge not, that we be not judged" was ironically, unintentionally self-mocking, since Lincoln had already passed severe judgement in the front part of the very same sentence.

Then—in a cleverly wrought passage that discussed God's role in merely hypothetical terms—he suggested that the War, brought on by slavery, was the Divine Will intervening in history to punish the nation for the South's sin.

> The almighty has His own purposes. "Woe unto the world because of offenses; for it must needs be that offenses come, but woe to that man by whom the offense cometh." If we shall suppose that American slavery is one of those offenses which, in the providence of God, must needs come, but which, having continued through His appointed time, He now wills to remove, and that He gives to both North and South this terrible war as the woe due to those by whom the offense came, shall we discern therein any departure from those divine attributes which believers in a living God always ascribe to Him? Fondly, do we hope, fervently do we pray, that this mighty scourge of war may speedily pass away.

This is a curious passage. In it, Lincoln spoke of the "Almighty" having "His own purposes." Yet the quotation was taken from the words of Jesus, in a speech to His disciples (Matthew 18:7). Why not come right out and use the "J" word? To be sure, orthodox Christians believed, then as now, that Jesus is God. But Lincoln didn't. It's barely possible that he saw the quote somewhere and didn't verify its source. However it is highly likely that he used "Almighty" because it sounded more like the Old Testament God, who was forever visiting disaster on those who disobeyed His commands, rather than Jesus, who tended to stress mercy and forgiveness. It was certainly a good quote for what Lincoln wished to say: that North and South alike had suffered because of the sin of slavery, but that the South ("by whom the offense cometh") had incurred the greater punishment.

> Yet, if God wills that it continue until all the wealth piled by the bondsman's two hundred and fifty years of unrequited toil shall be sunk, and until every drop of blood drawn with the lash shall be paid by another drawn with the sword, as was said three thousand years ago, so still must it be said "the judgments of the Lord are true and righteous altogether."

This address was delivered on March 4, 1865. In just over a month, Lee would surrender at Appomattox. The War was all but over, and Lincoln well knew the price Southerners had already paid for their attempt to leave the Union. Sherman and Sheridan—with Lincoln's approval—had made war against civilians; burned their houses and crops; slaughtered their animals; and ordered troops to shoot men, women, and children at random. Yet in the Second Inaugural, Lincoln suggested that these war crimes were somehow ordained by the providence of God.

As the Gettysburg Address illustrates, Lincoln knew how to use biblical rhetoric to justify his own political choices and their catastrophic consequences. For a man who though as little of Jesus as Lincoln did, in this address he made mighty good use of the red-letter section of the Bible—to curse his enemies and to picture himself as the instrument of God's true and righteous judgment. In so doing, he stood Washington's precedent on its head and once again revealed himself as the master manipulator of rhetoric.

Yet his ultimate affront to religious sensibilities occurred in his peroration, when—after using Scripture to scourge his enemies—he donned a cassock and became, in that white space between paragraphs, the benevolent dispenser of Christian grace, the peacemaker, the nurse of the nation that God had so sorely afflicted.

> With malice toward none, with charity for all, with firmness in the right as God gives us to see the right, let us strive on to finish the work we are in, to bind up the nation's wounds, to care for him who shall have borne the battle and for his widow and orphan, to do all which may achieve and cherish a just and lasting peace among ourselves and with all nations.

Small wonder he is regarded as our greatest president. You can fool most of the people all of the time.

12.

Bradford's Argument on "Continuing Revolution"

Mel Bradford always insisted—contrary to one of his mentors, Richard Weaver—that the argument from circumstance was superior to the argument from definition. To use a religious analogy, he believed that truth was only knowable through its imperfect incarnation, that as finite beings we could only understand God the Father through God the Son. Or to put it in philosophical terms, he was more a Thomist than a Neoplatonist.

With this temperament—this way of looking at the world—Bradford not only distrusted abstractions like "equality," but questioned their essential integrity when used as absolutes in the political realm. For this reason alone—and quite apart from the grim resonances it had for a latter day Southerner—Bradford could only see the Gettysburg Address as either a rhetorical parlor trick or else a dangerous exercise in blasphemy—someone pretending to be God the Father for theatrical effect, or someone who really believed he was God the Father. He saw in the biblical cast of phrases like "four score and seven years ago" or "our fathers" an attempt on Lincoln's part to cloak himself in the divine mantle of scriptural authority—to speak with the voice of God.

To such a charge, Lincoln's press agent might well reply, "Such a phrase was just Abe's way of catching the crowd's attention—a trope to wake up Grandma." Or, "Everybody talked like that when they made political speeches. People in the 19th century didn't take you seriously unless you sounded like a preacher." There's a good deal of truth in such statements, but you can't have it both ways. Either you trivialize the language of political discourse and say that, like a campaign promise, it is only good until sundown; or else you say that Lincoln's address is an eloquent and profound definition of the meaning of the American experience. If you choose the latter, then you have to deal with Bradford.

He was perfectly willing to take Lincoln seriously, not as a political philosopher but as a rhetor—a skillful and self-conscious crafter of language, less than Aristotle but more than Jimmy Carter. If you make this assumption, then you must be willing to submit to all its corollaries and implications. At this point, Lincoln is on his own, with none of the exemptions generally accorded to everyday discourse. Or, to put it more precisely—the Gettysburg Address is on its own. It can no longer rock along on the beauty of its own cadences or cuddle up in the warm blanket of some vague piety. It must grow up and take the GRE.

Thus Bradford finds in the address the prescription for a society based on unattainable abstractions like "equality"—and therefore a people whose expectations are doomed to remain unsatisfied, a Union forever in a state of becoming. He believes Lincoln invented this Union, at least for the popular imagination, and that his ideological construct is like a computer virus, always overwriting the concrete data of everyday experience.

At first glance, such a proposition seems extravagant, at best academic muttering that has little relevance to the real world, like the Kinsey Report. In fact, there is some evidence that what Bradford says can be proved in the discourse of realpolitik, where Lincoln's "new nation," reborn every Friday afternoon, thrives like a sunflower.

Consider the fact that George H.W. Bush—a New England rich boy with a middle-management soul—spoke throughout his cautious and unremarkable presidency of "America's continuing revolution." And what can we suppose he thought he meant by such a phrase, tossed off as casually and as confidently as a call for world peace? And why is it more respectable these days to commend the "continuing American revolution" than it is to endorse Mom and apple pie? Momhood is currently a dangerous idea to embrace, thanks to the feminists, and all pie, the health police tell us, is bad for the heart. Mr. Lincoln's Union spends tens of millions of dollars annually to prevent women from becoming moms, and poor Mrs. Smith is now compelled to put warning labels on her apple pies. Yet George Bush can talk about the "continuing American revolution" without a word of criticism from either the *Washington Post* or *National Review*.

Revolution? Against what? Against the current political regime, our representative form of government? Of course, George Bush doesn't mean anything so radical or so brave, nor do any of the hundreds of other politicians and journalists who enunciate this phrase carefully, soberly—as if they coined it. Somehow we are all revolutionaries together, and we are all revolting against the order we have created—so no one has cause to be upset. (It's like the old New Deal argument against taking the national debt too seriously: We owe it only to ourselves.)

Bradford tells us that the "American revolution continues" because, as Lincoln suggested in the Gettysburg Address, its goal is nothing less than perfection. This goal, he says, is a "millennialist impulse"—one that contradicts the "sensible inertia'" built into the history of the nation by its Founding Fathers. He characterizes Lincoln's vision in the address as one that labors to "abolish time, repeal contingency." He characterizes it as "this gnostic aggression against Being."

Here he is using Eric Voegelin's analysis of modern ideology to place the millennialist movement, and by implication Lincoln and those "secular puritans" who follow him. He goes on to say:

> Millennialism can mean no other thing today—and always moves from an ontological reaction against the distance separating, by definition, creation and

Maker; moves into either a "pulling up" or a "pulling down." With it we worship ourselves; falsify, and then forget our birthright. Variety, structure, measure, and any form of differentiated order are likewise millennialism's enemies—the original bill of things as written for our tenure in this place of test and trial.

There is something almost suicidal in Bradford's own rhetoric here. Invoking Voegelin incurs risk enough from certain quarters, but Voegelin is at least intellectually respectable. A phrase like "this place of test and trial" is not merely religious, but derives from a specific Protestant heritage, echoes the language of the two Great Awakenings, and is found in a number of hardshell Baptist hymns Bradford probably heard and sang in his youth.

In using such language, he knew the risks and chose to accept them. By implication, he was calling Lincoln a heretic and blaming him and his followers for the secularization of American society that has resulted in the breakdown of order and the redefinition of morality in our own time. It was no surprise to him that, by the 1960's, Christians were engaged in fierce theological quarrels over issues; or that, by the 1980's, mainline churches were beginning to look with fine impartiality on all forms of sexual behavior, including adultery and fornication, and to ordain lesbians—in almost every case, responding to an external egalitarian rhetoric that challenged the validity of Scripture and impugned the fairness of the biblical God.

It is important to understand that Bradford is not talking here about mere opposition to slavery—or, for that matter, to racial segregation, or to equal pay for equal work. In this essay, as in others on Lincoln, the substance of those issues is beyond his chosen purview. He is talking about the nature of the rhetoric and dialectic that Lincoln and others have used in support of their political goals. To suggest that he is motivated by racism or that this essay is an oblique defense of slavery is to resort to logical fallacies. His motives are irrelevant, and his argument is no more a defense of slavery than it is a defense of John Calvin. *Argumentum ad hominem* and *non sequitur,* as popular as they are in current political discourse, are still dishonest ways to respond to legitimate scholarly debate.

13.

Mel Bradford,
Old Indian Fighters, and the NEH

In politics, the dead can never rest in peace. The survivors fight over the bodies, the way the Achaeans and Trojans fought over the body of Hector. Mel Bradford died ten years ago [in 1993], and those of us who knew him best are finally reconciled to his death. However, when his detractors insist on exhuming his memory in order to kick him one more time, we find it difficult to remain silent. Thus, this reply to an article David Frum wrote recently for *National Review Online*.

In his commentary, Mr. Frum briefly discusses the attempt on the part of Mel's friends to see him appointed chairman of the National Endowment for the Humanities. The year was 1981. Mel and I were colleagues at the University of Dallas. I was his closest friend. At the time all this happened, Mr. Frum was a Yale undergraduate, hunched over one of the tables down at Mory's, humming the Whiffenpoof Song. So his article is clearly based on the campfire tales of old neocon Indian fighters.

He writes:

> But as the paleos themselves tell the story, the quarrel that erupted into view that day in 1986, began as a squabble over jobs and perks in the Reagan Administration—from the perception that, as [Sam] Francis

later put it, neoconservatives had arranged matters so that "their team should get the rewards of office and of patronage and that the older team of the older Right receive virtually nothing."

A quick reality check here: It is not in fact true that the ambitions of the paleos fell victim to neocon plots. Paleo Grievance Number 1 is the case of Mel Bradford, a gifted professor at the University of Dallas, now dead. Bradford had hoped to be appointed chairman of the National Endowment for the Humanities, but lost out to William Bennett. Unfortunately for him, Bradford came to the government hiring window with certain disadvantages: He had worked on the George Wallace campaign in 1968, and he had published an essay that could plausibly be read to liken Abraham Lincoln to Hitler.

First, for what it's worth, the Wallace connection was never a big issue. In a 1981 *New York Times* story, Irvin Molotsky reported that the neoconservatives' "criticism of Professor Bradford includes his support in 1972 of the Presidential candidacy of former Gov. George C. Wallace and his disapproval of Lincoln, which they view as especially inappropriate given Lincoln's role as the nation's first Republican President." So it was the neocons themselves who brought up the Wallace issue in the *Times*. And that's the last we heard of it.

In fact, we were surprised that they had missed the juiciest part of the story: Mel had been Dallas County chairman of George Wallace's American Party in 1968—a potentially more damaging involvement than his 1972 role in the Dallas County Democratic Party (which liberal columnist Ron Calhoun would later say Bradford had single-handedly destroyed).

When the neocons dropped the Wallace strategy, we knew it had failed. Perhaps they understood the degree to which Reagan's victory had depended on Wallace Democrats, who might be provoked to intervene on Bradford's behalf. And perhaps the neocon field officers decided not to press the theme of other-party affiliation because, according to our sources in North Carolina, Bill Bennett, Bradford's rival, had voted in the Democratic primary in 1980. To cover Bennett in this matter, a prominent supporter, a former Nixon cabinet member, had written a letter stating that Bennett had backed Reagan all the way. If our sources were correct, he hadn't even voted for Reagan in the GOP primary; and revelation of that fact would have exposed the former cabinet member's gracious fib.

Whatever the reason, the opposition never really tried to hang Wallace around Bradford's neck; and if any of those old Indian fighters remember differently, I believe they are mistaken.

The second charge—the comparison of Abraham Lincoln to Hitler—is a bit more complicated than Mr. Frum leads us to believe. Harry Jaffa, in one of his several debates with Bradford, praised Lincoln for believing in higher law. When Mel showed me Jaffa's article, I remarked that belief in higher law was not conclusive evidence of virtue, that Hitler had expressed the same belief in *Mein Kampf.* Bradford, in replying to Jaffa, made the point in a footnote. In reporting what happened next, I choose to omit the names of those involved, though I remember them well. Instead, I will use obvious pseudonyms to avoid the kind of ritual denials that would force me to name my Washington sources, several of whom are prominent in the conservative movement and still do business with the neocons.

The head of the Office of Presidential Personnel at the time was a California car dealer who, when the word "Lincoln" was mentioned, probably thought first of the automobile. Certainly he was ill equipped to follow the kind of complex and meticulous argument found in Bradford's reply to Jaffa. A man I will call "The Great Manipulator," a supporter of Bennett, took advantage of this intellectual paucity.

According to our sources, instead of saying that Bradford had compared Lincoln to Hitler, as Mr. Frum suggests, the Great Manipulator told the Car Salesman that Bradford had compared Hitler to Lincoln. "You see, this man admires Hitler. He even compares him to Lincoln." At some point in this conversation, we were told, the word "antisemitism" was used. The Car Salesman's pulse quickened. He read the footnote. By George, Bradford did admire Hitler.

The injustice of this slander, which came late in the game, finally broke Bradford's will to continue. I remember standing with him on the balcony of UD's Braniff Building a few minutes after we had received an account of this latest attack. For a moment, he stared out at the mesquite trees surrounding the campus, then shook his head.

"I'm through. If they want it bad enough to do something like this, then let them have it."

This wasn't the first time the Car Salesman had misread Bradford's work. Earlier in the process, he had summoned Bradford to the Old Executive Office Building and waved the professor's 15-page bibliography under his nose.

"The trouble is, you've published too much. Too many targets. Take this thing you wrote about homosexuals."

Bradford said he had written nothing about homosexuals. "What's this, then?"

The Car Salesman ran his forefinger down the lengthy list of items, one page after another, until he found the item he was looking for. Then he passed the bibliography across the desk and jabbed at a line.

"There."

The listing was an article on Bishop Richard Corbet[t]'s "The Fairies Farewell"—a light 17th-century lyric about the loss of belief in the supernatural.

Bradford burst out laughing—a tactical error. The Car Salesman was indignant.

Bradford attempted to placate him by explaining that the poem was not about homosexuals, but about literal fairies, the kind that fly around on gossamer wings and do good deeds—e.g., the tooth fairy. It was like trying to explain trigonometry to a cat.

After this incident, we wondered if the Great Manipulator had put the notion about homosexuals into the Car Salesman's head or if the Car Salesman had thought of it all by himself. One thing was apparent: With the Car Salesman in charge, Bennett's considerably shorter bibliography was an asset rather than a liability.

Mr. Frum writes further of Bradford: "Bradford could never accept that it was his own writings that had doomed him. As Oscar Wilde observed, 'Misfortunes one can endure. They come from outside, they are accidents. But to suffer for one's own faults—ah! There is the sting of life.' Easier to blame others and pity oneself."

When and where did Mel Bradford blame others and express self-pity? How about one example? He was appalled at the battle tactics his opponents had used, but he knew he had spent most of his adult life providing them with ammunition. Indeed, he understood better than anyone the liabilities his political opinions incurred—the academic appointments he was denied, the department chairmanship he had lost years earlier, the journals in which he could never publish, the conferences he was never invited to attend. (The University of Dallas trustees even delayed his promotion to full professor for a year because of his politics.) None of this surprised him.

Many years earlier—as a Vanderbilt graduate student—he had consciously made the choice that led inevitably to the succession of professional catastrophes that plagued his life. He had chosen to stand with the losing side, knowing full well what it had cost his intellectual mentors in the way of honors, academic advancement, and cold cash.

He did not, as others did, switch sides after the Reagan victory in 1980. In fact, he had supported Reagan in 1976.

Nor did he hold a grudge, as Mr. Frum suggests. In fact, when Bill Bennett was mentioned as a candidate to succeed Terrel Bell as secretary of education, Mel was contacted to see if he would speak out against his former rival. He replied that he thought Bennett would be a good choice for the job.

It was typical of his generous nature; but the response exasperated many of his friends, who, in this instance, wanted to see less of Jesus and more of Grendel. He had a magnanimous heart where adversaries and detractors were concerned, whether in intellectual debate, partisan politics, or campus quarrels. He forgave trespasses quicker than any man I've ever known.

So I find it singularly unfair that—ten years after Bradford's death—Mr. Frum, who never knew him, would turn him into a neocon caricature in order to make points in a current dispute. Indeed, I wonder if Mr. Frum really believes what he wrote on *National Review Online*. In a 1989 *Wall Street Journal* article, "Cultural Clash on the Right," he tells a somewhat different story:

> [I]t is true that bad feeling between loyalists who trace their conservatism back to 1984 and beyond ... and those who arrived at their conservatism later has festered ever since the great internal fight over the proposed 1980 [sic] nomination of M.E. Bradford ... to the chairmanship of the National Endowment for the Humanities. Lobbying by Edwin Feulner, president of the Heritage Foundation, William F. Buckley, Jr. and Irving Kristol persuaded the Reagan transition team to nominate William Bennett instead.

So which was it? Did Bradford's political activism and anti-Lincoln sentiments cause his downfall, or was it the persuasive powers of Messrs. Feulner, Buckley, and Kristol? The clever answer to that question is "a little bit of both." However, the more you think about it, the more that explanation fails to convince. If Bradford's acts and opinions alone brought him down, then why credit persuasion? And if persuasion turned the tide, then couldn't one reasonably blame the persuaders, as Sam Francis did?

Besides, I find "persuaded" too benign a word to describe what Bradford's opponents did to defeat him. Here are just a few examples, most of them reported to us by friends inside the Beltway.

Neocons enlisted the support of a University of Dallas colleague who furnished them with passages, violently wrenched from Mel's writings, which the Great Manipulator passed around the Old Executive Office Building. The collection was entitled "Quotes From Chairman Mel"—an arch allusion to a volume of quotes by that old paleo Mao Tse-tung. By an extraordinary coincidence, the colleague who supplied this information ended up working for Bennett at the National Endowment for the Humanities.

Bennett's partisans called the UD English Department and pumped the secretary for negative gossip about Bradford. She refused to give them anything—in large part because there was nothing to give. But they called her again and again, day after day, until she finally began hanging up on them.

According to our sources, the Great Manipulator padded up and down the halls of the Old Executive Office Building, telling everyone from the Vice President to the janitor that Bradford had a meager bibliography and that most of the items were from obscure Southern journals. In fact, Bradford's bibliography was almost as long as the Mississippi River—and included publications from all over the country. One of those obscure Southern journals was *The Sewanee Review*, considered by many to be the most prestigious literary quarterly in the English language. Another was *The Southern Review*, which routinely published works by Pulitzer Prize winners.

The Great Manipulator repeatedly warned the Car Salesman that Bradford would be rejected by the Senate in a nasty floor fight, thereby embarrassing the new President. Aware of this ploy, Bradford's Washington supporters, including the late Sen. John East, visited a number of offices and compiled a dossier of letters signed by, according to someone involved, at least 32 senators, pledging their support to Bradford—Democrats as well as Republicans. These letters were sent to the Office of Presidential Personnel and placed in Bradford's folder. A few days later, they were gone. (Washington insiders called it "stripping the files.") Bradford's supporters told us that the likely culprit was Sneaky Sal, who was an ally of the Great Manipulator and worked in the Old Executive Office Building. Undaunted, Bradford's people went around to all of the offices and again obtained signed letters. A few days later, Sneaky Sal apparently struck again. The second batch of letters disappeared. So a third time, Bradford's supporters made the rounds of senatorial offices and gathered signed pledges of support.

In the end, such tactics prevailed. Since Mel had been vulnerable because of his publications—Anti-federalist, pro-Southern, anti-Lincoln—perhaps an honest, straightforward opposition would have won the day for the neocons, as Mr. Frum, in his latest version, suggests it did. But they just weren't willing to take that chance. Hence the "gutter tactics," "hardball,'" "persuasion,"—whatever Mr. Frum wants to call it.

In 1981, a Washington supporter suggested that we do the same kind of hatchet job on Bennett—who, to our knowledge, had behaved well throughout the struggle and had never engaged in Bradford-bashing. Mel vetoed the idea. In the end, he agreed with Will Rogers, who said, "I'd rather be the man who bought the Brooklyn Bridge than the man who sold it." I can't help but wonder if Mr. Frum and all those old Indian fighters could possibly understand such a remark.

Twelve years after the NEH squabble, Mel Bradford died in a South Texas hospital during an emergency operation to repair a severely damaged heart. Alarmingly overweight, he had suffered a coronary while attending a conservative conference. When I heard he had been hospitalized, I called him. The surgery was scheduled for the next morning. His voice was strong, and he was in good spirits. We talked for about ten minutes. Both of us knew this might be our last conversation. (Earlier that day I had taken a dark suit to the cleaners.)

Then, just before we hung up, he said to me, "If I go out tomorrow, I'll go without any bitterness in my heart. I'm at peace with everybody."

He was not necessarily talking about the Great Manipulator or those who had participated in the various machinations to block his nomination. However, if they were on his mind that night, I'm sure he meant to include them in this blanket absolution. When you're about to die, you can't be bothered with irrelevant matters like the National Endowment for the Humanities.

But what about those of us who are left behind? How should we respond to these renewed attacks? The Christians among us have it on the Highest Authority that we are to forgive our enemies. Whether or not we have the duty (or even the right) to forgive the enemies of our friends is a more complicated question. If a friend is maligned or patronized when he is no longer present to defend himself, perhaps we should turn the other cheek. But then it isn't our cheek that's been slapped, is it?

I'm surprised that this matter has surfaced again. No one has anything to gain by keeping the quarrel alive. The neocons have all the power and visibility and resources they yearned for in 1981. The paleos have been marginalized to the point where their opinions, given voice by a shrinking number of publications, are depicted as scandalous by the left and by such people as Mr. Frum.

The neocons are too busy running the world to tilt with Mel Bradford.

The paleos, in the Era of Political Correctness, risk calumny every time they open their mouths, particularly in defense of the dead.

Besides, what we're really debating here is not substance but form, what is considered "proper" as opposed to what is intellectually true. Simply put, the neocons did things we were taught not to do. Apparently they were taught differently. Today, folks call that "diversity."

At this late date, the neocons' best rhetorical ploy is not to rewrite history but to say, "So what? We won, you lost"—precisely what William Tecumseh Sherman might have told Southern civilians whose farms he ordered burned and whose family members he ordered randomly shot. (It was Sherman who said, "The only good Indian is a dead Indian.")

That kind of response would silence us, since we would be left with no common ground on which to pursue the debate. But let's hear no more of noble Indian fighters and paleo self-pity. We could say a lot more on those subjects. And we will, if sufficiently provoked.

14.

Harry Jaffa and the Historical Imagination

In the 1970s, Mel Bradford and I were teaching at the University of Dallas, which offered a doctoral program in politics and literature. Students took courses in both disciplines. It was a well-designed curriculum and produced some first-rate scholars.

Bradford had long been interested in political theory, but the program probably encouraged him to read more extensively in this area and to write articles and (eventually) books on the subject. In fact, the time arrived when he had published more commentary on political matters than the entire politics department. His articles on Abraham Lincoln—only four—caused the greatest stir, since, in them, he explicated texts in a way that revealed a Lincoln incompatible with the iconic figure on the penny and five-dollar bill.

When Bradford had become, as he ironically put it, "unbearably distinguished," the head of the politics department arranged a formal debate on the subject of Lincoln and slavery: established scholar Harry Jaffa *versus* upstart Mel Bradford. Mel and I suspected that the true purpose of the occasion was to humiliate him in front of the UD student body and send him yelping into the bushes, tail between his legs.

I don't remember who kicked off the debate; but once under way, it took an unexpected turn. What was supposed to be a Jaffa-dominated exchange became, instead, a Bradford-dominated history lesson. Jaffa would offer abstractions about slavery in the

South, and Bradford would correct him by citing primary historical sources (tax records, census reports, studies of wills filed in county courthouses)—evidence unknown to the faculty of Claremont. The audience might well have concluded that Bradford had read everything published on the subject, while Jaffa had read little more than the Lincoln-Douglas debates and the Declaration of Independence.

Jaffa, unfazed by this barrage of erudition, continued to counter facts with generalities. He apparently agreed with fellow Straussian Henry Ford, who once said, "History is bunk." I am sure Jaffa's admirers believed he won the debate that night. I doubt that anyone else in that huge crowd thought so. The dynamic of the exchange between Bradford and Jaffa exposed for that audience the tendency of Straussians to dismiss any attention to the full historical context of a political document as "historicism," a form of relativism. Societies are transient; principles are eternal. It is dangerous to tie a document such as the Declaration of Independence to the time in which it was written. You might be snatched up by the Spirit of the Age and swallowed whole. Yet, if we are to understand texts, history—composed of the particularities of time and place—is essential, if only to clothe bare-bones abstractions with flesh and blood. Like God, abstract truth is best understood when incarnate. Facts worry principles into shape, kneading them like biscuit dough. If principles are true, their substance remains unchanged.

More to the point, people who ignore history while finding Truth in political documents presume that they can transcend their own temporal and cultural limitations. It is bad enough to believe that past political texts were written not for the people of that age but for the gods. It is even worse to presume that you are one of those gods. When Archimedes said, "Give me a fulcrum and a place to stand, and I will move the whole world," he knew he would never have to make good on his boast. Straussians, however, believe they have found such a place, where they can transcend the limitations of time and culture to do what Archimedes could only dream of doing.

Thomas Hoving, former director of the Metropolitan Museum of Art, tells of passing the museum's Tang horse daily and viewing it with growing suspicion. Acquired in the 19th century as an authentic piece from the Tang dynasty (A.D. 618-906), the horse—to Hoving's educated eye—began to look more and more Victorian. On a hunch, he had it tested and found that, sure enough, it was a 19th-century fake.

The piece had fooled earlier experts because they were prisoners of their Victorian sensibilities, unable to see their own unique age in the lines of the counterfeit horse. Because he was trained to do so, Hoving could see both the genuine Tang elements and the Victorian overlay.

Will scholars in the late 21st century be able to see the late 20th century bias in the godlike pronouncements of Jaffa and his disciples? Surely they will. Too many believe that all Dead White Males of consequence anticipated Francis Fukuyama in advocating some form of liberal democracy—the best Greek philosophers and historians, Shakespeare, even Machiavelli. Thus, the Ashbrook Center describes Leo Paul de Alvarez's argument in *The Machiavellian Enterprise* as follows: "As the 'first political philosopher to turn to the many instead of the few as the basis of rule,' claims de Alvarez, Machiavelli sought to replace the domination of the Christian Rome with a civil, secular, and egalitarian state."

This Fukuyavellian imposition of the Straussian political paradigm on the works of earlier writers is nothing less than a war on the past, with the ultimate goal to reduce it to rubble, plow it under, and sow salt on it. Yet, like the past, a text has an integrity all its own, a unique identity derived in large measure from the denotation of words, their connotations, and their historical context. If you are not attentive to these elements, a key word can undergo significant transmutation right before your uncomprehending eyes. Take, for example, the poem "Lapis Lazuli," by William Butler Yeats, which begins:

> I have heard that hysterical women say
>
> They are sick of the palette and fiddle-bow.
>
> Of poets that are always gay.

You can readily imagine what a current student at Brown University would make of these lines in a term paper entitled "Yeats and Female Homophobia." The poem deserves to be read in its original language rather than in the debased rhetoric of contemporary sexual politics, and that older language can only be recovered by adopting an historical perspective toward the text—easy enough to do with a poem this recent; not so easy, perhaps, in 100 years.

The typical Straussian refuses to submit to the formidable complexities of the past. After all, it is comfortable and self-serving to hear your own beliefs echoed in the voice of Shakespeare. So you treat the Bard as if he were living next door to you, mowing his lawn on weekends, fighting rush-hour traffic, listening to the Dixie Chicks.

Sometimes, however, you run across language that runs contrary to your Fukuyavellian thesis—and in the most embarrassing places. Take Harry Jaffa's problem with the rhetoric of Abraham Lincoln, who, he argues, refounded America as a nation informed by the principle of equality. Jaffa believes Lincoln hoped to create an egalitarian society in which blacks and whites would live together without prejudice. Lincoln's words tell a different story. Here is an excerpt from his debate with Stephen Douglas, held at Ottawa, Illinois, on August 21, 1858:

> I have no purpose to introduce political and social equality between the white and the black races. There is a physical difference between the two, which in my judgment will probably forever forbid their living together upon the footing of perfect equality, and inasmuch as it becomes a necessity that there

> must be a difference, I, as well as Judge Douglas, am in favor of the race to which I belong having the superior position. I have never said anything to the contrary, but I hold that, notwithstanding all this, there is no reason in the world why the negro is not entitled to all the natural rights enumerated in the Declaration of Independence, the right to life, liberty and the pursuit of happiness. [Loud cheers.]
>
> I hold that he is as much entitled to these as the white man. I agree with Judge Douglas he is not my equal in many respects certainly not in color, perhaps not in moral or intellectual endowment.

In the same speech, Lincoln reassured the crowd that Southerners would not use force to impose blacks on Illinois, which had earlier outlawed their very presence: "There is no danger," he said, "that the people of Kentucky will shoulder their muskets, and, with a young nigger stuck on every bayonet, march into Illinois and force them upon us."

As for Jaffa's egalitarian dream, Lincoln undercut such an idea in his 1857 speech on the Dred Scott case. Here, he came out in favor of shipping blacks off to Africa to prevent miscegenation. ("I have said that the separation of the races is the only perfect preventive of amalgamation.") He admits that "colonization" (an Orwellian term) will be a daunting task, but that the Power of Positive Thinking can work to overcome the obstacles: "Such separation, if ever effected at all, must be effected by colonization; and no political party, as such, is now doing anything directly for colonization. Party operations at present only favor or retard colonization incidentally. The enterprise is a difficult one; but 'where there is a will there is a way'; and what colonization needs most is a hearty will."

So how does Jaffa deal with these statements? He does what Straussians too often do when the text they have brought to obedience school turns on them and bares its fangs: They find hidden meaning in the work ("secret writing") or simply stand it on its head. The author seems to be saying one thing but is actually saying another. Passages that appear to be straightforward are, instead, ironic, and only the explicator can read the coded message tucked between the lines. Machiavelli was really a moderate democrat. When Mark Antony says, "This was the noblest Roman of them all," he doesn't mean a word of it. In a similar circumvention of the obvious, Jaffa says Lincoln made these remarks only because such rhetoric was necessary to be elected in racist Illinois. When Joe Sobran took Lincoln's statements about race at face value, Jaffa reproved him for not taking history into account: "To understand this however requires some historical imagination—putting oneself in the place of someone in an earlier age—something Sobran seems unable to do."

For a scholar with Straussian contempt for history, Jaffa has his nerve. It is not that he fails to make use of historical facts while creating his fairy tale. In his work, facts are more numerous than the sands of the desert. He recites names, dates, and events as readily as a bright third grader recites the multiplication tables. But his imagination is by no means historical. It refuses to submit to history. It is predatory. It possesses the past, driving out its true spirit, reconfiguring its soul.

Almost anyone can imagine that Lincoln might adapt his campaign rhetoric to the prejudices of those whose vote he was seeking. However, no one with a submissive historical imagination could attribute to a mid-19th century politician the kind of egalitarian sensibilities that Jaffa has attributed to Abraham Lincoln, particularly given Lincoln's comments on the subject of equality and his careful delineation of its limits. The real Lincoln, as opposed to Jaffa's 20th-century Lincoln, would never have been so moonstruck as to believe in the 1850s that he could actually implement such an anachronistic plan.

Also, if Lincoln lied about his racial views, can we not, through the exercise of our historical imaginations, conclude that he also lied about his opposition to slavery? After all, to run against

Stephen Douglas, he had to oppose its extension. Douglas had authored the Kansas-Nebraska Act, which overrode the Missouri Compromise and allowed slavery to expand. Had Lincoln not taken the opposite position, he would have had no significant issue to differentiate himself from the popular incumbent senator.

Frederick Douglass—Abraham Lincoln's contemporary and, therefore, a man who, in evaluating the Great Emancipator, had no need for an historical imagination—said at the dedication of a memorial to the fallen president:

> He was preeminently the white man's President, entirely devoted to the welfare of white men. He was ready and willing at any time during the first years of his administration to deny, postpone, and sacrifice the rights of humanity in the colored people to promote the welfare of the white people in this country. He was ready to execute all the supposed guarantees of the United States Constitution in favor of the slave system anywhere inside the slave states. He was willing to pursue, recapture, and send back the fugitive slave to his master, and to suppress a slave rising for liberty, though his guilty master were already in arms against the Government.

Would it not be a proper exercise of the historical imagination to accept Douglass's evaluation and admit that Lincoln harbored the prejudices of 19th-century white men from Illinois? Why not grant him a special insight into the injustice of plantation life, but stop short of turning him into a civil-rights leader, marching on Selma? The answer from Claremont is likely to be charges of bigotry, racism, and neo confederacy.

Years after the last Jaffa-Bradford debate, I dropped by the Free Congress Foundation in Washington to see Mike Schwartz, whom I had taught at the University of Dallas and who was then working with Paul Weyrich. On our way to Mike's office, we came into a room where Harry Jaffa was seated on a sofa, talking to a young woman. As we passed through, I heard her ask him, "But why would Bradford say such a thing?"

"Because," Jaffa replied, "he believes in slavery." Shocked, I stopped.

"Why Harry, I never heard him say anything like that."

"That's because you don't know him as well as I do," he said with a smile. "If you were to get him behind closed doors and give him a drink or two, he'd tell you the same thing."

Mike burst out laughing, remembering that I was Mel Bradford's closest friend and that I knew precisely what he thought about slavery, which he once called in print the worst tragedy in our nation's history.

Was Jaffa simply lying? I don't think so. Straussians don't have to lie.

They have the power to transform the written word into the image of their heart's desire. I presume they can do the same thing with people—remove them from their context, explicate them, transform them into what they really ought to be, as opposed to what they merely are. Jaffa knew in his heart that Bradford believed in slavery because whatever Bradford did tell him (behind closed doors after a couple of drinks) was something like secret writing, a sly way of saying one thing and meaning another. In the Straussian paradigm, Bradford had to have a whip in his hand, so Jaffa placed it there, just as he placed the "I Have a Dream" speech in the head of Abraham Lincoln.

Editorial Note and Acknowledgements

THE ESSAYS BY M.E. BRADFORD included in this book are arranged in two sections, chronologically within each section, to allow the reader a glimpse into the development of Bradford's thought on Lincoln and his reactions to other scholars' work on Lincoln over the course of his career.

The first of these essays, "Lincoln's New Frontier: A Rhetoric for Continuing Revolution," first appeared in two separate issues of *Triumph* magazine in May and June of 1971. The article reprinted in this publication is taken from the collection *The Best of Triumph* (Front Royal, VA: Christendom College Press, 2004) and is reprinted here with the kind permission of Christendom Press. An expanded version of this article was published as "Lincoln, the Declaration, and Secular Puritanism: A Rhetoric for Continuing Revolution," in *A Better Guide Than Reason: Studies in the American Revolution* (LaSalle, IL: Sherwood Sugden & Co.). "The Heresy of Equality," *Modern Age* 20 (Winter 1976): 62-77 originally appeared in and is copyrighted to *Modern Age*. Likewise, "Dividing the House: The Gnosticism of Lincoln's Political Rhetoric," *Modern Age* 23 (Winter 1979):10-24 originally appeared in and is copyrighted to *Modern Age*. Both articles appear in this volume with the kind permission of *Modern Age*. "From the Family of the Lion," *Chronicles* (December 1991): 30-31 is republished here with the gracious permission of the Charlemagne Institute. All rights reserved. The following essays were published in now defunct journals, or the copyright reverted back to the author given the passage of time since original publication, rendering these copyrights orphaned. A release was obtained from the person most likely to have an interest. These essays include,

> "Lincoln and the Language of Hate and Fear," *Continuity* 9 (Fall 1984): 87-108.
>
> "Against Lincoln: A Speech at Gettysburg," *The Reactionary Imperative: Essays Literary and Political* (Peru, IL: Sherwood Sugden & Co., 1990): 219-226.
>
> "Lincoln's Republican Rhetoric: The Development of a Political Idiom," *The Old Northwest: A Journal of Regional Life and Letters* 14 (Fall 1988): 185-212.
>
> "With the Lion and the Eagle," *Southern Partisan* 5 (Fall 1985): 23-24.

The essays of Thomas H. Landess were collected and published in Thomas Hilditch Landess, *Life, Literature, and Lincoln: A Tom Landess Reader*, edited by Clyde N. Wilson and Marybeth Landess (Rockford, IL: Chronicles Press/The Rockford Institute, 2015).

Special thanks to Clyde Wilson for suggesting the project and for the patience and services of Paul C. Graham and the good people at Shotwell Publishers for their help and patience. Also, thanks to Douglas Bradford for his assistance and insights.

A very special thank you to Catherine Spencer Devanny for her valued help in proofing most of the text. Any errors of transcription are mine alone.

About the Editor

JOHN FRANCIS DEVANNY was born in Maryland and received his Ph.D. in history from the University of South Carolina. For over 25 years, he taught a wide range of courses in the fields of history, literature, politics, religion, and economics. He plied his craft at a variety of schools including Catholic schools, an Episcopal school, a non-sectarian school, and the South Carolina Governor's School for the Arts and Humanities. His scholarly essays have appeared in several peer reviewed journals and anthologies. Jeffersonian political and economic thought is his focus, particularly John Randolph of Roanoke, but his work also includes forays into Southern literature and culture. He is currently an adjunct professor of history at Christendom College and an online adjunct instructor in history for Liberty University's graduate program. When he is not teaching or writing, he can be found in the garden; on a good day, he will be in the field or on the stream. He resides in Front Royal, Virginia with his wife Miriam, two of his four adult children, a useless if entertaining cat, and a spoiled Boykin Spaniel named Genevieve.

SOUTHERN BOOKS. NO APOLOGIES

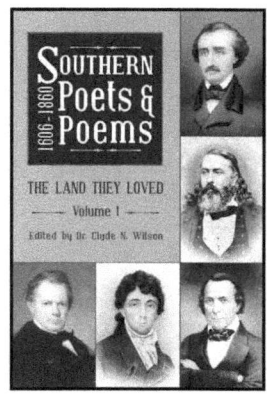 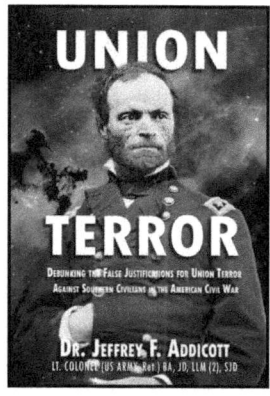 

OVER 90 TITLES FOR YOU TO ENJOY

SHOTWELLPUBLISHING.COM

JEFFERY ADDICOTT
Union Terror: Debunking the False Justifications for Union Terror

MARK ATKINS
Women in Combat: Feminism Goes to War

JOYCE BENNETT
Maryland, My Maryland: The Cultural Cleansing of a Small Southern State

GARRY BOWERS
Slavery and The Civil War: What Your History Teacher Didn't Tell You

Dixie Days: Reminiscences Of a Southern Boyhood

JERRY BREWER
Dismantling the Republic

ANDREW P. CALHOUN
My Own Darling Wife: Letters From A Confederate Volunteer

JOHN CHODES
Segregation: Federal Policy or Racism?

Washington's Kkk: The Union League During Southern Reconstruction

WALTER BRIAN CISCO
War Crimes Against Southern Civilians

JOHN DEVANNY
Continuities: The South in a Time of Revolution

JOSHUA DOGGRELL
Doxed: The Political Lynching of a Southern Cop

JAMES C. EDWARDS
What Really Happened?: Quantrill's Raid On Lawrence, Kansas

TED EHMANN
Boom & Bust In Bone Valley: Florida's Phosphate Mining History 1886-2021

JOHN AVERY EMISON
The Deep State Assassination of Martin Luther King Jr.

DON GORDON
Snowball's Chance: My Kidneys Failed, My Wife Left Me & My Dog Died...

JOHN R. GRAHAM
Constitutional History of Secession

PAUL C. GRAHAM
Confederaphobia

When The Yankees Come: Former Carolina Slaves Remember

Nonsense on Stilts: The Gettysburg Address & Lincoln's Imaginary Nation

JOE D. HAINES
The Diary of Col. John Henry Stover Funk of the Stonewall Brigade, 1861-1862

CHARLES HAYES
The REAL First Thanksgiving

V.P. HUGHES
Col. John Singleton Mosby: In the News 1862-1916

TERRY HULSEY
25 Texas Heroes

The Constitution of Non-State Government: Field Guide to Texas Secession

JOSEPH JAY
Sacred Conviction: The South's Stand for Biblical Authority

SUZANNE JOHNSON
Maxcy Gregg's Sporting Journals 1842-1858

JAMES R. KENNEDY
Dixie Rising: Rules For Rebels

Nullifying Federal and State Gun Control: A How-To Guide For Gun Owners

When Rebel Was Cool: Growing Up In Dixie, 1950-1965

WALTER D. KENNEDY
The South's Struggle: America's Hope

Lincoln, The Non-Christian President: Exposing The Myth

Lincoln, Marx, and the GOP

J.R. & W.D. KENNEDY
Jefferson Davis: High Road to Emancipation and Constitutional Government

Yankee Empire: Aggressive Abroad and Despotic at Home

Punished With Poverty: The Suffering South

The South Was Right! 3rd Edition

LEWIS LIBERMAN
Snowflake Buddies; ABC Leftism For Kids!

PHILIP LEIGH
The Devil's Town: Hot Springs During The Gangster Era

U.S. Grant's Failed Presidency

The Causes of the Civil War

The Dreadful Frauds: Critical Race Theory And Identity Politics

JACK MARQUARDT
Around The World In 80 Years: Confessions of a Connecticut Confederate

MICHAEL MARTIN
Southern Grit: Sensing The Siege at Petersburg

SAMUEL MITCHAM
The Greatest Lynching In American History: New York, 1863

Confederate Patton: Richard Taylor and The Red River Campaign

CHARLES T. PACE
Lincoln As He Really Was

Southern Independence. Why War? The War To Prevent Southern Independence

JAMES R. ROESCH
From Founding Fathers To Fire Eaters

KIRKPATRICK SALE
Emancipation Hell: The Tragedy Wrought By Lincoln's Emancipation Proclamation

JOSEPH SCOTCHIE
The Asheville Connection:
The Making of a Conservative

ANNE W. SMITH
Charlottesville Untold: Inside Unite The Right

Robert E. Lee: A History for Kids

KAREN STOKES
A Legion Of Devils: Sherman In South Carolina

The Burning of Columbia, S.C.: A Review of Northern Assertions and Southern Facts

Fortunes of War:
The Adventures of a German Confederate

A Confederate in Paris:
Letters of A. Dudley Mann 1867-1879

JACK TROTTER
Last Train to Dixie

JOHN THEURSAM
Key West's Civil War

H.V. TRAYWICK, JR.
Along The Shadow Line:
A Road Trip through History and Memory on the Old Confederate Border

LESLIE TUCKER
Old Times There Should Not Be Forgotten:
Cultural Genocide In Dixie

JOHN VINSON
Southerner Take Your Stand!

MARK R. WINCHELL
Confessions of a Copperhead:
Culture and Politics in the Modern South

CLYDE N. WILSON
Calhoun: A Statesman for the 21st Century

Lies My Teacher Told Me: The True History of the War For Southern Independence

The Yankee Problem: An American Dilemma

Annals Of The Stupid Party:
Republicans Before Trump

Nullification:
Reclaiming The Consent of the Governed

The Old South: 50 Essential Books

The War Between The States: 60 Essential Books

Reconstruction and the New South, 1865-1913:
50 Essential Books

The South 20th Century And Beyond:
50 Essential Books

Southern Poets and Poems, 1606-1860:
The Land They Loved, Volume 1

Looking For Mr. Jefferson

African American Slavery in Historical Perspective

JOE WOLVERTON
What Degree Of Madness?: Madison's Method To Make American States Again

WALTER KIRK WOOD
Beyond Slavery: The Northern Romantic Nationalist Origins of America's Civil War

Green Altar (Literary Imprint)

CATHARINE BROSMAN
An Aesthetic Education and Other Stories (2nd Ed)

Chained Tree, Chained Owls: Poems

Aerosols and Other Poems

RANDALL IVEY
A New England Romance: And Other Southern Stories

JAMES E. KIBBLER, JR.
Tiller : Clayback County Series, Vol. 4

THOMAS MOORE
A Fatal Mercy: The Man Who Lost The Civil War

PERRIN LOVETT
The Substitute, Tom Ironsides 1

KAREN STOKES
Belles

Carolina Love Letters

Carolina Twilight

Honor in the Dust

The Immortals

The Soldier's Ghost: A Tale of Charleston

WILLIAM THOMAS
Runaway Haley: An Imagined Family Saga

Gold-Bug
(Mystery & Suspense Imprint)

BRANDI PERRY
Splintered: A New Orleans Tale

MARTIN WILSON
To Jekyll and Hide

Free Book Offer

DON'T GET LEFT OUT, Y'ALL.
Sign-up and be the first to know about new releases, sales, and other goodies
—plus we'll send you TWO FREE EBOOKS!

Lies My Teacher Told Me:
The True History of the War for Southern Independence
by Dr. Clyde N. Wilson

&

When The Yankees Come
Former Carolina Slaves Remember Sherman's March From the Sea
by Paul C. Graham

FreeLiesBook.com

Southern Books. No Apologies.
We love the South — its history, traditions, and culture — and are proud of our inheritance as Southerners. Our books are a reflection of this love.

www.ingramcontent.com/pod-product-compliance
Lightning Source LLC
Chambersburg PA
CBHW050550160426
43199CB00015B/2605